CHASING IMPOSSIBLE DREAMS

An Odd (and often hilarious) Odyssey through International Sport

Jim Holt

CHASING IMPOSSIBLE DREAMS

An Odyssey in International Sport

Jim Holt

1

Hesiod Press

6307 12th Ave NE
Seattle, Washington
98115

"Chasing Impossible Dreams"

Hesiod Press

6307 12th Ave NE
Seattle, WA 98115
206-551-4210
E-mail info:chasingimpossibledreams@hotmail.com
Website: chasingimpossibledreams.com

PUBLISHER'S CATALOGING-IN PUBLICATION DATA
Holt, James P. 1960-
Chasing Impossible Dreams / James P. Holt
p. cm.
Includes bibliographical references and index
ISBN:978-0-615-29795-8

TABLE OF CONTENTS

Forward

This book is about my experiences in International Gymnastics. It is not a technical manual, but rather a reflection on my thoughts pertaining to some of the issues of the sport around the world, and mainly a compendium of some of the fun and crazy experiences I've had doing what I love to do....it's not a book about gymnastics really, but rather, about making connections, establishing contact with people of different cultures and viewpoints, and perhaps making some meaningful and positive differences through communicating values and attitudes.

It's about staying alert to the potential magic of any moment, because we never know what strange and unique experience might be around the next corner. We'll get to some background info shortly so that you can get a fuller sense of how I came to be involved, but first, let me explain what I do and why I do it.

There are 130 countries that are members of the International Gymnastics Federation and I tell people (only half joking) that 25 or 30 neither need nor want my help. Unfortunately for the travel-bug in me those 25 or 30 include France, Italy, Spain, Greece, China, Japan...in other words, most of the places that most people would like to go.

My" beat" is the developing world, what has often been characterized (or mis-characterized) as the Third World. While I would very much like to have some ongoing and formal affiliation (more on this in the chapter on the FIG Academies), I'm a free agent. I'll go anywhere, anytime, and work with anyone that wants me. What do I bring to the table? I wouldn't claim to be a "great" technical coach, although I think I'm competent. Strictly from a technical standpoint, I'm pretty good at constructing exercises that work to a gymnast's strengths, avoid his/her weaknesses, and are able to maximize start values with minimum risks. My greatest strength technically is in planning and preparation for major competitions. I'm very confident (and experienced) in the science and art of "peaking" athletes.

I've got an unusual background and skill-set in the world of gymnastics in that I've studied law and political philosophy. I understand how to integrate the various aspects of a business enterprise (I utilize the modern Western model for NGBs), and have invaluable experience through serving on the Board of Directors of USA Gymnastics for 8 years.

But my real strength and arguably unique contribution is in real passion and commitment to share and grow the sport anywhere I've the opportunity to try, and my absolute and unshakeable belief that anyplace in the world, if one can articulate a goal, one can have it become reality. This is not to say that everyone who wants to can be Olympic All-Around Champion, but what I do is build programs, and how I do it is simple. I tell people they can. I tell people that the secret to success is to "find an impossible dream, then go chase it." Sound crazy?

In 1989 I told a young athlete from Bolivia (an afterthought in the gymnastics world) which had never had athletes compete outside the continent that he and Bolivia could compete at a World Championships. He ended up competing at 3, helped a Bolivian girl compete at one, another Bolivian competed in 3 more, and in Athens in 2004, Bolivia had a woman compete at the Olympic Games.

In 1994, I gave the same speech to coaches and officials in Namibia (the country had only been independent for 3 years!). In 1997 and 1999 they were at Worlds and in 2000 at the Olympics in gymnastics.

In 1996 I told a 9 year old Yemeni boy that he could be his country's first ever representative to the Worlds. In 2006 and 2007 he was there. In 2008, he competed in Beijing as Yemen's first gymnastics Olympian.

Dream big. Dream impossible. It CAN come true.

One more thing- John Dunne in the 17th century at the funeral of Sir William Cockaine stated that: "No man is an island entirely unto himself…." Whatever I've accomplished has not been done alone. For most of my journey, my work, I've been supported, counseled, usually accompanied, and occasionally admonished by my wife Hannah. Hannah is an international level coach in her own right and has superior skills to mine in numerous categories that contribute to our effectiveness in building programs and inspiring gymnasts, coaches, and officials to "reach for the stars." This book, and the achievements recounted within would never have happened without her participation and contribution.

"There is no inevitability in history, except as men make it."
Felix Frankfurter

Chapter One

BOLIVIA

Viva Bolivia, home of the Incas! I love Bolivia, a land of contrasts and jarring juxtapositions unparalleled anywhere else on the planet. My first conscious thoughts about the country took place thousands of miles and several years removed from my first encounter.

I didn't know anybody when I moved to Oregon for law school, and developed a great interest in (and invested an absurd amount of time which should have been dedicated to studying!) "the movies". Portland had (pre-cable or videotape) a wonderful wealth of second-run and revival movie houses, and a couple television stations which seemed determined to run "obscure classics". It was a great time to be a 'film-freak'. In any event, one evening, I was sitting alone in the Mt. Tabor theater, and saw, for the first time, "Butch Cassidy and the Sundance Kid"....well, just about everybody has seen the film, but I hadn't at the time....so Butch and Sundance go through many of the adventures, and as we get to the final third of the film or so, Butch looks at Sundance, and out of the blue says: "Bolivia". Sundance (and of course ME!), look at him like he's nuts and my thoughts are "Bolivia? Huh? What? Where? You got to be kidding me!!"

One thing I've learned over the years is that one is probably better off never saying never....in other words, "Ya never know!!" It seemed to me utterly absurd (and was oh so hilariously funny in this wonderful film!) that anybody would even think of traveling to a place as off the beaten track and obscure as Bolivia.

So, *naturally*, years later, many of my most intriguing experiences have happened traveling though the (said lovingly) often-surreal and always appealing land of Bolivia!

A bit of background or How it all started

In the fall of 1989, Ignacio Morales entered the UW and joined the gymnastics team. "Iggy" had been a gymnast as a boy in Bolivia, but his family relocated to the United States and it had been 5 years since he had last participated in the sport. Morales wasn't the best gymnast on the team, but had an engaging personality and was eager to learn. At the time, (easily the subject of another book!), I was the Men's Coach at the Washington, ran a competitive age-group program on-campus, and was serving as co-Competition Director for Ted Turner's 1990 Goodwill Games.

I'm convinced that often, the subconscious part of our brain processes information and formulates concept and thought independent of our conscious mental processes. In retrospect, our goal to have the UW re-emerge after budget cuts as a recognized factor/power in the sport, combined with my enthusiasm and aspirations for international involvement (we had recruited a gymnast who had competed at the '87 Pan Am Games who spent two years with us then transferred to Arizona State), must have been factors for what followed.

It was a cool gray Saturday morning in Seattle. We were having a pre-season workout, and Ignacio was standing at the chalk tray in Edmondsen Pavilion next to the rings. Not thinking about anything in particular, I squinted for a moment, then turned to him and said, "You know what Ignacio? If everything happened just right, you could represent your country at the 1991 World Championships."

He looked at me. "What"? Suddenly, as if a veil had been lifted from my eyes, I realized what I had just said before it had even been a conscious thought...."Oh wow, you gotta be kidding me", I thought to myself. I turned excitedly to Ignacio..."Iggy, no I'm serious....the Worlds are going to be in Indianapolis in early Sept. of 1991. That's a little over 22 months away....we've gotta get ahold of the Bolivian Federation, start learning the Olympic Compulsories (through the 1996 Games, the Olympics were for All-Arounders only and compulsories were...well, compulsory so that a male gymnast would have a total of 12 separate routines on the 6 men's events)...as I went on verbally compiling a "to-do" or checklist, Iggy interrupted me..."You're crazy!" "No, no, no!" I replied, "believe it or not, we are going to DO this!"

Understand that little Bolivia, the poorest country in South America had never had a gymnast compete outside the 5 Bolivarian countries (Columbia, V enezuela, Ecuador, Peru, and itself) before, and now some gringo had the great (albiet wacko) idea of taking a very inexperienced gymnast and getting him ready to participate in the biggest meet in the World.

It turned out to be a long and interesting 22 ½ months, and one of the great moments of my life was on Sept. 7, 1991 when I marched out behind Ignacio Morales at the Hoosier Dome in Indianapolis representing Bolivia as it's first ever gymnast prepared to take his one touch on the parallel bars. Ignacio had worked his heart out to learn the compulsories and all the other demands that preparing for such an event imposed.

I had promised Ignacio three things: one, that he would NOT finish last (every gymnast's secret nightmare), two that it would be a peak experience of his life, and three that it would change his life in some positive, profound, and unforeseeable, but inevitable manner. Ignacio performed his exercises competently (best competition of his life to that date), and finished a proud 208th out of 213 male competitors.

And as a result, a relationship with international development and the Bolivian Federation was formed for me. I took Ignacio to two subsequent Worlds (more later), but suffice to say, our project helped establish communication with the Federation which a couple years later resulted in them requesting me through the FIG (International Gymnastics Federation) to conduct a coaches development course.

I was tremendously excited to travel and in February 1994, boarded a plane with my wife Hannah and we headed down to teach for 2 ½ weeks in Bolivia.

El Alto

There is one flight a day on American Airlines that leaves Miami at 23:00 hours or so and makes a graveyard flight to La Paz. It was and remains a unique flying experience. If you've ever flown a red-eye, you'll be familiar with the process of the lights being dimmed throughout the flight, and sometime, anywhere from oh 25-35 minutes before landing, a bell will ring, the flight attendants will say something over the loudspeaker about "good morning, beginning our approach, bla bla bla", the lights will pop on, there will be a general groan throughout the cabin, as people begin tossing their blankets on the floor, and yawning and stretching.

Well, that's not the way it happens when you fly into La Paz.

The cabin's still dim, the attendant says, "we're beginning our descent..", and I sleepily glance outside the window....WHAAAT???? There's farms a few hundred feet below us....I can pick out individual cows for criminy-sake....what the...and a few pueblos flash past us......and BUMMMMP!!!! We are on the friggin' GROUND for goodness-sake! You gotta be kiddin' me!!! I was (and be forewarned if you ever make this flight) in total shock it was so unexpected. Well, silly me, I had read the Lonely Planet guide to Bolivia, and of course knew that La Paz is the world's highest capitol city (about 35-4000 meters above sea level), but this landing was a real awakening (yes, I guess that is a pun). El Alto airport sits on the plateau overlooking the city, 13,200 feet in elevation, and therefore, we began our descent at what I assume is "standard operating procedure"., but the airplane runs out of air waaay early because we're landing in the Andes!!! Two minutes, maybe three max from the time that annoying little bell rings until you're on the ground. Put a stopwatch on it. Bet me.

Cochabamba

The city of Cochabamba is a little less than 200 kilometers by air from La Paz; it is located in the middle of the country and topologically resembles the cattle country in the American West. It is doubtful that there is any other flying experience quite like leaving La Paz, and flying East towards Santa Cruz or Cochabamba. As the airplane leaves El Alto, it gains altitude, and one finds oneself flying over some of the most rugged terrain on earth.. Approximately 10 minutes into the flight, the white and blue shadows of the craggy, ice-covered Andes drop away almost vertically in what seems like seconds, and miles below them, spread before us is a verdant green and brown plain...the contrast is startling, and incredibly beautiful...it's easily the most wonderful moment I've experienced looking out the window of an airplane. Let me amend that....the first time I flew into New York's La Guardia at night, the plane did a low and wide sweep around Manhattan on it's final approach...that was pretty special too!

My "Program Development" Course

I'm always intrigued at the expectations that coaches and officials have when contracting me to conduct a Development program. It's usually anticipated that I'll come in and teach them lots of gymnastics skills using "secret" drills and "special" techniques." That, of course, is the least important thing a young country (or club) needs.

Wherever I've been, in my first session I begin by explaining we're going to initiate an overall assessment. We're going to conduct an inventory of the problems, weaknesses, and challenges that (important) THEY perceive they face in developing their program....I always schedule 20-25 minutes...less and one will not receive a complete list, more and the groups will devolve into off-topical conversation. Groups are always puzzled, and a little hesitant to initiate this exercise because they a. have made the assumption that theirs will be a passive role in the project, and b. are unsure of where to start.

I remind them that it is THEIR Federation and that I'm there to lead and guide, NOT to dictate. That said, in order to get them moving in a direction, I always provide the first two problems/issues. Anywhere in the world, the top two problems are always: "a shortage of time and money."

Bolivia was the first country in which I had coordinated a full-blown program for development. When we walked into the classroom for our initial introduction with the 25 Bolivian coaches many of whom would eventually grow into close friends and colleagues, I looked to the back of the room and saw a familiar....tracksuit. I had never met him, but knew instantly that this was 8-time Bolivian gymnastics Champion, Walter Ari. Walter is a proud Aymaran Indian, short, powerful, with dark piercing yet friendly eyes, a strikingly powerful, albeit compact physique, and a hint of a very knowing smile below his long moustache as he looked back at me. Tracksuit? Walter had been Ignacio Morales first coach, and after his first Worlds, Ignacio had sent Walter the warm-up jacket that he had worn in Indianapolis. Subsequently, Sr. Ari, his wife Rosemarie (also a gymnastics coach and judge) became good friends with whom I still communicate.

After giving Walter a big hug, and explaining to the coaches the significance of the warm-up jacket, I broke the coaches into groups, and said to the group via translator (note: I speak conversational Spanish and have given subsequent courses in Spanish, but this first time I needed a translator): "I believe that your first two problems should be listed...yes, write them down on your lists....a shortage of "tiempo y dinero". I'd set our friendly translator up intentionally...I'd had lots of previous experience watching translators at work. Without missing a beat, she smiled and said to the group and I quote: "La falta de *time* y *money*". The group looked at her...I looked at her. "They know what I said". Suddenly, she smiled and giggled, and the group burst into laughter...The second of our collegial bonds had just been formed....I said to her smiling "Awww, I was just joking around and wondered if you'd catch it...I really appreciate your working so hard to help me."

After 20 minutes this (and all subsequent groups) come up with the same 10-15 issues. These issues can be divided into 3 specific problems:

1. a shortage of resources
2. a lack of communication
3. bureaucratic, administrative, or political problems and infighting

This is obviously a preliminary step in developing a long-range plan. In addition, it is crucial for as many persons as possible to have input. The more people that have input, the more one has made an investment, and one thereby increases the number of stakeholders.

The next step is to get a group to identify their long-term goals, both personal and national/Federation. In every country I've been to, people will, after prodding, state some sort of goal, usually an outcome competitive goal, and ALWAYS an objective far below what I'm going to suggest. The stated goal is *never* the real goal, but rather a cover, a (with all good intentions and perhaps not even conscious) ruse.

All people have "secret" dreams and ambitions. The reason that most people keep these dreams secret is first, that they either believe that their dreams are so unrealistic, that to admit that they really want these things is to basically judge themselves as being foolish or unrealistic. I hate the fact that people limit themselves in this manner. The second but not mutually exclusive reason is that individuals are reluctant to expose their "secret" dreams because they think their aspirations will be deemed by other people to be too "big" and therefore they will be embarrassed by the rejection or negative judgment of others.

It's a perfect set-up.... the Bolivians responded with: "We want to have good results in the Juegos Bolivarianos." I told them, "that is waaaay too small. Look at Walter in the back of the room. Stand up Sr. Ari. Bolivia has already been to the WORLD Championships twice…that warm-up is from the Worlds. The next goal should be to put Women in the World Championships, and then let's start working on getting full teams for both men and women there."

The next step, almost never explored in developing sports bodies, is the articulation of a timeline IN ORDER THAT an integrated project planning document can be created and implemented.

First critical question: how long would it reasonably take for the longest-long term goal to be implemented? As a general rule, in Olympic Sport, time is measured by quadrenniums or the times between Olympic Games. Then, therefore, an adequate long-term planning document will encompass 2-3 Olympiads or 8-12 years. Normally, if it's the first time I've visited a country, I'll settle for an 8 year plan.

Next, we work to create an organizational chart which will reflect the structure through which a strategic planning document will be developed.
I utilize a model formulated by Mike Jacki for USA Gymnastics in the early 1990s. Mike created divisions within his NGB, the "Internal" or gymnastics division, and the "External" or Marketing division.

I always focus on the external first...by this time, most coaches heads are spinning, but that's perfectly ok, because in this introductory phase, we're

a. challenging them to question their assumptions
b. altering their paradigm
c. changing their world-view

It is one thing to be able to articulate an impossible dream. It is an absolutely essential step. It is, however, in and of itself not sufficient to move individuals or groups to action. They need to be convinced that that dream is POSSIBLE, and the way that is done is to help them build the roadmap, so that they can actually see how it is feasible to move from whatever their status quo is, to the 'proverbial' mountaintop which would be the realization of their long-term "dream" objective.

If one is going to be able to visualize and understand the actual "how to", one needs to understand the road maps. I find it is easiest to focus on "External or Marketing Structure" as the primary starting point in building our strategic plan for two interrelated reasons. While coaches and officials usually anticipate development programs being about teaching gymnastics skills, it is necessary to provide a context in which those skills might be learned in order that they may relate in some meaningful way to the goals articulated. In other words, I tell the coaches to be confident, we WILL get to those topics, but that it is important to lay the foundations for the future actions of the organization.

External or Marketing Structure

This is the single greatest and most problematic hurdle for young or entry level Federations to overcome. Usually the individuals involved with the sport (in the developing world) fall into 2 categories: 1. coaches, who love the sport but have limited experience in the business world, and 2. 'administrators', usually from outside the sport who do not know anything about the sport, including it's international structure. These individuals are often politically connected through either a Sports Ministry or NOC (National Olympic Committee). A subcategory of 'administrator' which we have regularly encountered in the developing world is a parent of an athlete who has assumed the role of leader of the organization for any number of valid reasons, but ultimately the most important of which is to promote the interests of his/her child.

As I explained to the Bolivians, one's external or marketing structure is everything the organization does that relates to the public or in generating revenues. Depending on the conditions within a given society or country, there are a number of opportunities for activity from which an organization can derive benefit.

A sport organizations' two biggest assets are its' athletes and its' events. The two simplest ways to capitalize on these assets are sponsorships and events. While it is outside the specific scope of this narrative, I always try to discuss issues pertaining to "Communication", and in particular, media-tv, radio (particularly as way to promote events), and to suggest that Federations should consider opportunities through the internet to develop their programs. It is outside the scope of this narrative to discuss this in detail, but I raise it in discussing development with Federation coaches and officials in order to alter their paradigms and priorities pertaining to the growth of their sport.

Isle Verde

It's not there any more, but one of our favorite hangouts a few years back was a restaurant called Isle Verde. The beer was cold and cheap, the atmosphere warm and friendly, and the food was ample, cheap, good, and, it stayed open late! One of the oddest things about La Paz is that while it is a city with a population of 2.5 million, it feels like a small town, especially if you're the "new kid"...it's a very warm and friendly city, but you're quickly noticed if you're seen more than once.

One memorable evening after a long day working with the coaches, Hannah and I made our maybe 3rd stop into Isle Verde. We had been eating almost exclusively Andean cuisine, and felt like having something a little more familiar. We browsed the menu and ordered a medium pizza. Over in the corner, near the bar, there were a few tables from which we could hear snatches of both English and Spanish. Shortly, our pizza arrived. Medium? This was the largest thing I'd ever seen on a plate!

Although we were really hungry, there was no way we could come anywhere close to knocking down this monster. It was easily 2 feet in diameter, and thick, thick with cheese and ham. Well, we did the best we could, and as the meal started to wind down, a rather chubby gentleman from one of the tables wandered over. Paunch protruding from under his t-shirt and sporting a several days old collection of whiskers, he asked amiably in a Spanish-accented English:

"Are you gonna finish that pizza?" A little startled, but not offended, I replied,

"Why, no we're not." The fork he was holding in his left hand stabbed at the remains of the tray on our table. "Plunk, plunk, plunk!" He deftly transferred the remaining slices from our tray to the plate in his right hand, and in an instant,

the tray was bare and his plate full. "We don't like things to go to waste in Bolivia", he said with perhaps the hint of a wink as he turned on his heel and marched back to his table. We smiled at each other from ear to ear....what a great moment and one that would/could never happen in the good ole USA....

Oh the evening got better....a few minutes later, a 20-something-ish guy comes over sporting a Prince-Valiant-like hair-do. "You're Americans" he says in what was either a skewed Cockney or slightly mis-inflected Australian accent.

Why is it, wherever I go in the world, I'm always accosted by this statement rather than a question? Ummm, yeah pal, of COURSE we're Americans. Geez, we speak English with an American accent. Now naturally we never respond this way, and politely answer, "Why yes, we are, and might I guess that you're, what Australian?" "I am" he replied. "What are you doing in Bolivia?" "I'm a surfer"

"Excuse me?" "I'm a surfer, I'm a professional surfer." Ri-ight. Well, what the heck, maybe the guy IS a pro surfer, and after all, it's winter in the Northern hemisphere (oh wait, Australia's here in the Southern hemisphere too, so he could be surfing in Australia obviously). So I surmise to myself, maybe surfers do cross training, so naturally thinking of a complimentary dry-land training possibility, I inquire: "So, are you up at Chalkaltaya?" Chalaltaya is the world's highest ski area. Located about an hour-hour ½ outside La Paz, it's at 19,500 feet. "Where?" "Chalkaltaya, you know, skiing."

"No", he spoke a little more slowly, unsure if I was actually a functioning adult and as if to make sure that I was actually comprehending..."I told you, I'm a professional surfer." "OK", I responded as pleasantly as I could muster.

"It's been great to speak with you, and good luck with your training and competitions." A big grin "Thanks mate!" and he shook my hand and was off.

Hannah and I looked at each other. She gave me "that look"....the one that means, "What was that all about?". I looked back...."hey babe, I wasn't going to be the one to break it to the guy that Bolivia is a landlocked country smack dab in the middle of the ANDES!!" As far as I know (to paraphrase Herodotus) there is no surfing at Lake Titicaca either.

What a bunch of characters....so now, I reach for the bill, and then for my non-existent wallet which I have obviously absent-mindedly left back in our hotel room (Hannah hates it when I do that). So I somewhat reluctantly approach the bartender, "I'm sorry, do you speak English?" "I do" he replies in a German accent. "Is that a German accent; are you from Germany?" Note that I'm now the one asking the asinine questions! "Of course I'm from Germany!" (As if all restaurateurs and bartenders in Bolivia are German.)

I knew about Klaus Barbie and his famous table at another spot in La Paz, but really! What are you doing in Bolivia? "I came for the waters," he says with a straight face and wink, perhaps unwittingly, but presumably more intentionally quoting Humphrey Bogart as Richard Blaine parrying Major Stausser's interrogation in "Casablanca". "But Mr. Blaine", I respond in my clumsy approximation of Conrad Veigt's accent and intonation, "Bolivia is in the mountains." Suppressing a smile, he tops the exchange struggling to keep a strait-face, "I was misinformed." We both laugh. Hannah just looks at us.

"I've got what I hope is a small problem. I've left my wallet back in our hotel and can't pay the bill right now." "No problem," he replies, just bring it by the next time you're in the area."

Besides, I know you're the American gymnastics people working with the Olympic Committee...I saw you on tv last week." "Well, danke shoen." We laughed all the way back to the hotel; and of course paid up the next time we were there.

Calle Buenos Aires

The most dominant feature of La Paz is that it's a hole in the ground...as anyone who's been there can tell you, positioned high in the Andes, there are very few level spots anywhere in the city. It's steep, very steep, and perhaps unique in the world, the farther you go up, the poorer the area. The barrios surrounding El Alto host a large impoverished population as do the streets and alleys hovering on the hillsides above the main part of downtown. One of the most heavily travelled streets is Calle Buenos Aires.

Welcome to the heart of South America! On the sidewalks, fronting the small tiendas are countless vendors, usually Aymaran women in the traditional hoop skirts, buttoned sweaters and ubiquitous bowler hats, selling anything from soap, costume jewelry, bootlegged cds and dvds, to chestnuts, and fruit.

On Calle Buenos Aires, there simply is no way to walk on the sidewalk, so one is forced to walk in the street. This becomes complicated because the street is invariably jammed to a slow-moving crawl with honking cars, and diesel-spewing mini busses?

What to do, how to adapt? Easy....the only way for a pedestrian to safely negotiate the traffic jammed and crowded onto this winding and steep street other than to never venture here, is *to walk down the middle of the chaos!* One feels a certain giddiness (fumes from the gasoline?) strolling casually down oncoming and outgoing traffic with barely a foot or so clearance. One is in constant danger of being run down or run over. I don't know if Salvadore Dali ever visited here, but the genius who once memorably proclaimed "The only difference between me and a madman is...that I am NOT mad!" would feel right at home on Calle Buenos Aires!

Estadio Hernando Siles

One interest that has been a great starting point for personal contact over the years has been my enthusiasm for international soccer and its history. As the "world's game", soccer is a source of instant mutual interest between most males in the world. Anytime I get the opportunity, I try to get to a soccer match. I was particularly excited to have an opportunity to visit Estadio Hernando Siles, the National Stadium in La Paz. After all, I had twice represented Bolivian Gymnastics at the World level as a coach, and in 1993, shortly after our WC competition, Brazil came to Hernando Siles for a World Cup qualification match. Although mighty Brazil had never lost a qualifying match in the history of the World Cup, Bolivia's squad, led by midfielders Erwin Sanchez and the electrifying Marco Etcheverry upset Brazil 2-1 on an incredible (dribbling through 5 defenders!) run by Etcheverry, shocking the soccer world, and qualifying Bolivia to its second World Cup which was to be held in the USA in 1994. I was able to see the match from the United States live due to its being televised on Univision.

I was also eager to experience the 'carnival and fireworks' experience of sitting amongst the (usually crazed) fans of South American teams.

It turns out, that my request at Olympic headquarters was enthusiastically supported. A Libertadores Cup (annual South American club Championship) game between the country's two best teams, Bolivar and The Strongest (nicknamed Los Tigres) was taking place during my time in the country. I was so excited to head into the Stadium, but mildly disappointed (I shoulda just gone and bought a ticket without going through 'officialdom') that we were not going to sit down amongst the passionate followers of the two squads.

Because I was a 'quasi'-vip (I guess), I was escorted to the vip section of the grounds, which was nice, but....a little sterile compared with the atmosphere I was hoping to enjoy and experience. Nevertheless, here I was in South America, watching some fine soccer in a tight game...soon, half-time comes, and Christian Salizar got up and indicated that we needed to go out into the (crowded) concourse and get something to drink.

Well we no sooner got out there, then he grabs my jacket sleeve, and pulls me strongly towards a huddled group of people. “Jim, here is someone I really want you to meet.” One side of the group parts, and standing there is a distinguished looking gentleman in an expensively tailored grey suit, and a stylish red, yellow, and green silk tie. Without further adieu, Christian proudly introduces me to the (then) VP of Bolivia, Victor Hugo Cardenas. Sr. Cardenas election to the office of Vice-President was an historic occasion (and a ‘big deal’) in largely Aymaran-Quechwan La Paz, due to his being the first Aymaran Indian elected to such a high office in the history of the country. Like many of the South American countries, the heavy-handed legacy of Spanish colonialism created deep class divisions which remain and are primarily defined on ethnic lines...the lowest classes historically in Bolivia have been the indigenous tribes on the Andean Altiplano, and the Aymarans in particular.

By a happy coincidence, there had been a major profile on Sr. Cardenas published in the Sunday New York Times which I had read. “Sr. Cardenas”, I responded, “it is a real honor to meet you . By any chance, have you seen the New York Times piece that discussed your political career and policies from several weeks ago?” Sr. Cardenas, a broad smile creasing his face, rocked his shoulders slightly and said in a warm baritone and and flawless English, “Why yes I have...it was a very complementary piece, and I very much enjoyed speaking at length with the young lady reporter about a number of topics.” I told him how much I had enjoyed the piece, and after some pleasantries, I asked him a specific question about his policies on labor reform and its effect on indigenous peoples. While he expounded at some detail and length ,I could see in my peripheral vision the folks in his entourage looking at us, and commenting amongst themselves....while I couldn’t catch what they were saying, I could pretty much assume it was something along the lines of “Who the heck is this gringo, and what in the world does he have to say that would tie up or engage our country’s Vice President in some conversation in the middle of a concourse during a soccer match!” Shortly after, Sr. Cardenas and I shook hands (he rubbed my shoulder), and went on our ways.

Thomas N’Kono, the wonderfully animated Camaroonian goalkeeper (see 1982 World Cup v. Italy!) made several leaping saves to keep Los Tigres off the board in a 1-0 Bolivar win. What a country! Being in Bolivia is just so damn much fun!!

Taxi

Hernando Siles was approximately 3 kilometers from our hotel, and although it was a fairly nice late-summer night, we could have walked to the Stadium.

Since Christian and I were nicely dressed, we opted (wrongly, as it turned out) to get a cab.

If you're planning on getting anywhere in a hurry in La Paz, you generally need your own space-age jet-pack due to the traffic congestion. Needless to say, we got stuck in traffic, and not having my wallet (a disturbing trend?), we jumped out several blocks from the Stadium, and expressed our regrets to the cabbie, who unfortunately was not able to collect the fare. Thinking no more about it (although I most certainly SHOULD have thought myself the cad for shortchanging this gentleman out of what would be the equivalent of about U$ 1.00), we went on to the stadium.

Comes the dawn....we step out of our hotel on our way to the Olympic Center to begin this mornings activities and to my surprise (and sincere pleasure), last night's cabbie approaches us on the street...he removes his hat holding it in front of his chest with his left hand, and says very politely "Scuse Sr....en el noche ayer, Ud. fues en mi coche de alquiler..." I smiled (and maybe blushed a bit with embarrassment), reached for my wallet (which I actually had this time in my briefcase!) and pulled out several Bolivianos. "I'm very sorry senor about that....we were in a hurry, and..." The cabbie smiled and interrupted..."Entiendo Senor....futbol, no?" I laughed out loud. "Futbol, si si si! I am very glad that you took the time to find me..Is this enough for your trouble?" He looked down at the money, "No senor, lo es demasiado!" "No, it's good....you keep it! Buenos dias y gracias senor" I responded as we walked away. Two million people, and the guy can find me walking around a day later....

Believe it or not, it happened again a little later in the trip....Hannah and I were given directions to Walter and Rosemarie Ari's residence which was perhaps two kilometers from where we were staying. Avenida 16th de Junio is THE main street in the city...it winds all the way from the barrio of El Alto on the top of the altiplano, down through the deep gash that is La Paz, deep into the fissure of the mountain....virtually all other streets in one way or another are tributaries (and eventually capillaries that stem from this great artery of a road. To get to Walter's place, one winds through several small streets and turns that are (if you're not familiar with the city) "off the beaten path"....in any event, we're dutifully following directions, and I look up, and here, walking towards us from the other direction is the (then) President of the Gymnastics Federation, Sr. Jose Nunez, wearing his ubiquitous cardigan sweater! "Good afternoon Sr. Nunez!" we say greatly surprized. We know he doesn't live anywhere near here (as you'll read a bit further on)...."what are you doing here, are you coming from Walter Ari's." "No, I have a friend that lives in the area and I was at his place; I know Walter lives somewhere around here, but I don't know exactly where." We exchange a few more pleasantries, and go on our respective ways....Bolivia's like a small village sometimes!

Adventures in Inscription

Not that it's easy even now getting regular and good communication from less-developed countries or gym Federations (it should be effortless with virtually universal access to email, but it still isn't!), but it could be quite challenging "back in the day". I've coached (to date) 11 World Championships, and each of them, in their own way, had some special challenges. In a number (most of them actually), the biggest challenge has been the (in theory) simple action of getting the Federation and Athlete officially registered.

The FIG requires member Federations to submit Provisional, Definitive, and Nominative inscriptions leading up to World Championships. The Provisional Inscription is a notice to the FIG that a member Federation intends to enter the upcoming FIG Championships and is due in the FIG office no later than 5 months prior to the opening day of the event. The Definitive inscription communicates the projected number of gymnasts, coaches, judges that will attend the event as representatives of that Federation and is due 3 months prior to the opening day.

The Nominative form provides the names of all gymnasts and Federation persons that will be credentialed for the event, and is due one month prior to the start of the event.

At the present time, the FIG treats these deadlines as absolute, but during Yuri Titov's Presidency (1976-1996) (and presumably before, but I have no personal knowledge) there was a certain amount of flexibility. For the record, I believe that Titov's "case by case" policy served the international gymnastics community better than the current one, but I digress. The registration period for the 1994 Worlds took place in late 1993 and early 1994 (April World Championships), and was therefore just before the dawn of emails and attachments. Faxes were widely used for communicating, but "official" forms still had to be 'snail-mailed'. In order (and this is important) for an inscription to be accepted by the FIG, it had to be a. filled out completely, b. signed by the President (or a comparable Federation official), and c. have the "seal" of the Federation stamped or affixed to it.

Now to our (read: my!!) problem....I couldn't get Bolivia to communicate!! One more thing...all this took place PRIOR to my traveling to the country. While I had had correspondence with these folks for half a decade, because I gnacio Morales was going to school and training in the USA, I'd never actually met any of them face to face to this point. While I knew they had been supportive and sympathetic regarding Iggy's participation, for some reason, I had received no communication. For months(!!) I had written, and then fairly regularly had faxed them asking for confirmation that they had sent the necessary forms, and had received no communication back whatsoever. As we approached the deadline for the Definitive Inscription, and had received no response, I was getting desperate. The Definitive actually did have a "drop-dead" date, because it was the one upon which the FIG would conduct the order of competition draw 60 days before the start of the meet.

The 1994 Worlds were scheduled in April, in Australia. The original Definitive deadline was days away and I had received no word. In virtual despair, I took the liberty of faxing the FIG directly (a huge no-no in terms of protocol!) and copied the then-President, Yuri Titov), explaining that Bolivia was going to attend the event, but that there had been a communication problem and that we had had some problems getting the forms. Two days later, after not getting a response, in what felt to me (figuratively at least) like a trip to the gallows, I picked up the phone and called the FIG office and asked to speak with Norbert Bueche the General-Secretary. After he got on the phone, Mr. Bueche cut me off as I started my spiel, and informed me (as he usually did) that the FIG was structured such that it only took communication from member Federations and did NOT wish to have coaches or non-official Federation persons attempting to contact it. That said, he said, he had been in communication with President Titov about the matter, and that if the Bolivian Federation wanted an extension of the deadline the FIG would consider receiving a fax copy in order to get Bolivia registered, but that the original must follow by hard mail "immediately". I reminded him that mail could be slow from South America. He said he understood, and wished me luck. And the deadline for the submission of the fax was 72 hours. Thank you Mr. Bueche. Thank you very much sir! Click.

Now the execution has been post-poned 3 days...like Misha Auer's Boris Ziprovich character in "Destry Rides Again"(1939), I'm in an agony of "what to do, what to do..." Well hell, what would, say, Homer's Odysseus, "the man of many wiles" do? He'd *cheat* of course!

I've got no way to get any forms, and Bolivia isn't answering anyway....mmmm...Rob Paridis is the Men's Program Director of the Canadian Federation, and a good guy....I phone him, explain (a small part only!!) of the problem, ask him if he can fax me a copy of the 1994 inscription form, which he amiably agrees to do right away. Great. Now I've got a template. I take the fax copy, and snip the part where it says sent by CGF from the top. I go to my copy machine, and make a couple hard paper copies (just in case I make a little mistake or two as I prepare my elixer. Next, I rummage through my correspondence, and yup, here's a nice note from Sr. Nunez on Federation stationery. Now, here we go, off to Kinko's where I make a pristine color copy of Sr. Nunez letter on a transparent A-4 sheet.....niiice...his signature and the

Federation seal copy look perfect...umm-umm, now we're cookin'. I cut the seal off the transparency, and affix it to one of my Definitive forms, then make a copy of that, so that, now, I've got (what looks like a nice and 'authentic') Definitive form, with a Bolivian seal in what looks like purple ink. Next, I place Sr. Nunez's facimile signature under the Definitive form on top of an overhead projector, turn the projector on, and carefully trace Sr. Nunez' signature onto the form.

Oh yeah! No safecracker felt more pride looking at his work then when I finished checking this baby out. Perfect! Sooooo, then I check all the boxes, and fax my counterfeit form off to Moutier Switzerland and the FIG office.

The tricky part....I can't get this sent with a Bolivian postmark, and I sure as heck can't use some US flag stamp for the hard copy....of course....UPS, and I fill out the return address with the address of the Bolivian Federation, with a very small notation of a d/b/a so that a. UPS will take it, and b. nobody in Switzerland will be looking at the stamps. Plus, the folks at FIG should interpret getting a UPS package with Bolivia being serious about trying to stay in compliance. Man, am I one crafty dude or what? Whatta friggin' mess....whew!!!!

A slight digression....

For the reader that thinks, "Zounds, this person, if in fact, not a brazen lawbreaker, certainly seems to have criminal tendencies." Let me set the record straight through full disclosure. While I leave it to the reader to interpret whether the above indicates "criminal tendencies", I must confess to having a criminal record.

As previously mentioned, I attended college at Wazzu in Pullman, which is set at the far southeastern corner of the state of Washington. It's basically surrounded by farmland, and I'm certain that cows outnumber people in that part of the state…in other words, except for the university, it's very (v-e-r-y) rural…..kilometers and kilometers of rolling wheat….anyway, I was in my senior year in college, and had to stay in Pullman during the semester break 'cause it was right in the middle of the gymnastics season.

The campus is basically set on top of this great big hill, or a couple of them anyway…the town or what could be called the "downtown" was at the base of the hill…well, several of us one evening had gone downtown for some…refreshments….on the evening in question, for reasons I don't remember, we not only drove downtown (usually we walked), but I was the designated driver……..hmmmmm….please you do not want to hear the story of the first time I got drunk, which was most definitely NOT this particular occasion…but I digress….anyway, it's semester break, there's not a soul in Pullman (or I should say at the university) except for the in-season sports teams (everybody else went home to Seattle or someplace more…urban), it's

2 am, and I'm driving the group home…ummm, designated driver means I hadn't been drinking…soooo, the bar closes, the streets are deserted, and I start the car, drive up to one of the only 2 or 3 street lights in the whole darned town…I come to a complete stop, look both ways, and make a left turn <against the red light> onto a completely deserted one way street….well, completely deserted except for the cop in the parked (and dark) police car who saw me, immediately pops on his flashing light and pulls me over……

So anyway, here's this cop getting out of his car, had been on the WSU football team a couple years earlier, and he's writing a ticket for this silly "violation"…being a "smart-aleck" college kid, I try to talk him out of it…no way he was going for that…..so, I get the ticket, and have the option of paying the monetary fine or going to traffic court to argue the matter….naturally (for the record, I'm a smart-ass college student at the time), I decide to go to court…. Soooo, it's a couple months later (I requested as many extensions as I could get) and it's now early May, when spring is in full-bloom in Pullman(which can mean anything from a late-blizzard to sun-tan weather, sometimes in the same day!), and I'm in traffic court…I explain to the judge all the circumstances I've explained thus far (leaving out the "arguing with the cop" part), and in my conclusion pointed out to him that since there wasn't any harm, and since it was a minor <and technical> breach of the law, and since I was a "first time" offender, he should let me off with a "warning" (tell me not to do it again, but otherwise not penalize me)…..well, he said "No." "No, you're guilty and you have to pay the fine."

And I say: "well, your honor, I won't."

Judge: "You have to."

Me: "No sir, I don't."

J: "Yes, you do."

Me: No sir, I don't."

J: "If you don't pay the fine, I will have no choice but to sentence you to jail"

Me: "Ok, I'll go to jail."

J: "You don't want to do that."

Me: "Yes, I do."

Now I must go back a couple weeks….Pullman, as I've previously inferred is in the "middle of nowhere"…..I didn't even know where it was in the state until I actually was half-way across the state on my way to begin school there (another loooong story)….but anyway, in Pullman, about the only thing college students have for entertainment is activities put on by the University or general college hell-raising thought up by the college students themselves…there was this house near the bookstore up the road from the athletic complex near fraternity row that was rented by a bunch of football players (and a basketball player or two)…..it had a flat roof, and when the nicer weather started they had parties at the house (and sometimes on the roof!.....now I was not much of a partier in college, but somehow got invited to this bash they were holding one spring Saturday…it was punctuated by water balloon tossing (and especially launching balloons at the fraternity houses using surgical tubing and funnels (kind of like a catapault…..those babies could travel 100+ meters!.....)

Well, it was early evening on a spring Saturday, beautiful day, and probably 75-90 people milling around this place….drinking beer, a few long water balloons shot at the frats, music, but nothing really outrageous…now, the police in Pullman generally give students a pretty loose leash (for reasons which I've already more or less explained….)…and a police car pulls up and basically tells us all to cease and desist with the water artillery, or they'll have to write citations…. the topic on the roof turns to "transgressions" committed by people present, and it turns out that 7 or 8 people had already been to the jail for one reason or another….well, in addition to this "spirit of solidarity", my undergraduate major was "political philosophy", and my particular area of interest was (and remains to this day) radicalism, and particularly of the individualist stripe….the transcendentalist Henry David Thoreau once spent a night in jail in protest of a voting tax, and I thought that the experience might be a marvelous one…. …..so, I get the idea that instead of having to pay my fine, I could spend a couple days in the Colfax County jail.

(meanwhile, back at Court…..)

So the judge looks really pissed off at me, and says, "if that's what you want, that's what you're going to get"……and proceeds to sentence me to yes, you guessed it, a weekend in the Colfax County Jail. I was to report on Friday afternoon, and was to be released Sunday evening…

On the designated Friday, I go to the jail, a relatively compact 2 story building with offices on the ground floor, and the cell-block on the upstairs floor….they lock me into a cell, and I spent Friday night doing homework, and I had a bunch of books that I had brought along with me…..Saturday morning, I make the acquaintance of the one other inmate, some guy who had gotten into a bar fight and was charged with aggravated assault….."it really wasn't my fault…I'm only violent when I've been provoked and after I've been drinking heavily"….were you provoked? "Absolutely….and, to tell you the truth, I had had a few drinks……"

Right.

So anyway, late Saturday morning, they let Mr. Aggravated Assault out (he'd been there several days), and the one cop on duty asks me if I want to be a trustee…..which in the usual sense (i.e. incarcerations longer than a week-end) means the inmate gets 'special privileges' for good behavior……in my case it meant that if I was willing to spend Saturday afternoon cleaning the office, they'd lock me back into the cellblock (I'm now the sole resident) instead of my cell…I'd be able to walk around the whole cellblock (about 8 cells total) and they wouldn't have to make me dinner.....noodles and cheese 'cause I'd also have access to the cellblock hotplate.....well heck, ok, I'll do that...

Cleaning the office takes about an hour, not a whole afternoon, so I get to spend a lazy afternoon reading and looking out the bars of the cellblock at the rolling wheat fields of the Palouse (the area in which Pullman is stuck)....Saturday nite and Sunday more of the same,,,,quiet, lots of reading, nobody bothering me....at dusk, I call downstairs, "hey, when are you going to let me out, I'm supposed to be released..." well, after a couple exchanges like that, it turns out that they've misplaced my papers, and that they're not officially supposed to let me out without them, and the single cop on duty says, "sorry, we've got to hold you overnite until the judge signs a new release in the morning....well, I was having none of that, and honest.....just like Paul Muni in "I Was a Fugitive From a Chain Gang(1932), I take a metal cup, and start rattling it up and down between the bars....makes a helluva racket....well, after several minutes of this, I hear the cop at the foot of the stairs:

"You better cut that out!"

Right......sooooooo,

(remember, I'm in college),

I rattle the cup even louder, and reply: "what are you going to do....throw me in jail?"

Well, you can imagine how that was received by the forces sworn to uphold the law and protectors of all that is civilized and righteous, but my persistent rattling of the cup resulted in Inspector Clouseau cracking...the cop stomps up the stairs very angry, and opens the cellblock....in a low voice (it was obvious he wanted to punch me hard and repeatedly), he says: "listen smartass, I'm letting you out, but we know your license plate number and your address....we'll be waiting for you to screw up, and if you do......"

Well, I got the message, thank goodness I was going to be gone, graduated a couple weeks later.....

Ooops, forgot one part...that semester, I had a show on the campus radio station playing rock n' roll roots music and missed my shift....the station director called my house, and inquired of my whereabouts...one of my room-mates responded rather off-handedly, "...oh Jim?....he's in jail...."......needless to say, I got some odd looks when I went into the station the next week for my show.....

Well, one might conclude that with such a disrespectable, nefarious, and some might claim (rightly so) subversive background, that recidivism was predict-able, if not inevitable...*I still say it was all a misunderstanding!*

In any event, the package had been mailed to the FIG and I assumed that all was going smoothly and uneventfully..........sooooo, fast forwarding to "a few weeks later", and here I am, actually conducting the coaches' course in Bolivia. The second weekend we're there, Sr. Nunez, who turns out to be a wonderful guy...he's a teacher at the University, and has a very nice house deep in the "Valley of the Moon", in one of the most beautiful parts of the city....anyway, Sr. Nunez and Sra. Nunez invite Hannah and me, and several of the coaches attending the course to his house for a Sunday brunch. There's plenty of food, seemingly endless bottles of beer, and a couple large bottles of singani (the local and favored Bolivian 'hard-stuff') for later. Well, we are well into the afternoon, lots of overlapping and warm conversation, and Sr. Nunez, who had excused himself briefly, comes back to the large dining room table and sitting down, takes a small file folder out of his briefcase. After several minutes, he wordlessly slips 3 pieces of paper out from the folder and slides them across the table towards me.

I look down..........ULP!!!!!........and blink. Once. There's a (presumably unverifiable 'cause not many of us actually come back) story that the moment before someone dies, he/she sees his/her entire life flash before their eyes. Well, I didn't have my life flash before my eyes (hell, I didn't even die, although for a moment I wanted to right then and there!), but that was one loooong moment....face up, directly in front of me on the table, Sr. Nunez had spread:

1.a copy of the Definitive form that I had sent to the FIG,

2. a COPY of the form HE HAD SENT to the FIG (2 boxes I had checked were blank),

3. and a fax from the FIG inquiring as to what the hell was going on and why did Bolivia send in two different inscriptions?

In that what felt like a years-long moment (and in actuality was probably oh, 2 maybe 3 seconds), I struggled with my final summation in front of the jury...I remembered the old Steve Martin skit: "but Your Honor...I didn't know that Armed Robbery Was a Crime!", and Claude Rains plea at the end of "The Adventures of Robin Hood" (1939) as Richard the Lionheart confronts him with his attempted assassination: "...but Richard...after all...I AM your brother." Or maybe Marlene Dietrich "It took more than one man to change my name to....Shanghai Lily." Oops, that wasn't the end of the film and she didn't even die...out of time and without the imagination to come up with a colorful (however impossibly implausible) excuse, I cave in and throw myself at the mercy of the court....I tell the truth.

Although the coaches had not been aware of this situation, they are now looking at me curiously....hmmm, what's going on here, this seems like a very interesting moment....20 pairs of eyes serve as the Greek chorus as this plays out....

"Well Professor Nunez, you see, I wasn't able to get any communication, and I didn't know if there was some serious problem down here, and rather than have Bolivia miss the deadline"....the background timpani quickens, then abruptly stops..... as Toshiro Mifune pauses in that last epochal moment before he plunges the dagger into his abdomen, committing an heroic ritual seppuku in "The 47 Ronin", "..you see, well, I forged your signature and sent this to the FIG so that Bolivia would be able to compete."

Which spaghetti Western is it where Clint Eastwood as "The Man With No Name" is being hanged, the horse is kicked out from under him and the rope snaps? Well, Sergio Leone has nothing on Jose Nunez Ruis! He sort of smiles, leans back in his chair as he slides the papers back into his briefcase, and with a slow nod, looks at me (warmly?) and says, "Yes, I thought it was probably something like that." And with that, he pops open the singani and pours me the first glass. Drinks all around. Are you kiddin' me? I LOVE this guy!!

Oh, now that I think of it, here's part of the story that I almost forgot....when Federations fill out their paperwork for the FIG, it is always "boilerplated" that only "members in good standing" are permitted to participate in FIG events. Well, way back in 1991, you know, the first time ever for both Bolivia and me, we'd been working on making this crazy dream of Bolivia participating at Worlds for 22 months. It's now 4 pm on Sept. 6, the day before the morning Ignacio is scheduled to compete; we've just finished training for the day and are walking out of the training hall which is closing. The Opening Ceremony is at 7 pm, and we've got to get cleaned up. Ignacio, of course, will be in the ceremony as Bolivia's flag-bearer in the traditional parade of countries. I've been dreaming of tomorrow for almost two years and we are approached by Norbert Bueche the FIG Director General, i.e. "Everything Ultimately Goes Through Me" guy....Mr. Bueche, who got to know me the year previously when I was Gymnastics Competition Director for Ted Turner's Goodwill Games in Seattle, comes up and says, "Mr. Holt, it seems we have a problem."

A 16-lb cannonball just dropped into the bottom of my stomach...anytime somebody approaches you and says that "we've got a problem", it means YOU have a problem, and in this case it means I probably have a seriously serious problem. "Oh?" I say summoning up as eloquent a response as I could muster. "Yes, we have a problem. Your gymnast will not be able to compete tomorrow."

"WHAAAAAAAAAAAAT????" ....my mind screams? I apparently remain conscious, and I ask aloud as calmly as I can, "ummm, and what specifically is the problem?"

"Your Federation has not paid it's membership dues for this year."

"It hasn't? I'm shocked, shocked to find that there is gambling in this place..." (this is no time for great movie lines, I need to move on...)

"Oh?"

"Yes", says Norbert, "and without the dues being paid and the Federation being in 'good standing', your athlete will not be allowed to compete."
"How much does Bolivia owe?"
"400 Swiss francs. It's equivalent to approximately 300 US dollars.
I have no choice. I can't swim.
Butch to Sundance:
"Hell, what's the difference...the fall will probably kill you anyway"...
I jump...."Ummm, could it be paid now?"
Oh yes, certainly"
Oh, that water's cold, but I'm alive....!!
"Would the FIG take a check"
"Yes."
Norbert's Swiss. He's a 'the rules must be adhered to' kind of guy, the watchmaker type, but he's at heart a really good guy....
Ok, now I'm the King of Siam and being taught by Anna how to waltz (or perhaps more accurately, the minuet).
Lead on, herr Bueche, I'll gladly follow in lockstep....
"Would the FIG take a personal check?"
He's now got a twinkle in his eye and is almost, but not quite yet smiling.
"Yes."
It's 10 past 4 on a Friday afternoon and who knows where a bank is....
"Would the FIG take an out of state check?"
"Yes."

I'm still not smiling, I'm still in shock from the impact of the opening salvo, and Ignacio's been standing there listening the whole time, holding his gym-bag which has my warmup jacket and wallet inside. I turn to him, and say, Iggy, could you please give me my wallet. One more question for Herr Bueche.
"Mr. Bueche," "call me Norbert" he interrupts..."Norbert...do you by any chance have a pen I could borrow."
"Why certainly," and with what I think was a flourish, he reaches into the inside of his suit jacket and promptly produces one.
I open my checkbook and write him, or rather the FIG a check for $300.00 dollars out of my account.
"Thank you very much. "Good luck tomorrow" He turns to Ignacio for the first time. "And good luck to you in your competition." With that, he turns and walks off towards his next task....I breathe a sigh, a very deep sigh of relief.
Is there a moral to this story?
Yeah, the Bolivian Gymnastics Federation still owes me THREE-HUNDRED BUCKS!

Leopard Hunting

Late in our first trip to Bolivia, we finished with a couple days of clinics in the eastern city of Santa Cruz. Tropical and modern, the economic center of the country, Santa Cruz has some very nice neighborhoods in a climate similar to that of Southern California. We were put up in a house of one of the Club 7 gymnast's parents. Pedro and Carmelita were wonderful hosts, and real fun-lovers. A dentist by trade, Sr. Pedro and his wife took us out for a night on the town which ultimately turned into several stops at various "watering-holes". He was driving a 4x4 Jeep caravan, and perhaps second only to Hannah's Indy 500 impersonation in Santiago a couple years earlier (see Chile chapter), I don't think I've ever been more frightened in a car…

IF I hadn't been so drunk, I would have been even more frightened…If he hadn't been so smashed, it might have been even moderately safe, but as it was, it was insane that we were in a motor vehicle at all. At one point, Pedro came up to a stop light, (it's about 3 am and we're one of the few cars on the road), the light turns green and he's so bombed we sit all the way through this long green light, completely still until it turns yellow, then red again…Carmelita from the back seat: "Honey, next time the light turns green, maybe you'll want to go through it." So, we're trying to (somehow without having a serious accident) get the vehicle (and ourselves) back to their house, when Dr. Pedro is seized with an inspiration. He turns onto another thoroughfare, and after about 5 minutes pulls up in front of his office. "There's something I need to get." He runs (or rather stumbles lurchingly) through the front door…a light comes on, a light goes off, and here he is back out, clambering into the jeep.

He hands me a…..a, I guess it's a hide or pelt of some kind. What the? "What is it?" I ask, turning it over in the dark…it appears like animal hide of some kind, but on this side mottled fur….

"It's a leopard hide. I want you to have it. I shot it when I was hunting in the eastern part of the country a couple years back. Next time you're down here in Bolivia, I want you to come hunting with me! We'll camp out, drink some singanyi, and shoot us some leopards."

I'm not a hunter. This guy is seriously drunk. But, ever the diplomat, I certainly don't want to offend him or hurt his feelings. "Ummm, ok, that really sounds great. Thank you!"

From the back seat: "You are NOT going LEOPARD HUNTING in Bolivia!" Yes dear.

"Agitate. Agitate. Agitate."
Frederick Douglass

Chapter Two

BACKGROUND AND METHODS

I'm a gymnastics person. I do gymnastics, I coach gymnastics, I've written about the sport, and I've been involved administratively and politically at every level to which I've had opportunity or access. I love the sport and while I don't necessarily idealize it, I hope to be involved with it for the next 50 years or so.

How'd I get started? The usual...I was too short for basketball, too small for football, and too uncoordinated to hit a baseball. Ever seen the little fat kid with the crew-cut and glasses in the Gary Larson "Far Side" Cartoons? Yup, that was me. Oh, and I was a terrible high school wrestler (my one varsity season: 0-8-1).

So, as is typical in the Darwinian world of sport, I eventually stumbled across the one thing I could actually do with some competence which was gymnastics.

Through lots of repetitions, I eventually became a decent specialist on the Rings. One great thing about Rings is that you don't have to have any talent; basically all you have to do is squeeze hard and hang there....so it was something I could manage to do at the high school, and a little bit later, the collegiate level. Naturally, like most physically untalented people, it turned out that the best way I could stay involved in the sport was by coaching or helping people better (much better) than me do things I wasn't coordinated, kinesthetically aware enough, or gutsy (Kovacs? Me? No way!!!!) enough to accomplish.

Academically, I was always interested in the social sciences. As indicated in the Forward, I have always had a great interest in history and culture, and have been a voracious reader from six years of age onwards. Being widely read is an ENORMOUS advantage when one travels, because one is likely to have pretty broad anecdotal information which can help connect with people in a country or region where one is traveling. In addition, if you've got a solid foundation, it's relatively easy to do an intensive short-term research on a given region or place (Lonely Planet guides are my favorite "orientation" materials).

I would be remiss in not referring "armchair travelers" to a special tome. Easily my all-time favorite travel book (several editions, latest one 2005) is Robert Young Pelton's "*The World's Most Dangerous Places*". It's in it's own unique way, well, perhaps the best complement to Erasmus' "*In Praise of Folly*".

The subject matter? Exactly what it says! (Oh, and by the way although I make no claims to ranking with Pelton, but it does seem that many of the places I've been have been at one time or other....on his list.)

Formative background:

I'm certain that the secret to my success, however modest it might be is to find a way, no matter how many times you get knocked down, to "keep getting up off the canvas."

As a youngster, school came very easy for me, so "achievement" in that arena meant very little emotionally. For whatever number of reasons, excelling at sport was something that was always very important to me; on of the proudest moments of my childhood was being one of only 2 10 year old boys (5th graders) to "make" the 5th-6th grade CEO Little League Baseball team. In retrospect, I'm sure that I was placed on the team by the coaches, not because of my ability (I wasn't in the top 2 of the 5th graders, but can reasonably surmise that I fit in the top 3rd, i.e. the top 33% in the class), but because the coaches could see my desire and perceived me as "inspirational" which I did not agree with at the time and never have in my athletic career, although I came to understand how other people would "read into me" their attitudes and perceptions. I rode the bench during the year, but was immensely proud that I was a member of the team! I appeared in two games: first, I was sent up as a pinch hitter against a really fast pitcher from St. Leo's and was petrified, not of his pitching, but of FAILING. He struck me out on 3 pitches, and I never swung the bat; to this day, as if it were 5 minutes ago, I can see that third strike coming right down the middle of the plate and I froze; I have tried very very hard since that day never to repeat that moment!

No matter what else, no matter what it costs, you have to have the courage and resolve to swing the bat!!! Ganbatte! Do not let your fears keep you from trying....SWING THE BAT...Live life big....SWING THE BAT!

Lesson #1: don't hold back...swing the bat...go for broke....better to reach for the stars and fail, than settle for anything less

The second and final game I was in, I can't recall whether I worked the pitcher for a walk (I think so) or was put in as a "pinch-runner (note: I'm certain that I didn't reach base as a result of my getting a hit!)...in any event, there were two out, and on a 3-1 count, I ran for second and ended up stealing the base!! When the coaches asked me why I went on that count, I told them that a. the long throw down was hard for kids of that age, and b. given my speed (lack thereof) and the two outs, plus the possibility of ball 4, that NO ONE would even dream that we would be stealing, so I did! I was quite proud of being able to maximize my skills by thinking strategically. Of course, at the age of 10 (no Heinrich Schliemann, I!), I had not yet heard of Homer, the Odyssey, or Odysseus, but if there is a (albeit-fictional) lodestar that guides my destiny, I'd like to think that "the man of many wiles" looks with approval at my doings here on earth….

Lesson #2: think strategically….plan ahead

The following year was, concomitantly, the occasion of one of my greatest humiliations; as a 6th grader, we had a new coach who didn't think I could be competitive. We had "tryouts"…for two days I stood around ignored….without ever getting a chance to swing the bat, go up to the plate once, or even go out into the field to catch balls, I was ignominiously "cut" along with poor John Wood, the worst athlete in the 6th grade; I will never forget the shame and humiliation that I had been rejected without ever getting a chance, and ESPECIALLY because of my expectations based on my participation the year before….reflecting upon this, I can state categorically, that the knot in my stomach and the flush of shame upon being cut can wash over me emotionally today at the almost same level of intensity just by recalling this incident…..I have always resolved, (after crying all the way home from that final, awful practice) that no matter what, I'd try to find a way to "keep gettin' up off the canvas."

Lesson #3: no matter what, NEVER give in......keep fighting, one never knows when the breakthrough will take place…never, NEVER capitulate.

A bit later in college…..

I studied political philosophy with a minor in Economics and African-American studies, at Washington State University. I was and remain fascinated by the breadth and complexity of social and political structures throughout the world's history as our species has struggled to accommodate one another in a mutually beneficial (or perhaps more accurately, tolerable) manner. With all humanity's terrible setbacks and missteps, one might argue coherently that things are better in the present time than at periods in the past. In any event, while it was not my original vision, the confluence of my love of sport, and interest in cultures and politics eventually found an outlet, the subject of which, more or less, are the efforts I've made to contribute to international development of gymnastics and as a result of which allowed me to experience some of the odd and (mostly) wonderful encounters described herein.

One of the most significant aspects of my collegiate experience was that of the development of our gymnastics program during my 4 years there. In the 5 years prior to my freshman year, the WSU Cougars had finished last in the Pac-10 (8 teams in those years) five times consecutively. Most of the time, they weren't even close to getting out of the basement, and were not taken seriously by most other teams. My freshman year, there were 10 freshman (8 on partial scholarships and two walk-ons, me and a pommel horse specialist named Ken Hovermale). The coach brought the freshman in 2 weeks ahead of the upper classmen, and by the time the "uppers" arrived on campus, we had already formed our little tight knit band, and basically, because we had all just come from reasonably successful high school programs, and were excited to be "Pac-10 athletes, we more or less ran most of the laid-back and oh so cool older athletes off, because, collectively, we weren't going to stand being for being "bad". Our goal that year was to not finish last in the Conference. We ended up with one of the youngest teams in school (and perhaps Pac-10) history. The roster consisted on one senior, one junior, a late junior transfer, one sophomore, and us 10 freshman.

The specifics are outside the scope of this book, but suffice to say, we escaped the basement that first year (beat Stanford), and moved up the "food chain" over the next few years, including surpassing the longtime national power University of Washington, our school's bitter rival my senior year. The year following my graduation, WSU finished 12th in the nation and produced All-Americans in the All-Around and Parallel Bars; subsequently my Israeli teammate Dubi Lufi qualified to and competed as Israel's first ever gymnast at the Olympic Games.

For those readers unfamiliar with US collegiate sports, Washington State University, while a fine research and well respected land-grant institution is (in Division One Athletics) geographically in the most remote outpost in the United States. The nearest metropolitan location (although folks from the Puget Sound area would challenge that definition of "metropolitan") is Spokane, which is 90 miles (150 kilometers) distant.

Recruiting top athletes, and generating revenue is an extraordinary challenge for WSU given that it's Conference peers include schools located in Seattle (2+ million people), San Francisco (4-5 million), Phoenix (2.5 million), Los Angeles (who knows?). In comparison, the population in the 50 mile radius of Seattle is 54 (FIFTY-FOUR!) times larger than the comparable area surrounding Pullman.

Bottom line? In order to succeed, however one defines success, WSU has to find a way to achieve its' objectives with access to fewer resources....It's clear at Wazzu that one needs to find a way to "do more with less".

In retrospect, my experience convinced me that if Washington State can be competitive in the Pac-10, if Wazzu can produce "Rose Bowl" teams (1998 and 2003!) , then there's no reason that Bolivia, Yemen, et.al. can't be significant players on the international scene.

Lesson #4: a lack of resources is no reason to limit your vision, nor should it be a roadblock to success!

In 1974 there were 155 men's collegiate gymnastics programs in the United States; today there are 19. Universities in order to balance budgets hit on the unhappy tactic of cutting teams.

During the late 1970s I was both training and acting as Assistant Coach at the University of Washington. I was increasingly concerned and unhappy about seeing programs eliminated and told myself that if anything like that ever happened to a program with which I was involved, I'd do anything to make sure it didn't happen.

While I was in Ohio competing a the National AAU Championships in May 1980, the Athletic Department at the UW cut gymnastics from the varsity sports programs. When I returned from the competition, I met with the gymnasts, and swore to them that somehow, some way, the program would continue. The first two years were extremely challenging At that time, I dealt with (among other things) loss of varsity status, and its myriad of implications, fought to retain a location on campus, fought a new women's coach actively campaigning to get rid of it, had to develop a funding program from scratch because there was no previously known precedent in any sport I had to develop a competitive schedule with other schools, fight the UW administration for the right to remain in the Pac-10 (absolutely necessary to the program's survival, and accomplished by actually dealing directly with the Conference Commissioner in defiance of Athletic and Rec Sports Department policy and wishes!), re-establish relations with a disheartened and skeptical alumni, find/develop alternative feeder programs because the high schools which had traditionally been the source were being eliminated by the same forces which had changed the face of the UW program, and actually find bodies at the UW capable of representing it in gymnastics because all the former gymnasts had transferred schools!

From a very early date, I had a clearly articulated list of long range goals, including reinstatement, and at the end of that first summer, an inventory of my assets (a very short list), the most pressing problems we needed to solve, and a game plan on how we were going to get it done.. The very first steps were to develop a training program, ensure we had a place on campus to work out, and most importantly from the standpoint of a tangible payoff which would give other people a reason to participate in this crazy quest (by "conventional" standards) get the team to the 1981 Pac-10 Conference Championships. To accomplish that immediate and specific objective, we got a van donated from the father of one of the guys on the team (didn't have any funding that first year) packed 10 gymnasts, peanut butter, sleeping bags, and schoolbooks and drove 1583 miles and 29 1/2 straight hours from Seattle to Tempe Arizona; when we got to Tempe, it was 2 am, we had no hotel reservations (no money) and my mind had been racing for most of the entire trip regarding possible accommodations. I told the driver to head down frat row because I was "looking for the frat that had agreed to house us" at a quiet spot on a quiet street…I stopped the van, gambled that the frat door was unlocked, quietly got my team bedded down in the living room (couches and floor). We got a few hours sleep and I managed to get the team up, dressed, and out of there before any of the frat boys figured out what was going on. The team didn't find out until two years later the real story of that trip?!!!

The result? We finished a proud last at the 1981 Pac-10s, and began building for the future. (No one liked finishing last, but there was pride in the program's survival.

After a lengthy, almost decade long process to achieve true stability the Men's program continued to compete a full Pac-10 D-1 schedule against fully-funded teams. In 1985 Washington qualified a gymnast to the US Championships, in 1987 recruited an athlete who had competed at Pan-Am Games, in 1990 got first conference win in a decade (against Cal), and had USA National team members by the early 1990s. The specific events and strategies that enabled the program to re-invent itself outside of Athletic Department support and gridiron football subsidies are not important. What was essential in my formulation of a strategic plan of program building was the invaluable experience of as UW Hall of Fame Head Coach Eric Hughes once put it: "fighting a tank armed with a toothpick".

The experience ultimately, was wonderful training for working internationally to create long-term goals and build program structures with e-x-t-r-e-m-e-l-y limited resources.

In 2009, the University of Washington still has a men's gymnastics program.

Lesson #5: "Institutional" resistance is no reason for abandoning one's quest.

International Perspective-Formative

In significant measure my cosmopolitan inclinations are a result, of my early experiences. I was a child during the hey-day of the American Civil Rights movement and as a young boy, it seemed inconceivable to me that a country where everybody is supposed to be treated equal would discriminate against some of its' citizens. I think in large part due to my voracious reading habit formed early on in childhood, I've always had a fairly broad international perspective.

In addition, I had an experience during my secondary school years which profoundly affected me. The "Odd Fellows" (meaning political and religious dissidents) is a fraternal organization dating from the mid-19th century that has chapters throughout the US, England, and Canada (and I believe also has chapters scattered around Europe).

The Odd Fellows developed a working relationship with United Nations shortly after its' formation to establish and implement a cultural and educational program for high school students. Chapters from all over the world sponsor a student contest in each chapter city, and award the winner a trip to the United Nations in New York City. The students spend the daytime at the United Nations learning about the organization, participating in educational and group seminars, and spending the other parts of the day experiencing the wonders of the "Big Apple".

The summer after my junior year, I was the representative from Lincoln High School, and as part of the citywide contest, the candidates from the various Tacoma high schools were interviewed and questioned about various aspects of the United Nations. I remember being asked about Palestine being allowed to be a UN member, and I mentioned the challenge of sovereignty where two governments claimed the same space, but stated strongly that they should not be allowed entry due to Yassar Arafat coming into the UN armed with a pistol…in any event, the issue was not the specifics I guess of policy, but rather someone's interest and knowledge of the issues…I was awarded the trip!

So, the summer between my Junior and Senior years, I and 31 other kids (16 from Washington state, 8 from British Columbia, and 8 from Alberta) spent 24 days traveling by bus, first the length of Canada (from Vancouver to Montreal) which took about a week, then, south, and a week in New York at the United Nations, a couple days in Washington DC (where they made us wear jackets and ties in the middle of 35+ degree Celsius summer!!), and finally, west, across the entire US to end up back in Washington State.

The Odd Fellows pilgrimage is kind of a big deal…the Odd Fellows (I'm not a member nor was anybody in my family) have a LOT of chapters from all over and they have like 9 or 10 weeks where something like 200+ kids a week are at the UN…my week, there were over 200 others from all over the US; by coincidence, our group was the only one with any foreigners (even if "foreign" only meant Canadian)

While at the UN, we spent the evenings sightseeing around New York (my first time in that magical city!), and spent most of the daytime hours at the UN, engaged in various seminars, the majority of which evolved around a combination of UN activities, history, programs, and of course diplomacy and foreign policy (especially of the US's policies given that we were in New York and that the very large majority (everybody except the 16 Canadians on our bus) were Americans…. naturally during the course of our cross-continental bus ride across the breadth of the North American continent, several of the Canadians and I became fast friends….and, while in New York gravitated towards the same seminars (no, I don't recall whether that was because we were assigned as a group, or whether "birds of a feather flock together"….).

Since we were at many of the same seminars, and in a broad sense shared the same liberal perspective, one might imagine that our contributions to the various discussions tended to be relatively pointed(read: critical) regarding US activity around the world….well, it seems that these perspectives were not particularly well received by many who were members of other student groups there at the UN, and in fact, there developed a rather open resentment of the "stuck up, arrogant Canadian guys (including me of course)" who had the temerity to criticize the US government and hold up to ridicule (although we weren't aware nor was it our intent to do so!) American values and the American way of life..(at least as it was in the late 1960s). Somehow I got wind of this talk (all of which took place, naturally, "behind our backs"……

. Part of the organizational protocol at the UN, was a full-group (all 240 of us) meeting after breakfast at the hotel each morning in which the organizers would briefly review the previous day's activities, outline the schedule for the upcoming day, and ask for questions…….of which there were usually none…until the day after I had heard about this "talk" about "us" unpleasant Canadians…when the director asked if anyone had any questions, I stood up and said (paraphrasing): "I don't have any questions, but I definitely have a comment. I understand that there are individuals here that have been criticizing me and the other Canadians. For the record, I'm American, not Canadian, but that's not at all important. What is important is that this is the United Nations and I thought the whole point of being here is to experience the world of ideas and to be open to divergent points of view. It disappoints me that there are persons participating in this great conference that either don't agree with or don't understand that perspective….now for the record, I think the USA is the number one country in the world…. The idea of America is openness, tolerance, and above all the right to think, say, and do as you please. Now, America is number one, but I think Canada is a pretty great number 2 ….if you don't agree, then I suggest a little bit of introspection on your part."

I sat down…….and cripes, to my utter shock, most of the room stood up and clapped….and the director responded with something like: "This young man has put it very well….now let's remember why we're here and what the UN represents."

Un-be-lee-vable………

And further, totally unexpected and I was "floored" as the slang goes, at the end of the meeting, we all got up and started to leave, and all the Canadians are standing in a group, and come towards me and the guys are shaking my hand, and the girls are hugging (and in a few <very few unfortunately!> cases kissing me)........man, I haven't thought about that for quite awhile, but it really was an amazing moment that I most certainly didn't expect ....

In retrospect, even though I had significantly internationalist tendencies before the trip, the overall experience, and that particular "sharing of Canadian identity" during our time at the UN in some significant sense was a formative experience in the development of my "world view"

2. International perspective-philosophical background

The notion of persons identifying themselves primarily as being from one nation or another strikes me as somewhat absurd. I'm not simply a product of the United States, but am a citizen of the world. I'm a product of Western Culture am proud of and believe in it's traditions, values and history.

My world and social view have been strongly shaped by the entire arc of that history...I've been inspired by and passionate to learn as much as I can about the ascendency of Ancient Greece, its' contribution of rationalism, its' human-centric perspective, and its' wondrous artistic portrayals of men and women as they "might and ought to be". The epic works of Homer, Hesiod, Aeschelus, Euripedes, Aristophanes, and others uplift me. The development of philosophy and intellectual thought from Thales, Pythagoras, Herodotus, Thucydedes, Aristtotle et. al fill me with a profound admiration.

Middle East

It is a source of amazement that so many people have virtually no knowledge of the history of intellectual thought and the transmutation of Greek Culture into Europe. It seems to me an almost unfathomable void for persons interested in virtually any aspect of modern life. It is particularly stunning to me that in contemporary times, with a "trumped-up" conflict seemingly existing between the West and Islam, that 'mainstream' commentators either ignore or are oblivious to the fact that there would BE NO Western Culture as we know it without the astonishing contributions of al-Farabi, al-Kindi, Ibn-Sina, Ibn-Rusd, Ibn-Khuldun and the other giants of the Islamic Golden Age which not only translated the Greek into Arabic, but built upon Greek thought and tradition. It was in fact the Muslims who made possible the reintroduction of Greek thought in the European Middle Ages which profoundly influenced the re-birth of rationalism and independent inquiry in Europe (see: Albert the Great, Peter Lombard, Thomas Aquinas).

It distresses me to see Western commentators either infer or directly accuse Islam of its' backwardness or primitiveness (with respect to it's conservative cultural values or its "anti-democratic" political orientation).In reality, the Islamic world is having extraordinarily interesting internal discourses as it struggles with adapting and adjusting the values and mores of its religion and culture to modernity. In perspective, it was only 400 years ago that Giordano

Bruno was burned at the stake, and that the European "West" was undergoing the same kinds of metamorphoses that Islam confronts in the 21st century. We are kindred peoples and spirits, albeit, culturally, a bit out of synch with respect to timeline.

Latin America

Unless one digs below the surface and looks to origins (and the long-view), the cultural and economic developments of the Latin American peoples can be easily oversimplified and misunderstood. It is difficult for outsiders, particularly North Americans who generally assume that because we're all "Americans" and that the timelines of development are so close together, how pernicious and harmful the Spanish occupation of South America was to its' indigenous peoples(see Chilean chapter). While the Native Americans of North America are justified in claiming their ways of life were changed forever and that their cultures were damaged beyond repair, the combination of a almost virtually medieval Spanish court controlling a continent combined with the repressive tendencies of an Inquisition era Church, the development of political and social rights in South America has long-lagged the North.

Africa

In Africa, without understanding that most of the continent's nation-states are only (or less) than half a century old, and noting that that those countries were drawn on maps in a broadly arbitrarily fashion by the departing colonial powers(see "Nigeria" chapter), it is impossible to grasp many of the challenges and issues facing the peoples of the continent. Further, recognition of the very strong and ancient tribal identities is essential for understanding some of the root causes of problems. We'll discuss this in more detail later in the book, but it understand that "Africa" is many different "Africas"...Africa is BIG...there are 52 nation states, and within those countries, there are a thousand and more tribes, each with their own histories, traditions, and, yes, conflicts and grievances amongst each other. (see Zimbabwe chapter for specific discussion).

3. International perspective-philosophical values

I'm a byproduct intellectually of the Age of Enlightenment, and live in a post-modern world of doubt. My primary socio-political influences stem from the works of such thinkers as Hugo Grotius's concepts of Natural Law, John Locke's (1688) attack on the "Divine Right of Kings", and the Founders of the American Revolution, in particular, Thomas Jefferson, Patrick Henry, and Thomas Paine. I am convinced that the greatest socio-political statement ever written is simply:

We hold these truths to be self-evident, that all men are created equal, that they are endowed by their Creator with certain unalienable Rights, that among these are Life, Liberty and the pursuit of Happiness.

And that, without getting too philosophical, technical, or even wordy (difficult as that might be for the reader to believe I'm capable!) is what I try to communicate through the vehicle of gymnastics.

What Jefferson is saying in the American Declaration of Independence from England is that each person has "unalienable" ,meaning they can't be touched, they can't be altered, they can' be taken away...not by you, me, governments, public opinion, religion, or anybody. ALL persons have the right to live the kind of life they want, to pursue their goals in the way they perceive best, to strive for and ATTAIN happiness. Dream your dreams, take risk, go for it! What the hell, why CAN'T Yemen go to the World Championships and Olympic Games in gymnastics?

The reader should note that mankind collectively has progressed (my word) from a tribal, to city-state, to feudal, to regional, and in the last 3-400 years national identity….as recently as 1865 in the United States, people were arguing the primacy of "states rights" over the one that has prevailed, National identity. Ultimately, while "nationality" has arguably been the foremost "identity" in the 19th and 20th centuries, in the long-view whatever the ultimate position (or disposition) of nation-states, it appears that we will ultimately be global and interconnected. That's in part how I view my work in gymnastics.

In my international coaching and consulting capacity, I champion the cause (without stating it explicitly) of self-determination, self-actualization, and individual achievement. As absurd as it might seem to use international sport as a vehicle, it is nevertheless a venue in which I thrive, and for whatever the reasons and circumstances, have utilized as an opportunity to advance my ideas, help the people with whom I interact, and also have a whole lot of crazy fun….

Working in international sport is incredibly frustrating, unless one has the proper political connections, not particularly remunerative, and ALWAYS a friggin' BLAST!!!!

For the record (and with apologies to Lysander Spooner): I believe in and am an advocate for:

1. Liberty:

people have the right to run their own lives according to their own dictates, in their own times, according to their own judgments…..everybody else, stay out….

2. Self-determination:

don't let your parents, your teachers, your government or anybody else decide what you should want to do, or do! "dream an impossible dream….then go chase it!" While we all (or the least deluded of us) understand that not ALL dreams come true, I try to share with people the notion of believing that dreams are possible and that they can happen in reality.

3. Egalitarianism

I'm in favor of Egalitarianism, but temper that with a respect for and desire to have a merit-based identities based on objective results…..in all of Olympic/international world sport, it troubles/pisses me off that the institutions charged with administering the various activities invariably refer to themselves as "the national <or international> "governing" bodies….no word, no thought pertaining to "service" or "stewardship", just govern and rule….

4. I'm an strong proponent of **Skepticism**. I am methodologically distrustful of "belief" without the evidence to back it up, I do not believe in holding my opinion, ideas, or destiny to a "higher power"…

5.i'm an advocate of **Secularism**, and take objection to the notion that we need to find a way to mitigate the difference between belief and skepticism.

I'm philosophically opposed to (no wonder the FIG and USAG are perhaps nervous about me):

1. Authority:

…"hey pal, who the hell decided that you knew more, or were more qualified to decide what's best for me (or for the Federation) than me.?"

2.Hierarchy:

…a system based on a descending order of well, orders….a system based on an ascending series of capitulation of judgment

3. Centralization

I'm opposed to authoritarianism and centralization of authority. I believe that the best social structures are decentralized. I'm suspicious of "certainty" without (is there ever any?) rigorous and air-tight evidence….

4. Bureauracy:

the execution of hierarchy as described above….I don't like it (see Goodwill Games experience, among others)

5. Tradition:

….now, that said, I am in no way opposed to a knowledge of, respect for, and love of history….Newton said (somewhat self-promotionally) " I stand on the shoulders of giants"…whether this is true in sport or not can be debated, but…

as I wrote in another context, "we owe our progenitors and posterity the best within us." My criticism here is not a lack of admiration for previous achievements, but the unquestioned valuation of the past because "it's the way things have always been done."

"Gee Jim, then why did you get involved with something as 'regulated' international sport?"

I have a vision of what's possible, a strategy on how to do it, and tactics which sometimes apparently fall afoul of the powers that be (in the FIG) given the present structure of sport.....Maybe I got involved because I'm an idiot, or a dreamer, or a Quixotic delusionist.....bottom line, I love the gymnastics, and I'll be damned if I'm going to give it up to the either limited-imagination apologists who uphold the status-quo in order to keep their (ultimately nominal and silly) "authoritarian" positions, or to defend their small (actually tiny/trivial in the "big picture" scheme of things) positions...

A well known women's gymnastics figure derisively refers to these people as "FIGlets". By that dismissive term, she refers to people who somehow have been elected to the volunteer positions in the International Governing body, and soon morph into these pompous, entitled figures who act as if their judgment is better than everyone else....sort of like the US Congress come to think of it....

People can make informed decisions pertaining to their own lives when working in the developing world. We shall encounter in the chapters to come the historical and philosophical influences which have resulted in "a/the Culture of Limitation". In almost every part of the world, individuals are socialized from the earliest age to defer (and ultimately capitulate) to "authority" to the notion (usually unstated and often unconscious) that somebody else knows better than you and (always unstated) can define the parameters of one's activities and establish both objectives and limits. I reject this categorically, and utilize sport as a means of both implicit refutation, and I work to show that sport can be a vehicle by which individuals that they can liberate themselves from this pernicious doctrine....Some specific examples and case histories will be discussed throughout the various chapters of this book.

4. Tactics

Slight digression: relatively early on in my coaching career, I got involved in the administrative aspect of the sport by volunteering to be State Director, which is an unpaid position between the US National Office, and the clubs and coaches in the state. I was very involved in trying to grow gymnastics within the boundaries of Washington, and at one point was (although I didn't perceive it that way) hectoring the other coaches and club owners in a way that wasn't particularly productive. I got a phone call from the then Regional Director, Hideo Mizoguchi, who in essence called me on the carpet and told me to "cease and desist". He basically informed me that I didn't know what the heck I was doing, and that if I really cared about making things work, I'd come down to Eugene Oregon and spend a weekend with him. I think he was surprised when I said ok. It was probably the most important "road trip" I ever took.

Over cornflakes one morning, he got to the main point. "Jim, you're intelligent, but your not acting very intelligently. These are good people you're working with and they really care about the sport and about kids. But, for the most part, they don't have your experience or your ability to envision things in the long-term. They don't understand you or where you're coming from, and if you can't find a way to communicate, they won't listen, and they certainly won't follow." He then hit me right between the eyes with something I"ve used since that day....Mizo said: "Jim, if you want people to follow you, you have to tell them as often as you can find reasons to do so, that *you need them, you LIKE them, and that they're doing a good job!"*

I've never been hit by lightning, nor knocked off a horse, but St. Paul couldn't have been struck more impressively than the way those few words knocked some serious sense into me!

One aspect of 'national identity' that I find fascinating is the generally unconscious impact of geography, and in particular, landmass in one's national "orientation. To a citizen of the Netherlands (as an example), the subconscious notion of "country" is one mirroring "The Netherlands". In contrast, to an American, the total landmass of Holland is a little more than half the size of the state of West Virginia which is the 41st largest state in the USA. It felt a little strange for Hannah and me, the first time we drovc across the Netherlands, to think we could get through an entire country in a few short hours!

If one has not been to the United States, it's difficult to understand how "big" relative to most of the rest of the countries in the world the USA is.

Whenever I have an opportunity to engage in a conversation with someone from a foreign country, I try to learn about their perceptions of the United States. Our different geographies and histories have shaped in significant part our different values and perceptions. My job is to find common ground in order to facilitate communication and interaction.

"So have you been to America?" If the answer is yes, then the conversation will flow organically from there..."Where?" and so forth. In my experience working in Development, the vast majority of people will not have been to the USA.

Therefore, my question after "No, I haven't" is "What do you know about America, or what do you think about America?"

Wherever I go in the world, I hear the same three things, and I hear them in the same order, almost every time: people always tell me that:

Americans are arrogant.

America is a violent place

Americans know how to get things done.

I love to discuss the above views and engage in discussion....

1. Americans are arrogant.

"You know, you're right. Americans can be arrogant, but not in the way you think. If you mean you've encountered Americans traveling in your country who seem to act arrogant, it's possible that they are, but have you ever considered the fact that they just may not be aware of how to best behave because they don't know your country's culture? America is a really big country, and most Americans don't often travel abroad. And the issue with languages? Well, somebody living in Iowa has to travel 12-1300 kilometers to get to the nearest foreign country...and then has to speak Canadian.

The reality is that what is perceived as American arrogance (I say) is a confidence or pride based on for example our "national myths". If you'd been to America, you could experience this notion of a melting pot. You know, it's always been interesting to me that the Japanese, for instance, think that their ethnic homogeneity is one of their greatest national strengths and that, in the US, the belief is exactly the opposite...not about Japan, but that America's greatest strength is it's heterogeneity and diversity. Moreover, Americans are keenly aware and frankly, proud of the fact that throughout it's history, the people who came to America from across the seas were not the wealthiest, most highly positioned, or privileged. Mostly, America is comprised of the dispossessed.....our Statue of Liberty calls out to the world, with the words inscribed upon her base:

> *Give me your tired, your poor, your huddled masses yearning to breathe free, The wretched refuse of your teeming shore, send these, the homeless, the tempest tossed to me....*

I try to explain that Americans don't feel "superior", but rather that their homeland at its best represents a beacon of hope for the whole world, and that they have pride in that.

2. America is a violent place

"Yes, America is a violent place, but not in the way you think, nor for the reasons you probably think it. Life in America is NOT like you see in the movies. We've got problems, but it's not cops and bad guys spraying bullets all over America's city streets day in and day out. Let me say that Americans have a lot of guns...but there's an historical reason for it. Remember, that America was founded by a revolution. It had to pry itself away from the British Empire through force of arms. The second Amendment of the American Constitution recognizes the right of it's citizens "to keep and bear arms". Now as odd as this might sound (to the rest of the world), at least try to understand that this comes from a suspicion of governmental power and expressly recognizes the right of the people to resist (and overthrow) oppression. I don't ask you to agree, but at least to try and understand. Now there's a little bit more about this I want to communicate. In most places in the world I travel, I see houses surrounded by high brick walls, often with broken bottles strewn across the top; now I know there are courtyards inside, it's an architectural convention in many places, but to an American, it can look kind of threatening. In most of the United States, houses don't have fences or walls around them...they have a lawn of grass. From the sidewalk, you can walk directly up to the front door...oh by the way, the windows don't have any bars on them, they're just windows...anyway, in most of America, unlike many other parts of the world, you just walk up to the front door and knock, and then go in....it can be violent yes, but not in the way that you think.

3. Americans know how to get things done.

I agree, but it is NOT because America is a wealthy country with lots of resources or that all Americans are rich because they're not. It's a mind-set...maybe an unsophisticated mind-set, but Americans know how to get things done because they believe things are possible. Let me give you an example...everybody knows and admires John F. Kennedy right? Well, in the late 1950's when the Cold War with the Soviet Union was at it's height, you may know the history, the Soviet's launched the satellite Sputnik into space. And everyone in America went crazy, because now the Soviets were ahead of us technologically, and might be able to put nuclear rockets up there, and all kinds of crazy paranoia...and the US responded by ramping up its' technological research and development departments, heavily pushing math and the sciences in school...so just about the time that the whole thing started to settle down, the Soviets put a dog into space, and the US went nuts again....and about a year after that, the Russians sent Yuri Gagarin, a MAN into space who actually ORBITED the earth....Americans were besides themselves, worrying about how this was possible and how was it that we were ever going to catch up.

Well, in May of 1962, this whole thing was thought so serious in the USA that President Kennedy went on live national television to deliver a speech on the state of the "Space Race"....his speechwriters had written, "we will send a man to the moon and return him safely to the earth sometime in the future." JFK, without telling anyone, looked straight into the camera and announced to the American people, "The United States of America will send a man to the moon and return him safely to the earth sometime in this decade." Everybody at NASA (the Space agency) just about had a heart attack! The clock was ticking and the gun pointed straight at their collective heads...they had 8 ½ years left to pull this thing off!! And on July 20th, 1969 Neil Armstrong stepped onto the surface of the moon.

The point of this story is that Kennedy put the United States out onto the proverbial branch of a tree and then proceeded to saw the limb off. ***The only option* (from his American perspective*) was success.***

It's important to share with people that "Americans are crazy." And if you're willing to be crazy, you can get things done too...it's an **adapted** mindset, it's NOT genetic.

3a. "Americans know how to get things done....redux....

The one other example I enjoy bringing up and describing comes from the 1982 film, "*Star Trek: Wrath of Khan*". In Star Fleet Academy, the Kobiyashi Maru exercise is a test with a "no-win situation." In the history of the Academy, the only midshipman that ever 'beat' the test is our hero, James T. Kirk. (note: Trekkies might point out that coincidentally, our fictional 23rd century hero Kirk was born in…Iowa.)

> Spock: The Kobayashi Maru scenario frequently wreaks havoc on students and equipment. As I recall you took the test three times yourself. Your final solution was, shall we say, unique?
> Kirk: It had the virtue of never having been tried.
> Lt. Saavik: Admiral, may I ask you a question?
> Kirk: What's on your mind, Lieutenant?
> Saavik: The Kobayashi Maru, sir.
> Kirk: Are you asking me if we're playing out that scenario now?
> Saavik: On the test, sir. Will you tell me what you did? I would really like to know.
> McCoy: Lieutenant, you are looking at the only Starfleet cadet who ever beat the no-win scenario.
> Saavik: How?
> Kirk: I reprogrammed the simulation so it was possible to rescue the ship.
> Saavik: What?
> David Marcus: He cheated.
> Kirk: I changed the conditions of the test. I got a commendation for original thinking. I don't like to lose.
> Saavik: Then you never faced that situation. Faced death.
> Kirk: I don't believe in the no-win scenario.

Now the point of these stories is three-fold.

First:

I wish to establish a connection with people, and do so in a way that creates a give and take, and an open-mindedness about each other's point of view.

Second:
I want to provide a sense of perspective, particularly about where I come from, and how it relates to how I think and act.
Third:
Because I am not comparing or judging, but sharing what I passionately believe to be possible, I'm attempting to empower them (without saying it directly, which can come across as judgmental and preachy) to believe that these ways of looking at the world can be theirs too. There are no guarantees in life, and success certainly isn't certain, but the belief in success is essential in making it possible to succeed.

The most important thing I can share with the world is to plant seeds and whenever possible, nurture them so they might flourish. In the words of Mikhael Bakunin (in a slightly different context), "I shall continue to be an impossible person as long as those who are now possible, remain possible!"

I've had many more projects fail than have succeeded (see "disappointments" chapter), but I think/hope I've made some difference (however modest) in the areas in which I've striven to be involved….

My approach can be reduced to a couple of well-worn clichés…

First, "dream big", and be specific.

Second, and ultimately, I'm convinced that the secret to "success", however one defines it is to "keep getting up off the canvas"…

"Risk! Risk anything! Care no more for the opinion of others, for those voices....So be the hardest thing on earth for yourself. Face the truth."
Katherine Mansfield

Chapter Three

CHILE

Chileans are arguably the proudest and most individualistic people in all of South America. They brag that they were the last to be defeated by the Spanish Empire (true, but whether it's a measure of the geography –the westernmost part of the continent being attacked by invaders from the east), or their fierce resistance to outsiders is a matter outside the scope of this narrative. Certainly the (apocryphal?) story of the Chilean tribal king, who, in conflict with the Spanish was captured and to make an example of him in front of his countrymen had has hands chopped off and returned to his people....whereupon his Queen-wife strapped daggers to his stumps and sent him back into battle as an example of resistance to the invaders fires the Chilean imagination of their history and heritage. In addition, the achievements of Bernardo O'Higgins, and the fact of Chilean independence almost a full decade before the victories of Simon Bolivar are permanent sources of Chilean pride in the same vein as the national myths (they might be true, but they are stories pertaining to the national mythology nevertheless) of the United States. No doubt about it, the Chileans are a fiercely proud and independent people!

I have had numerous lengthy discussions with South American colleagues over the years regarding both the commonalities and differences between our historical and cultural experiences. My South American friends to a man (person!) always complain about citizens of the USA referring to ourselves as "Americans". In South America it is a point of honor (and contention when speaking to a Yank) that they are Americans as well. "How come you people think of and call yourselves the real Americans. We're American too!"

It is helpful in understanding and making effective communication with our neighbors to the South to compare and contrast the colonial experience of North America (colonized by the English and to a lesser extent French), with the Spanish conquest of South America. The verbs are consciously chosen. There are 3 significant and fundamental differences between the historical experiences of the 2 Americas. While it is true, that the North American colonists subjugated the indigenous peoples, they did not enslave them. In Bolivia, for example, for centuries, the Aymarans and Chechuan Indians were taken by the Spanish and basically enslaved in the silver mines of Potosi. So much silver was extracted from the ground over the 16th, 17th, and 18th centuries, that it is said that it would have been possible to build a road 3 meters wide from Potosi to Madrid. Again, the North American Indian peoples were treated abominably, but on a relative scale, they were not systematically brutalized and exploited in near the manner of the South American experience.

Readers should note that in addition to the difference in cultures between the Spanish in the South and the English/French in the North that South America was colonized over a century before there were serious European inroads into the North.

A second significant difference in the experiences of colonization is that the political evolution of Spain lagged far behind most of the rest of Western Europe, and in particular the English and French. While both of those countries were profoundly changed by the evolution of individual political rights based (however tentatively) on the concept of Natural Laws governing the universe, Spain clung to it's conservative monarchy. While there are extraordinary artists and other cultural figures that have come from Spain, it wasn't until perhaps Frederica Montesey or Benueventura Durruti in the 20th century that Spain had any political theorists of note. England? Hobbes, Hume, Burke, Berkeley Locke, Winstanley, Gibbon, Smith, Bentham, Mill, Huxley… France: Descartes Bayle, Montaigne, Diderot, Voltaire, Rousseau, Proudhon, Fourier…the lists in those two countries is virtually without end….Spain simply has nothing comparable. Ergo, the political foments that transformed England, France, and the concomitant histories of their colonies, were not felt in Spanish dominated South America.

The third and intimately related factor that distinguishes the Southern American colonial history is the role of the Catholic Church contrasted with its relative absence and complete lack of influence in the North. I've long joked that the two most conservative organizations on earth are the Catholic Church and the International Gymnastics Federation." Catholicism, especially Spanish catholicism was/is profoundly conservative. The cultural mores and limitations served the interests of the State and despite the gradual independence movements by the various nation-states of the Southern Hemisphere, the cultural diversity and individual freedom of choice were much ameliorated by the hegemony of the Church. The Church that the peoples of South America experienced during its' formative centuries was that of Torquemada NOT John XXIII.

On a certain level, it doesn't matter if somebody in Chile or Bolivia is unfamiliar with the history and values of my culture ….what really matters, and I believe is, my unique selling proposition, is that I am able to translate my values and attitudes into a , well, formula is too pat, too mechanistic a word, but I'm able to share my views through the "other's" filter….. example: in Bolivia, I use Simon Bolivar to explain independence and resourcefulness….this is an extremely crude and simplistic example, but used consistently, imaginatively, and flexibly, it creates a bridge of understanding, common ground, and gives me a certain "street cred" wherever I am; it's been the underlying foundation to whatever I've managed to contribute to international development.

Luis Salizar

is one of the most intriguing and interesting people that I have encountered in my sporting travels. Luis hails from the small resort town of La Serena, and has through two decades of effort, been instrumental in transforming Chile from a invisible gymnastics backwater into a country that regularly places in the South American results, and in the 21st century has sent full teams of both men and women to the world championships.

Luis, who announced his "retirement" from the Chilean national scene in 2007 is mid-60ish (who knows for sure?) in age. He is short (5'4'?), paunchy, balding, with a wispy sort of beard. His background is shrouded/clouded in mystery…. As a young man, he was very active in Socialist political causes, and was a strong supporter of Salvadore Allende in the elections of the early 70s. When Allende was deposed in a military coup by Augusto Pinochet in 1973, Salizar, along with so many Allendenistas were forced to leave the country under potential penalty of death. Luis spent almost 2 decades as a political refugee in Fidel Castro's Cuba, where he attained the background and knowledge to become a gymnastics coach of high level.

One of the more interesting (and intense) meetings that I've ever had the opportunity in which to be involved revolved around Luis's first trip to the United States; I had a gymnastics school at the time, he was training two girls to compete at the Worlds (it turned out that they did not), and at a time when Chile was transitioning from the Pinochet regime to the democratic (this is early 1990s) President Lago administration, in Seattle, the Chilean Consul was a gentleman by the name of Kerry Monterey….Sr Monterey was an appointee of the Pinochet regime and actually resembled the late General, a tall, patrician man with an impeccable brown, pin striped suit, gray tie, and late 60ish sandy gray hair….I don't recall the precise reason for Luis needing to speak with him, but nevertheless, we dutifully trudged into his office in downtown Seattle. My Spanish at the time was in the nascent stages, so it was with difficulty that I followed the dialog, but the undercurrent of tension and enmity was v-e-r-y clear. Sr. Monterey apparently had a dossier on Luis (I had no idea I had fallen in with such "a disreputable character"!)….Luis in turn, could barely conceal his loathing....when our interview was at an end, we entered the elevator, Luis was almost shaking from what I perceived might be tension and what I subsequently concluded might well be anger....when we got the ground floor, Luis stepped smartly out of the elevator, walked rapidly down the hallway towards the front door of the office building, and 3 steps after pushing through the revolving door, spit a large gob of saliva onto the sidewalk...."Criminal....el homre es el criminal."

Luis ran the gym school "Escuela Gimnasia de Chile" in La Serena for many years. A former President of the Chilean Federation, he was responsible, after Marcelo Toledo's initial foray into international gymnastics for Chile regularly (in 1987) and thereafter, joining the international community and competing at the World Championships. After his 6-week stay in th USA where he picked up a respectable level of English proficiency in a very short time, he pioneered the development of preschool apparatus in the Southern Hemisphere, was the driving force behind the organization of the First World Club Championships (more below), and in essence, forced Chile to be heavily involved at the international level. Luis is a rascal, a troublemaker, a great friend, and an important figure in the history of South American Gymnastics.

Estadio Nacionale

As I have previously alluded, there are few better conversation "ice-breakers" (especially among men) than soccer....find a Bulgarian anywhere in the world, and ask him, "Hey, who was that tall guy with the dark hair who scored that header in the come-from-behind win against Germany in the quarterfinals of the 1994 World Cup?" (even if you know the answer) and the Bulgarian (ANY Bulgarian) will instantly recall and respond, "Lechkov in the 78th minute, just after Hrisko Stoikov rattled the net (not necessarily the word they will use) to tie the match!"

I of course, presumed the same was true of Chile....we had been picked up (late) from the airport, and were driving into Santiago....members of the welcoming group (and Luis as the then President) were sitting with us in the car...we went past the grounds of Colo Colo, arguably the premier team in Chile, and a little bit later passed, as one of the committee members identified it to me "That's our National Stadium." I looked at the outside walls as our vehicle swung past, and asked, "would it be possible to stop and go check it out?" Well, that apparently was no problem, and shortly later on a beautiful mid summer (late January) day, the 6 of us were wandering around the perimeter, and subsequently through a tunnel and into one of the sections of the stadium...a typical bowl, seating oh, I'd guess 80,000. I turned to one of the members of our group and said, "Brazil 3, Czechoslovakia 1." "Pardon me?" in response. I repeated myself "Brazil 3, Czechoslovakia 1." "What's that?" was the reply....the other members of our small group were now looking at me. I smiled…"Surely you recall the score of the World Cup Final. Brazil 3, Czechoslovakia 1." More looks….I said, "As I recall, Brazil, led by the great Garrincha because Pele was injured due to a consistent program of fouling by their opponents, beat the Czechs in the 1962 World Cup Final IN THIS VERY STADIUM. Doesn't anybody remember that?" I finished with a straight face. Well, our Chilean friends, a bit abashedly admitted, no, they hadn't recalled that particular bit of their sporting history at the moment apparently thinking my comments, somewhat out of context (although I'll be darned to figure out how it could possibly be "out of context in the very venue in which it took place!!!!!?), but yes, that event had happened and by the way…how is it possible that a gringo, an American from a place that had no history of soccer and no appreciation of soccer could POSSIBLY know that?

Rings/scaffolding

When we entered Luis's facility for the first time, I was nonplussed to say the least…they had the rudiments of a pit, but nothing remotely resembling what might be acceptable in the US or Europe,…large chunks of foam crammed against very (v-e-r-y) small pieces, and abutting the sides and bottoms of a very shallow pit.

Perhaps the arguably most intriguing (terrifying, and even though I've got dowell grips, there is no way I could even consider getting up onto this apparatus….he had a "rings-stand" constructed of (literally) some painting scaffolding, with a couple of ropes looped over one of the round metal beams and a couple rings hung at the bottom of the loops. It is conceivably possible that somebody could do a few strength hold moves on this rickety and unstable piece of equipment, it's a 50-50 proposition as to whether somebody could actually hold a handstand, and there is no way hell that anybody could actually do a dislocate felge handstand or any other reasonably accomplished swinging element in a safe manner.

Cabbie

We're in La Serena, driving through town and enjoying the scenery….driving our cab is a swarthy gentleman right out of the "Carlos the Jackal" school of type-casting…..our cabbie is a dark haired, balding gent with a thick (but not beaded) growth of beard….his hair is greasy and matted …we get to where we're supposed to go, and he stops…..now, it's hot out and he's been driving all day…kind of sweaty or pitted out one might say….La Serena is basically known for two primary things….first, it's a resort town with a lively night life…lots of discos dotting the coast and are lit up at night with hot music and young people out for a great time…It is also the home of the astronomical observatory "Cierro Tololo", and there (for years) has been an ongoing tension between the commercial interests of recreational and tourist development, and the scientific work of the astronomers who, with some powerful observatories and telescopes just an hour away from town up in the Andes are vehemently opposed to the continued expansion of "nightlife" due to it's negative impact on the ability to see the stars…..in any event, we were being housed in the American astronomer's compound, and the compound had developed a very distinctive black t-shirt with gold emblem and lettering on it. Hannah had inquired, and apparently there were no longer any of these shirts left. As she has put it, "My oldest son Todd was attending the US Naval Academy at the time, and I thought it would be a great present for him if I could find one." Flash forward to our cab ride, and yes, our rather oversized cabbie was, yes, wearing one of the Tololo shirts. Hannah was sitting in the back seat. "Excuse me sir, I've been looking everywhere for a shirt like the one you are wearing….do you by any chance know of a place where I could find one?" We pull up to a stop sign. Wordlessly, the cabdriver strips the shirt up and over his head and tosses the stretched and sweaty (and smelly) thing back at Hannah almost hitting her in the face…."Here" he says.

"Why thank you very much…" she replies with as much diplomacy (although I detect a dubious note in her voice) as she can muster…..So she's sitting in the back seat with this sweaty stinky shirt on her lap, and our cabbie is sitting, sweaty hairy chest, pot belly and all exposed behind the wheel. What the hell…I'm wearing some (long forgotten) gymnastics shirt with some emblem on it…..I strip off my shirt and hand it to the cabbie…"Fair is fair….we really appreciate this, and I'd like you to take mine in return." "Well, thank you very much!" he responds warmly, and taking my shirt (which is approximately 5 or 6 sizes too small for him, stretches it almost to the ripping point and pulls it up and over his head, and almost like a "reverse-moult", pulls it laboriously down his trunk where it stops two or three inches short of his belly-button as his ample girth strains the fabric (and our oh so sensitive eyes at such an amusing spectacle. So, we finish our ride, Hannah with a sweaty Cierro Tololo commemorative t-shirt, the cabbie with my 1987 Pan Am Games shirt, and me, shirtless in La Serena…..hilarious.

La Serena-exibition

After spending a couple days in Santiago, and doing an informal coaches clinic, we flew to the resort town (approximately 400 kilometers north) of La Serena to participate in the 1st Annual World Club Championships… It should be noted that, relative, to the "big time" in international gymnastics, this is a pseudo-event, not sanctioned by the FIG, and as I came to understand, was simply a marketing ploy for the local officials an business-people for the La Cerena Community. That said, they did a helluva job. There were posters positioned all over town…They had attracted gymnasts and club programs fro all over South America, a team from the Soviet Union featuring Nikolai Andrianov's son, and of course, us as North Americans....moreover, it subsequently turned out there was continental-wide television being broadcast throughout the 5 day event.

We arrived at the venue on Wednesday evening the night before the start of the competition....unbeknownst us, there was an exhibition taking place at the venue. Completely surprised, we were informed that our athletes <no preparation, no warm-up> were expected to participate. As we walked into the (approximately 4500 seat arena), we hear this rumbling, this inchoate as we moved closer, roar. I smell, not quite smoke, but an acrid odor, almost like chordite or expended gunpowder. We turn the corner in the concourse, walk through a tunnel, and like a huge wave breaking over and on top of us, in this darkness, there is a wall of noise, and boom!, a burst of light....We have stepped into the main arena, and (it's supposed to be an exhibition for goodnes-sakes, there is a more than capacity crowd...in South America, ushers don't bother to clear the aisles in most sports venues...we had maybe 5000, maybe 5500 people crammed into the arena...all the steps in all the rows were filled with people sitting in them....

Instead of regular lighting, the gymnasts were being required to perform routines with spotlights shining brightly (blindingly?) on them. The noise? Just a cachaphony of crowd noise as these folks rhythmically alternated between chants, songs, and just a rather unfocused roar. The smell? Unbelievable....they've been shooting off fireworks (!!!!) inside the building.....now this is what the whole South American experience is supposed to be about! Perhaps Robert Crumb's Mr. Natural had the best and most cogent turn of phrase: "The entire Universe is completely insane!" man, "I love Chile!!!!! "

It should also be pointed out that this event took place on "South American time". The start of the exhibition (and the 3 days of subsequent qualifying competition STARTED around 21:30 hours (9:30 in the evening!). I know that there are exceptions, but for the most part, judges in this part of the world are very conscientious about getting their evaluations correct and correspondingly, take their time n doing so ....ergo, the competitions ran late....v-e-r-y late....the earliest we finished in the 4 evenings we participated was 1 am, and on Friday night, it was 1:45 am when the final routine was completed. La Serena is a great resort town, but even there, getting started with the night-life at 2 in the morning was a bit problematic....plus, we were exhausted by the evening's events anyway.

As in many international competitions, controversies pertaining to scoring erupted. Luis Salizar was particularly aggrieved at what he perceived was unfair (low) scoring directed at his girls in the competition. After the second evening, he called the coaches and delegation heads together to discuss the matter, and went off on a long complaint about how poorly organized the event was and suggested that we collectively could take the event back from the organizers in order to make it fair. While the lengthy format, long sessions, late late nights, and erratic judging were creating a level of "willingness to listen" amongst the delegations present, it gradually became clear to me that Luis was overplaying his complaints and that there was a hidden agenda that was driving his unhappiness. Luis had been Federation President a couple years before, was not happy that he had been replaced, and although his club was the premier one in La Serena, he resented the fact that this event had been usurped by the "city fathers" and local businessmen, and that he had been kept more or less out of the loop. In any event, the real agenda was he wanted to wrest control (or at the very least make a statement) from the event sponsors and the Chilean Federation. I like and respect Luis, but had no interest in being any part of some local internecine warfare.....at a point in the evening (it was now about 3 am because this thing was convened after the Friday competition), Luis asked for comments. I responded by saying, more or less, "I know we've all had concerns....but as foreign guests (read between the lines here: "as gringos who I know you'd like to see fall on our faces even if you like us personally"), I'd feel most comfortable letting the people who are running the meet, run the meet."

No sooner were the words out of my mouth than the longtime Cuban coach Hector Ramirez chimes in: "I agree with Jim. Let's get out of here and get to bed." General laughter around the room....meeting adjourned.

Hannah-Lada

Shortly after I first met Hannah, she came out to Seattle to conduct a clinic for my (then) age-group girls program She was from a Dayton Ohio suburb. During that first trip, she made several references to how bad, how intense the traffic was in "the big city of Seattle"...I wasn't sure how to read all this, but what the heck...she's a small time gal, maybe the I-5 corridor during 'rush hour' might seem a little overwhelming....I mean, after all, what do I know? Well, turns out, once we get to South America, well, Santiago is big...it's a big capitol city of a large country...the metropolitan population is at least 3 times the size of MY little provincial hometown Seattle.

One afternoon, we were short of drivers...just about "rush hour"...the vehicle of choice in commandeering us around was an old mid 80s Soviet "Lada"...kind of a poor (very poor) man's version of a Datsun....in any event, I was not comfortable driving standard transmission vehicles, so Hannah volunteered to get behind the wheel of this broken down old beast...so off we veer, from the side-roads of Santiago into the main thoroughfare...wow, there were a LOT of vehicles careening from side to side on this stretch of highway, and it seemed like the majority of them are convys (vans), crammed with passengers, some of whom (very few of whom) are seated inside, and a whole lot (read: damned near everybody!) are hanging (precariously it most certainly appeared to me!) off the side, running boards, back, and even top of the vehicles…what the f---? It's not like we are in sub-Saharan Africa or anything,

Santiago is a sophisticated, almost "European" metropolis ….no matter, "rush hour" traffic in downtown Santiago is INSANE….a 4 lane highway has 6 vehicles abreast, racing along at 50-60 (or more miles an hour)….so what happens when Hannah gets behind the wheel of that Lada? She dropped the manual parking brake into "off" position, flipped the gearshift into drive (maybe popped the clutch, it all happened so fast I don't recall exactly what happened, and vrrrrooooom!, she swung that Lada into traffic like she was pulling out of a pit-stop at the Indy 500.

Jeez, until that moment, I had totally forgotten that she had grown up in Indianapolis, and (probably) was an old hand at "open-wheel" and Formula One racing! Well, sitting in the passenger seat (no seat belt, we're in South America for goodnessakes!) was a harrowing experience as she careened down the road dodging cars and blasting the horn…not that she was doing anything unusual in context, mind you….all (oh say half-MILLION) other vehicles surrounding us were doing the same thing in an impromptu version of roller-derby (or maybe demolition derby)….I was sure I was going to die when she roared past one white convy…honest to god, we were so close that I could reach out and adjust the mirror on the thing as we went by…..oh, and if the collisions in Santiago wont cripple or kill you, the exhaust fumes ultimately will! VRRROOOM!!!!

Never let 'em see you sweat dept.

During my final days in Chile, the organizing committee had decided to reward all the organizers and officials with a "farewell" banquet at a local Santiago restaurant….As I shall describe in a number of future episodes, there is (at least I feel) a strong impetus for foreigners, i.e "me" to find a way to connect and to fit in with my (to me) foreign hosts….whenever I'm in a restaurant with hosts from a country I do not (or at least try not) to order from the menu. "What would you like to eat?", I'll be asked…."Oh, I'd like something typical from this region…could you please order for me?" ….well, part of the fun of that is that the local folk will ALWAYS (or almost always) try to pick the most disgusting cuisine available in order to watch the "outsider/foreign guest" (in this particular case, the "gringo") squirm….oh, what fun and frivolity!....gimme a break guys, you think you're a knight up on the chessboard with a move advantage….no way, you've just been suckered into "Jim's contact/connection/uber-diplomacy class #101."

Slight digression: during college, I once ate a tree-frog on a bet at a kegger, but that's a whole other story…

In any event, the folks at the table took me at my word, and ordered me a meal…..the waiter came back to the table, maybe 20 minutes later, and distributed the various dishes. There was beef with salad, for a couple others, a large and nice, what in the European West would be considered a "meat-pie" (i.e. empanyada)….accompanied by a number of other, well, more conventional meals….

Slight digression: the "booze" of choice in Chile is "pisco", a grape-based alcoholic beverage which, at least in my subjective experience is one of the most noxious/toxic/ and lethal concoctions ever devised by man…..it might be acceptable if you've had a single glass (or maybe glass and a half), but when one gets down to actually drinking it with colleagues, well, one quickly descends to slurring one's words, which and of itself would not be a problem given that you've (or at least me) is already butchering the language…pisco is a bitch….have a little too much, and in the posterior portion of your skull, the next morning feels like you've had an ice pick stabbed into your brain….one of the most ugly, debased, nagging headaches I've ever had….I just wanted to die, it was so nasty…"pisco"…the booze that makes you want to swear off booze forever!!!!"

In any event, the food came to the table…lots of what looked like for everybody else goodies, and for me, a bowl of soup….a bowl of cold soup, and in fact, a cold bowl of raw seafood soup….yummy!

The bowl was set in front of me…tomato based, and included a large number of raw seafood delicacies…. I spied a couple of anchovies, several clams, a few mussels, some raw oysters, 3-4 shrimp, and several at the time unidentified species of south American seafood… It was a wonderful bounty, an exceptional feast….not that anyone at the table would completely understand my agenda but I most definitely understood that there was a payoff if their little gambit was adroitly played.

It was obvious to me that most of the good folk sitting around the table had never partaken of this particular dish, nor was there any intent to do so….all eyes are "furtively" on me…how is the outsider, the gringo going to react to this challenge …?

I grab a spoon, and start wolfing the soup down….realizing, I am almost the only person eating, everyone else is "sneaking furtive glances at me)…..Folks look over at me…."how do you like your meal?"….I know they are hoping I'll gag…"Very nice, good food, thank you for ordering it" I respond.,…hesitation….they're not entirely sure how to respond…"You really like it?"

I get a whole lot of faces peeking down the table at me…."never let them see you sweat is my motto…" "Of course, I respond, this is great…" I take a big spoonful of raw fish and tomato based liquid and slurp it down…remember, this is RAW FISH I'm slammin down with a spoon….a few minutes of desultory conversation amongst the Santiagans, then they try one more time….surely (albeit covertly) disappointed, and certainly approaching resigned: "You're really enjoying it?"

Now is the time for the killer comeback…"It's great!" I say, "and I'm really glad you ordered it for me…"it's just the ticket"…"as you probably know, Seattle, my home town is a harbor city on an inlet just in from the Pacific Ocean….and we have seafood at home all the time…and due to our close relationship and relative proximity to Japan, we have THIS KIND of seafood all the time….plus, when I was in college, I roomed for a year with a bunch of Japanese exchange students…

Crestfallen (more or less) heads rotated from directed at me towards front and center, people looked down at their plates and resumed their individual meals.

There's more….as I have previously alluded, I'm a voracious reader…you might conclude from reading this missive, that I'm a voracious producer of (possibly irrelevant!) words as well, but it's been a longstanding habit of mine that I need to read something before I can go to bed and get to sleep…when I got back to Luis Salizar's apartment that night (that's where I was staying when in Santiago), before I could settle in, I needed to read something, read anything…turns out that that particular domicile had little (no, actually nothing, zero, lada, negativo!) in the 'printed word' department….i was thrashing around, trying to get to sleep, and couldn't due to my "reading deprivation". I turn on the light, rummage through my luggage trying to find something, anything that I could have my eyes scan ink on paper….in desperation (or call it last best option) I start reviewing the "travel advisory" that I had received from the US State Department prior to embarking on this trip….rather mindlessly reading down, I chance on the admonition, "ALERT: there have been scattered reports of cholera in regions of the country (the country of course, being the CHILE I was currently visiting!)….it is believed that this outbreak is caused by contaminated seafood….UNDER NO CIRCUMSTANCES should anyone visiting Chile ingest or eat seafood at this time. WARNING: raw seafood is particularly dangerous and should be avoided at all costs."

Go figure……oh yeah, after turning out the light, "I slept like a baby."

El Rancho Rodeo

One thing about Luis Salizar's apartment….it not only didn't have any books, but it was located in a part of town that seemed, well, pretty well cut off from anything remotely resembling "real life" or some any of possible social interaction…..

One evening, Luis and his wife had some sort of commitment and were out, leaving Hannah and me to our own devices….now we have previously discussed (and most travelers are familiar with) the difference between the

"Northern European" daily activities, and that of the Latin/Mediterranean cultures…..in other words, if the Danes are in bed at 22:00 hours, the Spanish and Chileans are just about ready to go out to dinner….there was no food in the Salizar's place, and around 10 or so, Hannah and I…….

Brief digression: throughout this book, I try to emphasize the empathy and flexibility I have as a diplomat and traveler…I feel comfortable and relish adapting to my surroundings and circumstance (well, not always comfortable, but I like to adapt to the challenge)….well, whatever my mind feels and believes about this is a different issue/perspective than what my stomach feels….in South America, as most people know, one has a light (if at all) continental style breakfast, a mid-morning snack (empanyadas), and the main meal of the day is lunch (supper in the old days of the American mid-west and West)….after (an increasingly rare) mid-afternoon siesta, the workday continues, and in the evening, a light "dinner"…..

All well and good, but each of us travels (apologies to Linda Ronstadt), to the beat of a different drum. For me personally., I've never really cared for breakfast, and try to skip it whenever possible…in addition, I've never been much of a "lunch" person….i find that putting food into my stomach in the middle of the day makes me sluggish…and when I was working out and competing in gymnastics, I always felt heavy after eating at midday, so over the years it became something I avoided…also, and this is just a personal idiosyncracy,

it always felt like a "reward" to me if I were able to more or less abstain from eating during the day, then be able to eat and enjoy whatever I wanted at night.

Well, of course in South America, it's very different, and my tummy wasn't agreeing with the change in culture/timeframe….I didn't want to eat in the middle of the day, and again, on this particular evening, around 10 pm, I was starving, and there was nothing to eat….with no viable alternatives (we didn't feel comfortable "phoning out for pizza" given that we didn't know a. where we were in the vast sprawl that is Santiago, or b. where the nearest pizza place was due to "not knowing where we were in the vast sprawl that is Santiago, lol!"….in any event, I was starvin' and we needed to get out and find some grub!

We went down to the street from Luis's apartment, and walked out into a completely dark street…no lights, no cars, no people, and remember, we didn't know anything about Santiago….the nearest restaurant, fast food place, or even corner grocery-store could have been 2 blocks or 5 kilometers away….we walked down about a block and a half….and saw a light, or rather, a series of lights….approaching, we saw a non-descript (remember, there wasn't another thing in the whole street!) entrance ringed with lights, "El Rancho Rodeo"….not knowing what it was, but having few (read: NO) other alternatives in mind, we walked through the portal….)

Wow....it turns out that "El Rancho" is indeed a restaurant, no it's more like a large ballroom that happens to serve food....and check it out, there's a stage over at the front of the place overlooking a large, it's like it's a 1940s ballroom floor....in our wildest dreams we didn't anticipate a "floor show" at damned near 11 pm on a week-night....we were one of only two or three couples in the place....the waitress came up and asked what we wanted.....I looked down, ordered a beer...."no senor, we don't have beer here....would you like pisco?" Ummm, sure....it takes about 15 minutes, but our drinks arrive, coincidentally (or not so as it ultimately turned out) there are few more people trickling into this totally out of the way dive.....

We sip our drinks, look around, and incredibly (or at least it seemed to us odd) that on stage, a group of musicians take up their places and launch into an enthusiastic set...now we're cookin', it's not my particular favorite kind of music, but they are lighting it UP!!! Wow, how did we stumble across this cool spot?

No idea, but ya'know what? They do about a (seems impossible, 'cause it ain't Springsteen) about a 2-hour set...nice stuff! We're groovin' to the tunes, more or less oblivious to the what turns out to be steady influx of customers....somewhere along all this, the waitress comes back and wants to take our meal order....I look at the menu, and say, "I'll have the "Argentinian platter"...I had no idea what it was, but I was hungry, and what the heck...

The band leaves the bandstand...it's now 1 am in the morning, and my tummy is burning a hole in my interior core....well, the noise level (to me) imperceptively rises, and as I look around, most of the tables in the room are (inexplicably) filling up.....what the hey, there's a flurry of activity, and lo and behold, belive it or not, thre is ANOTHER band/musical group mounting the bandstand...!!!!!

Its' now about 1:40 am, and it appears the party is just getting started....our meals arrive....turns out that Argentinian platter, (we all know how meat-oriented the gauchos from thePampas are) is all about beef"..........on my plate is no salad, no vegetables, no plant-life of any kind, on my plate is (I counted!!) six different kinds of beef and meat...round steak, t-bone steak, pork chops (nope, that would be pig, or maybe I don't clearly recall) who knows what other kind of steak, and, what the hey, "chitluns"............I had a 6-course, and approximately 3 hour and 6 ziillion arterioscholosia dose of what the heck, we're here and going to make work ......

Anyway, this SECOND group appears on the bandstand, and it turns out to be a combination saiya and rock n roll band...they get the place jumpin right away, and there is lots of pisco flowing through what has become a crowded night club partying like it was new years eve in the middle of nowhere in Santiago on a week-nite! Wow....after about an hour and a half of hot music, the band takes a small break....the "MC" gets on the microphone and starts talking to the crowd…

”Where are you from?” he asks a couple….”oh, we live in (some suburb of) Santiago?” And why are you here? And so forth….he works 3 or 4 couples, Including a young people from Peru who were on their honeymoon…..

We’re sitting near the back of the room….I guess I don’t look very Latin….he puts one hand over his eyebrows, shading his eyes as he peers out at us…gesturing, he points directly at me and asks: “And you?” Los Estatos-Unis! “Really?” comes the reply….we don’t get too many North Americans here….what are you doing in Santiago?” “We’re here working with the Gymnastics Federation and the Olympic Committee.” The whole room has turned and is looking at us….

“Well, welcome to Chile, and thanks for coming to El Rancho Rodeo.” The band comes back, starts up, and our table is suddenly swamped with men asking Hannah to dance, and women practically dragging me up from my chair to get out on the dance floor…..for the next 2 hours, we are out “cuttin’ the rug” with all the cool cats and kittens getting’ down at Rancho Rodeo…..it’s dawn when the party finally breaks up and we start back towards Luis’s apartment….we turn and look at each other…did what we just experience really happen? Amazing.

"An idea that is not dangerous is unworthy of being called an idea at all."
Oscar Wilde

Chapter Four

MISCELLANEOUS NONSENSE

Goodwill Games (1990)

One of the really nice perks of being involved in an international event is the opportunity to meet some of the "greats" in the field. At the Goodwill Games, our organizing committee was able to arrange a boat cruise for the members of the FIG Men's Technical Committee, a group of 7 brevet judges, nominated by their Federations and elected at the FIG Congress following the Olympics every 4 years. One of our volunteers was able to get a 105' antique yacht donated for a 3 hour cruise for the group. Approximately 20 volunteers, their spouses/significant others, and members of the FIG Executive and Men's Technical Committee embarked on a cruise around Puget Sound the evening before the beginning of competition.

At one point during the evening, I saw Yuri Titov, the then FIG President standing with Boris Shakhlin and Karl-Heinz Schocke, both members of the MTC. Titov and Shakhlin are among the most famous and decorated gymnasts in history and were teammates on the Soviet National team for a decade. Shakhlin was the Olympic All-Around Champion in 1960, and Titov was World AA Champion in 1962. Karl-Heinz was the East German National Coach during that period, and had subsequently been on the FIG Technical Committee (and was at that time, President) since the 1960s. I approached the trio, and at a momentary lull in the conversation, made eye contact (neither Boris nor Karl-Heinz speak English), and gestured to Shakhlin,

Slowly lowered my head, and closing my left hand, I put a fist on my hip. I then leaned forward slightly, and dangled my right arm freely. I wouldn't describe myself as a "student" of gymnastics history, but am very interested in the subject and find the exploits and achievements of our forerunners extremely interesting. I've got a fairly extensive video collection (this pre-dates "You Tube"), and the great Soviet teams of the 1950's through the early 1990's are featured prominently. I had been watching an old film of these great athletes and took particular note of Mr. Shakhlin's manner of presentation. Shakhlin was famous for his unique pose in his moments of final concentration prior to saluting the judges and beginning his exercise.

Karl-Heinz immediately understood what I was trying to communicate, said something to Shakhlin, who smiled, then shook his head "no." He then proceeded to in essence mirror my stance, but with both fists on his hips.
I then smile, wagged a finger at him "no, you're mistaken"...and resumed the position I had initially taken. He smiles, shook his head 'no' again with furrowed brow and a pursed lip smile, then repeated the double hip pose. I responded with a second finger wag, and resumed my original pose, but pivoted on my left foot and held the position with my back to the three gymnastics legends. Shakhlin was renowned for turning his back to the apparatus momentarily and holding his body in this position.

I turned back to back to the three and Karl-Heinz is flapping one hand with a delighted smile, and Titov, shaking in an almost childhood glee, as if he'd just discovered some completely unexpected treat, puts a meaty hand on his old teammate's shoulder and gesturing in my direction says to Shakhlin, "he's right you know...that's exactly how you did it!" Schocke chimes in with his concurrence, and Shakhlin, submitting to the memory of the majority, drops his head in mock submission, then approaches me, gives me a big traditional Russian hug and (sloppy) kisses on both cheeks. Whatta great moment!!

Bureaucrats

One of the things I hate the most about "officialdom" is that people who have "official" positions tend to think that the world revolves around them, their position, and "the functions of the office." It is exasperating, to someone who is committed to the growth of the sport and providing opportunities to individuals who might not otherwise have them to have to (more than occasionally apparently!) bang antlers with

a. the pillars of precedent and restraints of "regulations". I will speak of the FIG in other parts of this book....

b.as a citizen of the world who happens to reside in the USA, I've had a number of issues with USA Gymnastics, the organization that proclaims itself as: "The Governing Body of gymnastics in the US." I've always thought the emphasis should be placed on the organization being a "service body". There are some very good people that work in the USAG office in Indianapolis, but oftentimes, there is a sense among them that THEY are the sport in the USA and that everyone around them either aren't very qualified, aren't very intelligent, or by virtue of the fact that they aren't salaried staff, don't have the right to suggest policy.

I was the Competition Director for the Men's Competition at the Games, and therefore was officially a member of the local organizing committee. The Games as people may recall were a brainchild of CNN television mogul Ted

Turner, and as such, the LOC had a semi-autonomous affiliation with Turner's network.

Along with the athletic competition, the 1990 Goodwill Games celebrated a "cultural" exchange, and in particular with what was the (dying remnants although it wasn't clearly understood at the time by most people) then Soviet Union.

One of the branches of the cultural exchange was a group that worked to bring former Soviet Olympic athletes to Seattle, and house them with local families. This particular project had nothing formal to do with the athletic portions of the Games, and certainly nothing to do with USA Gymnastics. We had the opportunity to meet and get to host the Soviet gymnastics Olympians Mikhail Voronin and Elvira Saadi at a couple of informal events.

I believe it was after the first night of competition, I had just returned home, and (being the Competition Director) got a telephone call from the head of maintenance in the Tacoma Dome….one of the custodians had been servicing one of the women's restrooms, and found a purse. It turned out the purse had a Soviet passport in it, and did I by any chance know how to contact one Elvira Saadi?

Well, as a matter of fact I do, please hold on to the purse, and either I will pick it up first thing in the morning, or I will make sure that Ms. Saadi and the family she is staying with will come and identify themselves and it for you. Thank you very much for the call, and yes, one or the other of us will be there first thing to pick it up. Yes indeed, thank you for contacting me.

Oh, I need to back up….prior to actually meeting Mr. Voronin and Ms. Saadi at the event, I received a phone call a couple weeks prior to the Games from a lady who (it turns out) was part of Elvira's host family. "Mr. Holt, I'm Mrs. So and so, and I'm hosting one of the Soviet Olympians. The name I've been given is Elvira Saadi, and I was wondering if you might know anything about her?"

Now I didn't exactly put it this way, but Elvira Saadi? Are you kiddin', she's one of the great names in gymnastics and especially Russian/Soviet gymnastics history. I went to my personal library, photocopied some material and pictures (especially from a nice book titled "Soviet Gymnastics Stars" and sent it off to the woman. Soooooo, she knew all about her houseguest before they ever met.

Anyway, I phoned her, explained the situation, she (and Elvira!) expressed gratitude that I called; they were obviously relieved that the purse was found and secure, and would be down at the Dome to pick it up the following morning. Next morning, I got a phone call. It was from one of the officials at USA Gymnastics (I won't name her because my point is not about this specific individual, but rather the mindset of "officialdom"). She was quite irate to have learned of the incident regarding Ms. Saadi's purse, and was somewhere between indignant and actually angry that I hadn't bothered to report it to them.

"Ummmm, actually, I'm sorry for any inconvenience, but the Tacoma Dome maintenance person phoned me, and since I knew where Ms. Saadi was staying, I called them and solved the problem."

"That's not the point. You should have called us."

"Well, what would you have done differently?"

"You should have called us."

"If you don't mind my asking so, why?" It wasn't a big deal, I knew where to contact her, and got her purse back with a minimum of hassle."

(Scolding now) "You should have called us."

(now my hackles are starting to rise, 'cause I don't like the whole "we're in charge" mentality anyway…."Hey….Saadi belongs to a cultural exchange group that has nothing officially to do with the competition; I was put in contact with her host family weeks ago…what is the problem?"

(revealingly) "WE are the National Governing Body."

"So what? You don't have jurisdiction over Ms. Saadi or the Cultural Exchange group."

"We are running this competition."

"With all due respect, so what? The cultural exchange is peripheral to the meet, and as a member of the organizing group, I was contacted and took care of it."

"We should have been informed. Elvira Saadi is a guest at the competition."

"She may be, but whether she's Ted Turner's guest, TBS's guest, the Goodwill Games Committee's guest, the LOC's guest, or whomever's guest, it strikes me as odd that she had a problem, I took care of it with a minimum of fuss, and instead of thanking me, you're giving me a hard time about it. I apologize for not contacting you if it makes you feel any better….if you need to discuss this further, I'll be at the event tonight."

"click."

Typical bureaucratic nonsense…..

"What the Hell"

Eberhard Gienger was World Champion on the Horizontal Bar in the 1970s and was twice an Olympian and Olympic Medalist from Germany. He has long been one of the most popular and traveled gymnasts in the sport's history. I got to know him pretty well during the year he lived and trained in Seattle in the late 1970s, and although we had kept in touch over the years, I hadn't seen him in a decade. With the Goodwill Games (and the Men's Technical Committee of which he was a member) coming to Seattle, I was excited at the opportunity to renew an old friendship, and hopefully find some time outside the "gymnastics commitments" where we might be able to get together to socialize.

Herr Gienger is a great guy. He is one of the most charming (realllly can turn it on for the ladies!) and fun people I've ever been around, and a guy who LOVES to put people on the spot...especially in a public setting. Eberhard is also widely known as one of those "adrenalin junkies", somebody who likes/needs to do new and (to the uninitiated at least) "dangerous" things. He's long been an avid skydiver, and at the Games took great pains to show (and great pride in) everyone he encountered a video of himself performing giant circles, goodness only knows how many thousand feet up in the air, on a high bar bolted to an (in flight!) helicopter. After several giants, he releases the bar and performs an octuple or dectuple (I lost count!) backwards somersault before finally 'popping his parachute."

It's a Friday night in late July. We have just concluded the first evening of the men's competition, and a number of officials, judges, and coaches are standing in a group near the scoring table just down from the Pommel Horse podium chatting about the meet. Eberhard turns to me and says, "Jim, I've found a jumpsite just a little South of the arena and I'd like you to go skydiving with me on Sunday morning." Geez, that'd be great, I think to myself. He's from out of town, I've got a car, the meet doesn't start till mid-afternoon...this would be a great opportunity to get together and 'catch up'. So I say, "Sure....I'd love to drive you down there." With the trademark Gienger twinkle in his eye and (my adjective) devilish smirk, he pulls the pin from the grenade and tosses it at me..."I don't want you to drive down with me....I want you to JUMP with me." Suddenly there is complete silence....every head in the group swivels in my direction, all eyes boring into me....they're all ears.

"Uhhh, ok." Whaaat? Did that just come out of my mouth??? If life was a cartoon, and in this moment I most certainly wanted it to be, I would be desperately grabbing those words and trying to claw them back into my mouth. I wanted to slap myself! I'm now stuck! If, for any (certainly reasonable reason) I don't go through with this, the gymnastics community is going to be on my back and teasing me for the foreseeable (and maybe for years 'cause this is the kind of thing that becomes 'urban legend') future.

He's not done, and he wants to make sure that unlike Houdini, there's no way for me to wiggle out of this...so now he hits me with the bazooka..." That's wonderful" he intones....a three beat pause...then, and remember, everybody's listening with great interest,"...but maybe you'll find some sort of excuse between now and Sunday." Dum da Dum Dum!! My tummy hurts, and I suspect I'm not going to get a lot of sleep in the next oh 36 hours or so (not that I'm counting it down already or anything!)

Well, I got it on Saturday several times from him, always in front of people..."you sure you're going to go through with it?" "You're sure that some sickness isn't going to hit you tomorrow morning." This guy is relentless. Oh yes, and lots of comments out of my presence to others around the arena.

Rudy Magdeleno, a judge from Southern California who came up to volunteer for the event approaches me: "Are you really going to go parachuting with Gienger?"

Mark Pflueghoeft, the Coach of the University of Wisconsin who's staying at my house during the meet: "Jim, are you nuts?"

Sunday morning rolls around. I'm stuck sure as shootin', so like the guy walking the last mile (minus the priest or the possible reprieve from the Governor), I drive down to Tacoma (the gymnastics competition was held in the Tacoma Dome), pick Eberhard up, and we head down to the Kapowsin airfield. The plan is for us to do a tandem jump, you know, where the "non-parachutist" is attached to the real jumper?

We arrive at the airfield, go through a brief tutorial on what exactly I need to do and when, and without a whole lot of extra discussion, get our gear on, Eberhard checks the 'chutes, teases me a bit again, and he and I, along with several other jumpers, get up into the plane....shortly later, we near the drop zone, and are approaching 11,000 feet in altitude. Eberhard double checks the harnesses, "we're at 11 thousand feet" the pilot announces, and one of the Kapowsin jumpers pops the door....I don't remember clearly the next few moments exactly...he has always maintained that as soon as the door popped open, I started dragging him towards the door...I just remember seeing that door and feeling like I was in a tunnel.....suddenly I was at the door and felt the cold steel of the doorframe as I gripped it....as instructed, I rocked, one, two, three, and suddenly was OUT of the plane with a brown and green quilt of ground far far below me.....un-be-lee-va-ble.....now, if you've never jumped out of an airplane before, you're not sure of what the sensation (other than probably anticipating that horrible sinking feeling in the pit of your stomach and a highly elevated heartbeat) will feel like....wow, the first sensation that hits me is air hitting me in the face....second, falling through space is LOUD! With air rushing past you at (quickly and beyond) freeway speeds, it's really loud!

Uh-oh, something feels very very wrong, I don't feel right....oh, right, I've got to assume the correct position; a free-fall is exactly the opposite of the standard gymnastics posture...you are supposed to arch your back, pull your heels towards your butt, then cross your arms....this stabilizes you in a horizontal drop position during the fall....I still doesn't feel right...I know I'm forgetting something....oh yeah....it's important to breathe....in the initial excitement (read: trauma!) I've been holding my breath....whoosh, I let the first one out, and very consciously, force myself to breathe....man, this still feels wrong, really awkward....hey dummy, you're all tensed up...I've got just about every muscle group contracted, stiff as a board.....I think of "Dottie the Wondercat" back at home, and relax....woah...wow....I can feel the tension drain out of me like a wave washing away....

It may have only been a few seconds, but that sequence felt like long long minutes....intellectually I understand that Eberhard is just inches above me, hovering and in control, but it feels like I'm falling alone.....now that I'm stabilized, breathing, and reasonably relaxed, I survey my (such as they are) surroundings....the sun is out, it's a warm summer morning (probably 9:30 or so) with just a trace of cirrus clouds "dustbunnying" across the sky, I look over to my left, and there's Mt. Rainier, almost close enough to touch....here I am, almost 2 miles in the sky, falling through space, and surrounded by impossible to improve beauty.....it is a moment that I will remember exactly and treasure for the rest of my days......

It feels much longer, but after about 50 seconds, unbeknownst to me, Eberhard pulls the cord to deploy the parachute....Crack, crack, crack, crack, yoowwwwwch! Ooooogfhhh! Being in an alien environment, I hadn't known what to expect.....if I knew then what I know now, I would have stretched (s-t-r-e-t-c-h-e-d) extensively at the airfield before getting into the plane. When the chute pops open, you get a very very fast deceleration, which especially when you are not expecting it and can anticipate it, and in my case, results in cracking nearly every one of my vertebrates!!! I was sore for the following week.

All of a sudden, with the canopy spread above me/us, it's totally quiet, excepting a very light rustling of the fabric and the sound of my breathing....the contrast with the 'freight train-like noise of free-fall is both startling and reassuring....for the next 2 ½ minutes or so, we rather blissfully float towards the beckoning verdant below....Gienger decides to get playful....in control of the directional cables, he pulls us sharply to the left, then to the right, creating a semi-circular swinging movement that I find distinctly unpleasant...."woooaahhh", "hey, can we just kind of go down quietly?" I hear him laugh, his head inches above mine...."no problem" he reassures me, and for most of the rest of the drop, it's nice and smooth....now, as we get to oh, 500 feet, I start to get a little concerned...this has all been a very interesting experience, but now, we (or rather Eberhard) has got to negotiate a landing....at 100 feet, I can feel the ground rushing up at us at a much faster rate than I am a. comfortable with, or b. would have been able to control if in fact I was jumping alone and in control (or lack thereof) of the chute....well, just a split second before the bile starts to raise in my throat, we decelerate as Gienger pulls down on the directional cables, and, as instructed, we make a perfect baseball slide into the grass in the middle of the drop-zone. What an incredible ride!

Gienger executed a few more jumps before, in the early afternoon, we drive back to the venue, We go up to his room to change into our jackets and ties, and he gets to the venue a few minutes before me. Now, as much as the guy loves to tease, he's a wonderful and warmhearted soul, who, in this case, informed virtually EVERYBODY, that indeed, I had jumped.....I walk into the arena, and if not quite swarmed, am accosted by goodness knows how many people...."Did you really jump with Gienger? No, I mean really." "Sure." "Are you out of your mind, did you really jump?" "Well, yeah,", I respond in feigned "what're you talkin' about, was there ever a doubt?' expression.

I guess my favorite reaction was from my old college coach Bob Peavy who was there as (for me an honored) volunteer....he didn't say anything that day, but weeks later I got a postcard....it read: "yeah....what the hell...I just decided to go up in an airplane with Gienger....and jump out.....what the hell...." Whatta guy! Whatta day!

Hungary

The World Championships were held in Hungary in October, 2002. As I rode the bus across the country from the International airport in Budapest to the host city, Debrecen on the Sunday afternoon I arrived, I couldn't help but feel a melancholy that permeated this ancient land. As we passed through village after village, one could see couples, mainly older couples, out for weekend strolls, passing the old markets and the fields, barren with leafless trees as what promised to be an early winter approached. Looking out at the topography, the flat plain that is middle and this part of eastern Europe, my minds eye can see the armies that have passed across (and dominated) this place. The Ottomans in the 15th century, and of course more recently, the Nazis and then in return, Stalin's hoards.....through an accident of history, the people of this land have settled between two historically fierce rivals, and have been battered and buffeted by the winds of history. It is startling to me in a sense, to experience the vitality, earnest generosity, and sense of fun that make up a large part of the Hungarian spirit.

Wherever I have traveled, I've employed "soccer" as a device by which I can make immediate contact with people and begin a conversation or experience.

Jorge Pedraza, my Bolivian gymnast and I had commandeered a taxi to take us from the hostel in which we were staying and head to one of the training halls for workout. The cabbie was an older man, I'd guess in his late 60s or early 70's. He had gray, almost white hair, and a 3 or 4 day stubble of beard on his chin. A wrinkled white shirt, open halfway down the chest revealing curly white chest hair, and two gnarled hands gripping the steering wheel. Jorge's in the back seat, and I'm with the driver in front. Now I don't speak a word of Hungarian, and I know he doesn't speak a word of English because I tried, and the only way to communicate where we wanted him to take us was by pulling out a map of the city which we had received in our delegation packet, so, how to make contact? I think for a moment...then, I reach into my briefcase, take out a piece of paper and a pen, and on the paper, I print

ENG 3 : HUN 6

As the cab comes to a stop in compliance with the next stoplight, I show the paper to the cabbie.

For those who aren't cryptographers of soccer line scores, ENG is England, and because it's placed first, we know that England is the home team; HUN is obviously Hungary, and if this is a real game, anyone looking at it would know that Hungary beat England 6 to 3 in a game played in England.

Well, the cabbie takes one look at that paper, glances over at me, and erupts like a Roman candle....he starts jabbering and gesturing in rapid-fire Hungarian, gets a huge grin on his face, and well, the light turns green, he's got both hands flying around in the air, and it takes several honks from the car behind us to get him started again...uhh, that is, the cab moving again, because he's just raving away without letup. I was expecting a positive response, but nothing quite as flamboyant as this!

For the non-cognoscenti, the 1953 match between Hungary's legendary "Mighty Magyars" team and the English National team is one of the most important and famous matches in the history of soccer. England, the nation that gave birth to the world's game, had never been beaten at home in an international match. Hungary came into a packed Wembley Stadium and DESTROYED the English in a devastating display of offensive firepower. This one game permanently changed the balance of power in world soccer, and has been known ever since as one of the seminal events in the long history of the sport. So of course I expected our cabdriver to react to my little scribbling.

Coincidentally, I had had the opportunity a couple years before to meet and speak with one of the players from that game. At the FIG Congress in Portugal, Bill Slater, the (at that time) head of the British Amateur Gymnastics Association was a delegate. Known professionally as one of the foremost proponents of education, and particularly physical education in the British Isles, Dr. Slater, in his younger days was a professional footballer, playing right back for Wolverhampton Wanderers and the English National team. He was a defender for England that day, and told me that yes, the Hungarian team of the 1950s was arguably, the 1970 Brazil side excepted, the greatest soccer team in history.

I wait for the cabbie to come up for air and breathe....as soon as he stops talking, I look at him and smilingly say: "Push-kash", which of course is the approximate pronunciation of Ferenc Puskas's last name, the legendary Hungarian striker with the deadly left foot who so decimated the English on that long-ago day.

In perfect synch our driver starts bubbling again (I don't speak the language but understand he's waxing poetic about the giants that bestrode the pitches of his youth...)....one more... "Hideguti", I probably butcher the pronunciation, but he gets the idea, and off he is again (presumably) extolling the virtues of the lynchpin of the Hungarian midfield, Nestor Hideguti.....

Shortly afterwards, we arrive at our destination, Jorge (who has been wordless but watching the fun with interest) and I get out of the cab, and unexpectedly, so does our driver....I've been through this before in different circumstances, so I'm not entirely surprised, but quite pleased when he comes over to me and gives me a big hug, kisses me on both cheeks....yeah, I almost get "beard burn", he takes my hand and gives it a furious shake, holding it between both of his. I reach into my briefcase, take out my wallet to pay him, and he waves me off with a wave of his hand and a smiling sideways shake of his head...... he's refusing to take my money!!

These crazy experiences and moments never get old...to this day, I can only vaguely imagine what happened when he got home that evening: "Honey, you are NOT going to believe what happened at work today....I picked up these two guys in the cab from the gymnastics, you know? Aaaaand............". It makes me smile just thinkin' about it!

Age (pronounced Aw-(hard g)gee

One evening after podium training, a number of coaches and judges from various delegations had gathered at one of the local "public houses" and were exchanging stories over goulash and beer....I was invited to "sit-in" by some folks from the US and English delegations, and to my very happy surprise, one of the gents at the table was Age Storhaug. I had seen him, of course, at meets before, but I had never had the opportunity to meet him or talk with him. Storhaug is simply, a legend in the sport. He was the "main man" in the 50s when Norway was still a gymnastics power, and subsequently has been both National Coach, and coach of the seemingly immortal (or at least ageless) Espen Jansen (39 years old, still competing through the '07 Worlds and suggesting that he'd be around for the next quadrennium as well).

Age's most unique claim to fame was his "world famous' barn. Apparently, his family owned a farm, and he did his gymnastics training (good enough to be a high level international and European Champion!) in the family barn. I was excited to have the opportunity to ask the man himself about this....soooo, as soon as there seemed to be an appropriate window, I chime in, "Hey Age, I've always wanted to know the story of your barn..." Well, apparently he either hadn't told the tale for awhile, or having an enthusiastic (me) and numerous (all the other folks at the table) audience, he extolled:

"Well, for many years, you know, even into the 1960s the barn was known throughout the world, or at least Europe as a place where "serious" training took place...I don't claim it seriously, but I honestly believe that the first "landing pit' in gymnastics history was the "hay bales" in our barn....we'd stack oh, 4-5 feet (he actually said 1-2 meters) of hay on one end of the horizontal bar, and do dismounts into the haystack…it's a nice soft landing as long as there are no needles stuck in the hay you understand", he'd say with a laugh and a smile…

Slight diversion: according to Espen Jansen, Age is arguably the most impressive polymath in the international gymnastics community….he speaks 13 (!!!!!) different languages….according to Espen : (NOR, SWE, FIN, RUS, ENG, ESP, POR, FRA, ROM, ITA, GER, DEN, hell, I forgot the last one, maybe the guy speaks Swahili or Urdu, what the heck…anyway, Espen told me that once Age had to go into the hospital for about 10 days for some unspecified procedure, and to ward off the "boredom", he decided to teach himself another language…

Yeah, right. hand ME a dictionary and a cassette tape (or is it now cd's or computer programs?) and in a week I'll be fluent in Mandarin….right….. moving right along, Augie is sharing the (relatively late) history of his barn and how even track and field athletes would migrate to Norway to commune with him and the athletes that had congregated around it …

(Another digression…)

track and field ("Athletics") and gymnastics have much more in common than the generalist might presumably assume. Both disciplines are ultimately focused on the maximal results ("Citius, Altius, Fortius") in the most economical manner….the primary axiom of gymnastics is the primacy of the economy of line or motion, in other words, the fewest angles, muscle groups, body parts one utilizes in order to execute a given element, the better. Example?

A back somersault in a straight-body position is better than a somersault with a piked (bent at the waist) or tucked (bent at the waist and knees) axiomatically, not because it's harder to do (although it is), but because of the principle of economy of line….one of the great Athletics coaches of the last half-century in the USA was Ken Shannon of the University of Washington.. His specialty was the field events the throwers and multi-disciplinary athletes…shot, discus javelin, hammer, pole vault, and decathlon…..

Every Autumn (North American off-season) he scheduled a six-week microcycle where all his throwers would do gymnastics in the gymnastics room. His decathletes and weight-men would spend 6 weeks doing gymnastics and then return to the gym every other week during their competitive season for "cross- training".

My favorite comment was from one of the UW's better decathletes who would tease me: "you know Jim, we track and fielders are of a higher evolutionary order if you come to really think of it….we've graduated to using implements, whereas you gymnasts seem bent on returning to the trees!"

Any gymnast who has ever gone to an "Ape House" at any zoo in the world and stood in front of the "gibbon exhibit" and looked at those rock n' rollers swing their (uncoached!) giants, Tkatchevs, et, al. will understand that this guy knew EXACTLY (and was correct) in what he was talking about! Ok, for those who endlessly yap about the "artistic in "Artistic" gymnastics, I will concede, gibbons have TERRIBLE (and therefore arguably deductible!) toe-point.

Oh, one more arguably irrelevant experience....
Hannah and I are in China, World Championships 1999. One of my 3 (or 4) all-time favorite women gymnasts is the magnificent red-haired, beautiful (and beautifully explosive) Russian powerhouse, Yelena Prudonova....it was obvious that a person of no less distinction than Leonid Archaev loved her...(loved her in the sense that he loved the power and amazing athleticism of her gymnastics specifically)....for those who don't have access to YouTube (or simply don't have the "institutional memory"), Prudonova, a staggeringly beautiful girl, was simply the most explosive and powerful woman gymnast seen to date in the long history of the sport.

What was the single most incredible skill thrown at that competition? Yelena was (remember, we are talking a decade ago in a time when the commentators are always talking about contemporary gymnastics as "the New Age")....Prudonova was and is the only woman in history that has competed a handspring double front salto vault. She hit the floor, stuck the landing with one small step, and scored 9.6.........out-friggin-rageous!!!! To everyone who admires the athleticism of gymnastics, and understands the near impossibility of making that skill (especially with the constraints inherent in the <then> "women's vault" horse, it was a staggering, astounding achievement. The judges, in their conservative (some, me included might argue 'benighted and/or deluded") viewpoint, deducted for what they perceived as "execution" errors...now to be fair, it was not the most, if one weights economy of line (i.e. smooth and straight and flowing body lines/angles) as the determining factor in the evaluation of exercises and skills....that said, Yelena was transcendent...in qualifying, she ran down the runway, and exploded off the horse completing 2 ½ rotations, and landing in a low squat with 1 small step. 9.6. ridiculous.....anyway, the competition over, and all the delegation busses have left....we are acquainted with Kermit and Jean Davis, the tour guides of the International Gymnast tour group from many previous evens (Hannah had traveled with them to China in 1984), and their bus hasn't left yet....we approach, and ask if we can "hitch' a ride, well of course, gymnastics, even at this level seems, ultimately to be a small family, "c'mon aboard, we'll make sure you get to where you need to go..."

We move to the back of the bus, folks on the tour looking at us curiously what with our Namibian National team warm-ups and all...The fans/tourists are discussing the meet...."Hey, what did you think of Prudonova's vault?", one of the tour-goers eventually asks....a voice in the dark, as the bus wings its way across the streets of Tienjin...."I can't believe they didn't' take more off on that vault....did you see how low she landed....she landed in a deep squat which should have been a serious deduction."

WHAAAAT?????? Sometimes gymnastics pisses me off...here's the most amazing skill thrown in the entire competition, and the woman doesn't even get a medal because she's being deducted for having her legs apart while rotating, and landing sort of low. Ridiculous.

Anyway, back to Age....it turns out, he's telling the tale, that he and the boys in his town actually had a gymnastics training hall that they worked out in the late 1930s. In 1940, the German Army invaded the town....everybody is listening intently as he explains: "Well, the regular German soldiers weren't particularly welcomed in our town, or our country for that matter, but they were just young men doing a job to which they'd been assigned. It wasn't until a couple of incidents between Norwegian Resistance and the soldiers that the Nazi S.S. came to town and prohibited all public meetings or gatherings. That included our training hall. "

(Note: ironically, students of gymnastics history will recall that gymnastics was persecuted in Germany in the 1840s because it was considered a para-military and potentially politically radical movement!).

It should also be noted that Age quietly but dramatically understated the circumstances during that period. Norway was thought of by Hitler to be one of the likely spots for the Allied invasion, and kept almost 200,000 troops there. Despite the Quisling administration's collaboration, the Norwegian Resistance kept up a determined campaign of sabotage and were ruthlessly repressed with German retribution on just about any(and often no) pretext.

"In any event," Age continued, "we were young men who wanted to continue our training and fitness, so even though we could potentially receive the death penalty if we were caught, we managed to remove all our apparatus from the hall over a period of a couple weeks during the night, and transported" interrupting, I insert: "You mean smuggle?" He smiles..."yes, if you prefer....we smuggled our apparatus out of the hall and into my family's barn without the SS noticing. We trained there for a number of years, and after the Germans left, we.....I interrupt him again..."after the Germans left? After they left? Age, what were the Germans (I've got this big smile and incredulous look on my face because of how casually he's describing all this) doing in Norway in the first place and what caused them to leave???"

He smiles again..."well, I'm sure you all know something about the War." Uhhhhh...yeah...(I mean "hell yeah!!!!!"). I just never really thought of, it never occurred to me about what it would be like to do gymnastics with a *death sentence* hanging over you if you were caught.

"after the Germans left". Right.

"so, " he concludes, "after the Germans left, we moved the equipment back into our training hall."

"What ever became of your barn?" "It's still there....we milk cows in it." Amazing.

Commonwealth Games

As recounted a bit later, Hannah and I coordinated a training camp for the Nigerian Men's team in Seattle prior to the Victoria Commonwealth Games.

One of the best things about the Commonwealth Games (we were, as far as I know the only Americans (CJ Johnson the UIC coach representing Barbados excepted), to be credentialed for the event. Ron Smith, the English international judge always refers to us as "You colonials." in any event, we were up in Canada representing Nigeria at the Games....after a days training or competition, it is common for officials from the various delegations to meet for food, libations, and conversation....the members of the British Commonwealth comprise 59 different countries, and one thing that's great about this particular event is that virtually everybody speaks the same language, thereby facilitating easy fellowship and communication.

Note: that is not to say that, for example, the North Korean women's team doesn't laugh and enjoy me doing a silly dance while we're entering the "farewell banquet" in Stuttgart, but the language barrier limits the conversation/interaction somewhat...

Back to Victoria: The gymnastics crowd had basically picked one of the pubs in central downtown Victoria as its' main gathering point. On the evening in question, there must have been oh, 20-25 of us situated around a long extended table, pitchers of beer and burgers scattered throughout. Hannah and I were surrounded by a number of people we knew from various countries and events, and of course some new acquaintances and colleagues as is always the case.

Directly across from me, perhaps coincidentally, perhaps not was the (then) Canadian Men's Program Director Rob Paridis, a great guy and good friend...at one point during the general conversation, without it being directed at me, I hear him refer to someone (or Federation) who are looking for someone to help assist in "some project". Immediately my antennae go up....now, unbeknownst to me, Rob knew perfectly well about my passion for international development...no, better stated, of course I knew that he knew, but...I didn't know (at the time) that his comment was intentionally meant as "bait" to focus my attention....like the flounder (that he likely presumed me to be), or the heroic Chinook salmon (I might have perceived myself to be), I snapped at the bait..."what, what, what are you talking about? You said

something about somebody wanting some assistance....some smaller country...can you tell me anything about it?"
"Well," he casually responds, it's no big deal...there's a Federation that is looking for some help in a project they're contemplating, and they asked me if I had any ideas about who might be able to help them."
"And....and?" I pressed....what did you tell them....Rob, you know this is what I love to do...could you possibly put me in contact with them?..."
I don't know if Rob Paridis had ever seen the film, "A River Runs Through It", and while he has a broadly passing resemblance to Brad Pitt, he played me here like a big ole fat trout snapping at a line....which was his precise intent from the beginning....of course

"Well Jim, there's this small and inexperienced Federation which is looking to put together a competition it's an international meet, and they've never done anything like this before...I can tell you is that I've been approached, and that these people are looking to find a suitable candidate who might be able to help them build their program by coordinating this international event...."""
I abruptly interrupt:..."Rob, ...tell me more, what did you tell them?"

Now, I guess because of the insistency of my enthusiasm, I've managed (which otherwise I would prefer NOT to do) to attract attention around the table....while I'm grilling Rob regarding this situation, I'm at first vaguely, then a bit later acutely aware that all sorts of folks, whatever their particular conversations, have turned their heads and are focused on the conversation between Rob and me.....the master fisherman continues to play with his victim, errr, "prey"....

At this point, I feel a hand on my arm....Hannah has been here before...she is not objecting necessarily, but the hand communicates clearly, "hey dummy....this is a set-up...it might be a great opportunity, but take a deep breath..."She is the voice of caution and reason as I plunge heedlessly on....
"C'mon Rob, tell me everything..."

By now, most of the table around us has stopped their chit-chat and is now looking with interest on our conversation....

He's snagged the hook (although like the dumb fish I am I don't know it yet)....
Broadly oblivious to the numerous pairs of eyes observing me curiously, I blunder on ....he looks to his left and right....he makes sure that he has the ENTIRE table's attention...."well, Jim," he intones leaning forward conspitorially, the fact is, I WAS approached by this Federation, and they are looking for a few months to along term commitment...."
"And".... I flop around helplessly as Rob reels me in....
......"and their gymnastics is at such a low level....(all eyes on the table <including mine> are now on Rob)....“...that even YOU could help them!"

the table explodes in convulsive laughter.....chagrined, I smile, but, inform him that if in fact he's serious, I'm ready and willing to go, ready and willing to meet with this person right here in Victoria.

Talk about a win-win-win.....so we did meet....more on this project (and its' ultimate permutations) in the "Namibia" chapter.

Peresopolis

I have to laugh (actually, no I mostly cry!) at many of the foreign "policies" of the United States Government....it never has made the slightest bit of sense to me for governments to refuse to talk to one another (oh, that's mature...didn't most of us grow out of that around the time we got to second grade?),,,..but America, of course, doesn't talk to Cuba or Iran....moreover, we (I hate using the collective when it doesn't apply to me, but for better or worse, I am a legal 'citizen' of the USA <and of course a "citizen of the world" by personal exclamation>) not only won't have relations with certain countries, but we rather enthusiastically demonize them. Instead of rivals perhaps jousting over spheres of influence or natural resources, we designate countries we don't like as "enemies" or silliest yet (ever?) Axes of Evil.

In September 1994 I was lecturing at the US Regional Congress in California. I was approached by a young gymnast named Freddie (or Farhad) Behahin who asked, "I understand that you've had a lot of international experience, know a lot about Rings and that you worked with Paul O'Neill." The former is presumably true, and the latter is definitely the case. I collaborated with Paul (see chap 12) and helped him prepare for the 1994 Worlds where he won the Silver medal on Rings. "Yes, I worked with Paul, it was a great experience although we didn't win the World Championship". "Well, I'm a ringman at UCLA and I want to compete at the Worlds." I respond, "hey, that's really a worthy goal, but it's kind of a tall order....you see, next year's Worlds is going to be the qualifying meet for the Olympics and there won't be specialists...I think the 1996 Worlds which will be held in Puerto Rico will be for specialists, but the USA will only have one spot for a specialist, and even though Paul was second at 1992 Worlds in Paris, there's a guy named Chris LaMorte who in my opinion is even better than Paul, and for you to qualify to the World team, you're going to have to be better than both of them."

Freddie looks at me.

"I'm Iranian"

"What?"

"I'm Iranian"

"Pardon me?"

"I'm Iranian"

........long pause as it starts to sink in....

"You mean, like Persia?"

"Yes."
"Ummm, what kind of passport do you have?"
"Iranian."

I get this huge grin...."Well, why didn't you say so? That makes a huge difference, no problem, there should be no problem" (I'm thinking to myself, "except for all the absurd and pointless and inevitably messy bureaucratic hurdles everybody in Iran is going to throw in your way")....all you have to do Freddie is contact the folks in the Iranian Gymnastics Federation to send in the appropriate registration forms which they call inscriptions to the International Gym Federation at the appropriate times. I'm sure with a little lead time Art (Shurlock) and Yefim (Furman), (the UCLA coaches) can help you with that."

"They've already told me they're going to be too busy working with Chainey and Steve (USA Olympic hopefuls) over the next couple years. I was wondering, hoping actually, that you might be able to help me."

"Persian, huh?" "Yes."

Well, Mr. Behahin, I'd love to help you. "What you need to to is talk to Art and Yefim, and if they tell you it's ok with them, I'd be glad to help you and get you prepared to go to San Juan for the Worlds. We've got about 18 months."

So, Freddie got the coaches at UCLA to agree, and he and I set about putting together a working plan. UCLA during the 80s and first half of the 1990s was one of the dominant and most respected teams in US gymnastics history. UCLA produced Olympians Kanati Allen (1968), and 1984 Olympic Gold Medalists Peter Vidmar (Silver AA, and 2 time NCAA All-Around Champ), Tim Daggett, and Mitch Gaylord. They had numerous other National team members, Olympians, and NCAA Champions prior to their funding cut in the late 1990s. Coaches Art Shurlock (himself an Olympian in 1964), Makoto Sakamoto (1964 and 1972 US Olympian and 7-time National All-Around Champion), and later, Yefim Furman (Soviet National team member and alternate 1972 Olympic team) were and remain among the most highly decorated and respected men's coaches in the United States. It was (and remains) an honor for me to be considered by them to be a peer (even if I'm really not), and it truly humbled me that they graciously and enthusiastically supported my collaboration with Freddie.

During the quadrennium leading up to the 1996 Worlds (and more significantly from their perspective, the 1996 Olympic Games which were to be held in Atlanta Georgia, Art was primarily focused on UCLA's Chainey Umphrey (who ultimately made the USA Olympic team)and Yefim's primary focus was on the wonderfully talented Steve McCain,(who made the team in 2000). Because of their focus on the US athletes, the coaches honestly did not feel that they could do full justice or expend the required energy on Freddie's behalf, and therefore, were happy to let me work with him. This kind of thing (contrary to whatever negative opinions I've expressed in terms of the politics and pettiness of much of our sport) is the real and welcome counterweight, and why in part, I love the sport and respect the people that work within it so much. Art, Makoto, and Yefim are among my all-time favorite and most respected people in gymnastics.

A (hopefully brief) digression:

Earlier this year, Hannah and I had an opportunity to meet Larry Banner and his wife Marti during a trip to California….although I had known of Larry's gymnastics accomplishments for many years, I had never had the opportunity to meet him. Larry, after decades away from the sport in a set of circumstances too convoluted to go into here, took over as "webmaster" for the US Gymnastics Hall of Fame website. The old "Helms Hall of Fame" had been formed in 1959 and was taken over by USAG in 1996, but there had been relatively little research done on the inductees. Larry, taking over in about 2005, went about, passionately, laboriously, and almost comprehensively documenting in extensive detail the accomplishments of the inductees; moreover, he sleuthed and published an incredible repository of photographs of all 260 persons who had been inducted into the Hall of Fame.

His personal story (Larry is a UCLA grad, a 2-time <1960 and 1964> US Olympian and a member of the US gymnastics Hall of Fame) is understated in the "history" section. It turns out that Mr. Banner was virtually a "shoo-in" to make his third Olympic team in 1968 (ranked 2nd going into the final trials), but decided to forego his Olympic opportunity in order to be present at the birth of his and Marti's first child which would be taking place during the Games in Mexico City. Further, and to my complete astonishment, Larry told me he suffered from polio as a child…he indicated to me that due to the atrophy of the muscles of his back that it was extremely difficult for him to perform a back handspring in a tumbling pass….in a time where gymnastics is perceived by many people as requiring level approaching physical perfection, the notion that someone afflicted by polio as a youth could ultimately make an Olympic team is almost unfathomable.

It gets (depending on one's perspective) weirder or more sublime….gymnastics apparently wasn't Larry's first or best sport. He was recruited to UCLA on (of all things) a gridiron (i.e. American) FOOTBALL scholarship….in high school, he was an all-state defensive back. It turns out that due to the ineligibility of freshmen during his years in school he spent his initial college year at a junior college which fielded a football team….after intercepting a pass during a scrimmage, he was carrying the ball downfield and was subsequently submarined by the top player on the JC team, fullback Don Shinnick who went on to become an All-American and Rose Bowl captain at UCLA and who enjoyed an illustrious 12 year career as a linebacker for the Baltimore Colts. Larry's knee was blown out on impact by the powerful and aggressive Shinnick, and upon recovery, he focused on his gymnastics skills, and the rest, as they say, has become history.

Larry was not a teammate of Art Shurlock at UCLA (Art attended school as an undergraduate at Cal), but was on the 64 Olympic team with Art.

I shared with Larry perhaps by favorite Art Shurlock story. Shortly after the 64 games, Art was named Head Coach at UCLA. In addition to the great athletes named above, he coaches such luminaries as Tony Pineda (2-time Mexican Olympian and NCAA Champ), US National Team members Mark Caso, Chris Caso, Curtis Holdsworth (NCAA PH Champ and Pan Am Games competitor), Robbie Campbell, David Moriel (NCAA HB Champ), Brian Ginsburg (America's Cup Champ), Alex Schwartz (NCAA R Champ), Luc Tuerlings (Belgian National Champ and Worlds Competitor), and countless others. UCLA won the NCAA team championships in 1984 and 1987....throughout this amazing run of success, Art remained the unpretentious, gracious, and supportive person that he has always been.

In 1981 my first UWashington team at the Pac-10s, as I have previously described, was a bunch of wonderful guys, but a rag-tag bunch that would challenge the 1962 Mets or the 1899 Cleveland Spiders (or the 2008 Detroit Lions) for the title of the worst team ever....I was extremely proud that we had managed to get to the Conference Championships, but (although I never divulged this to the team until this day should any of them ever have the opportunity to read this), I was acutely aware of how bad we were, and was extremely embarrassed (or perhaps better put, profoundly sensitive) to how we were being perceived by the gymnasts who had so recently been my peers and the coaches who until we actually showed up at the event had been my role models not my colleagues.....

Art seemed to sense my unease....at one point during the warm-up, UCLA was throwing every skill in the Code on high bar (I mean, Mitch Gaylord who has two skills in the Code of Points named after him was competing for goodnessakes!), and Daggett and Vidmar, well, needless to say, our little group was overmatched and overawed....Art was sitting on one of the benches in the Pavilion at Arizona State and he called me over....I had no idea what this was about....

Art said, "Jim, I know you've got some challenges...but I want you to know that these are going to be the best times of your life....you're doing good things for the right reasons....don't dismiss the importance of this experience....when you look back on it, this will be the best time of your life."

I looked at the man like he was crazy....he's got a team with the some of the best gymnasts the United States has ever produced....he's going to win the Conference Championship and may very well win the National Championship, and some of his guys will be on the Olympic team in 3 years...he's got the support (and a paycheck!) from the UCLA Athletic Department, and he's telling me that I've got it good? What the f---?.........it turns out, that sage Shurlock was absolutely dead right on in his assessment….ultimately, it's not about the prestige, where one finishes, or even about the money…..in the end, even on such a small ("off-Broadway)stage as "gymnastics", what have you done to make a difference in the lives of the people around you……

"Fast forward": given this magnanimous, generous, giving spirit, was there any chance that Art Shurlock would stand in the way of one of his relatively "minor" gymnasts (i.e. floor and rings specialist Freddie) not having the opportunity to achieve his aspirations? Of course not….Art (and Yefim) graciously agreed that Freddie could collaborate with me and that it would be a great thing for Freddie, UCLA, and Iran to participate in the 1996 World Championships, albeit with a different coach….

As mentioned before, Freddie and I coordinated a training plan…he came to Seattle and lived with Hannah and me in the summer (between school quarters) of 1995, and at the end of the year 1995 Farhad (Freddie) took UCLA's winter academic winter quarter off and moved back up to Seattle to live and train with me and Hannah in preparation for the 1996 Worlds…..

It was a great experience having him in our home….over the years, both before and after we got together, Hannah and I had had a great deal of experience hosting "foreign" students/athletes in our homes….when she lived in Ohio, Hannah and her family had hosted students from Japan, China, and Spain, and I had (pre-Hannah) had a number of college gymnasts in my house and had been for a year the legal guardian of Mike Williams, originally from Couer d'Alene Idaho, who eventually made the US National team and to this date is the ONLY American to compete a triple-salto on the floor in competition….

Freddie fit into our household very well…it was wonderful for me to discuss the realities and nuances of Iranian politics. Freddie's family, as many expatriates, were not enamored of the conservative Islamic revolution that had taken over the country in the 1970s, and led to, in his personal case, his abrupt and clandestine departure from the Islamic Republic of Iran at the age of 12 in the 80s.

Freddie worked his tail off…he got his routines polished and ready to compete at a high level in San Juan. One of the things that we worked on, but ultimately were unable to achieve was a maltese cross with a 180 degree variation….in other words, a 2 second hold position in which the arms were parallel to the body parallel to the floor and which the body was rotated 90 degrees (in other words) hips facing the floor and ceiling, rather than abs and back….unfortunately, although it has not been officially recorded into the Code of Points, there was a Malaysian gymnast who performed this skill in the preceding(1995) Worlds...given that Freddie would not have the skill named after him in the Code since he wasn't the first to perform it, we dropped it from his exercise and replaced it with a hold skill that he could perform with greater assurance of completion without execution deductions.

None of that is really important in the long run....what is most important is that this young man's dream of competing at the World Championships was realized and it actually came true. Freddie trained in Seattle with me, traveled to San Juan and he represented Iran with honor and class. Freddie finished in the top half of all the competitors on floor and rings, and was recognized by the media with a profile in both the International Gymnast magazine (the oldest <1956> and most widely respected throughout the sport) and World of Gymnastics (the official FIG publication).

For me, (albeit not for Freddie since his focus and perspective <appropriately)>was on his having the opportunity to participate), the most significant aspect of this collaboration was the reinforcement for me of my perspective and philosophy that governments "usually" get in the way of real human accomplishment, but there are ways in which people can unite, circumventing the restrictive policies of nations. In this case, despite the fact that the United States of America and the Islamic People's Republic of Iran (charter member of the "Axis of Evil, remember?) did not (and as of this writing do not) have diplomatic relations), it was possible for an American to be the 'official' coach and "Chef de Mission/Head of Delegation for the Iran "team" at a World Championships."

There are (at least) 3 reasons that contributed to this arguably unique set of circumstances...and by unique, I wish to emphasize, that over a decade later, relations between the USA and Iran are at best problematic....on the sporting level, it should be noted that the US (at least) press made a HUGE deal of the albeit simple and (it should have been) non-controversial soccer World Cup group match between the two countries in France in 1998....it was a simple matchup between two teams that had been drawn into the same group, and the US press approached it like it was some hugely significant international summit...silly.... (Iran won by the way)....

Regardless, what for me of personal significance, is that some bureaucrat in Tehran, in order for Freddie to achieve his dreams, whatever the other objectives might have been, was willing to "sign off" for an American (a citizen of the "Great Satan" officially) to represent, to be the official "voice and face" of Iran at the World (!!!!!) Championships. To fully put this in perspective, Freddie's father Hamid was a multiple-time national champion in Iran and a brevet international judge. I have no idea what the true level of his influence was, but I'm certain that Hamid had a profoundly significant impact on the willingness of Iran to inscribe his son as their representative to the Worlds.....Hamid was able to come to and attend the Worlds the day of Freddie's competition and took over from me as Head of delegation on that date

Lao Tse's assertion "When a leader's work is done, his aim fulfilled, his people will say....we did it ourselves." applies not only to the bromides of history, but to the "real world" experience that we, well, experience.

Aside:

Given international politics, I wasn't sure exactly how I'd be received in my capacity as an official representative for Iran at the event.

There was a welcoming luncheon for judges and officials in San Juan...I attended as Head of Delegation for Iran....I was approached by an American colleague (remember, I was a two term USAG Board member)..."Jim, who are you representing this time?"

I'm not always sure if this is an honestly curious question, or some sort of mildly dismissive "why do you bother working with these non-entities" put-downs that I sometimes (arguably mistakenly) think....

"Iran"

"Yeah, right!" was the rejoinder....

"Iran"

"Sure...do you think I'm some kind of idiot"

"No honest, I'm coaching Iran."

"No way."

"Look at my credential"

the US judge/official in question reached across the space between us and grasped the plastic badge dangling in front of my tie (I was wearing slacks, blazer and tie for the luncheon)....

"Holy crap....you're coaching Iran!!!!?"

"Ummm, yes."

"Hey..." to some unnamed USAG officials,,,,,"you are not going to believe this..."

Believe it... in international sport, there are often officials who transcend the nonsense of political issues.....I have no idea if Hamid Behahin had some inside connection with the Iranian Olympic Committee and Gymnastics Federation, but it is a wonderful testament to all that is best within the human spirit and family that there were individuals in Tehran who were willing, in order for a young Persian man to realize his dreams, to permit an American to be for that brief moment in time, an "official" Iranian......

I do not know for certain, but I believe that I actually met the individual responsible for inscribing me for San Juan. Hannah and I were on the staff at the 1996 Olympics and FIG Congress in Atlanta subsequent to the San Juan Worlds. Iran was represented by a member of their Olympic Committee Mr. Hassan Ramajanian Poor. Mr. Ramajanian Poor kept mostly to himself, and didn't seem to have breadth of contacts and acquaintances amongst the various delegations. Several (but trying to not be too forward) times during the course of the Congress, I approached him and asked if he needed anything, and if so, I was available to assist him in any manner he deemed necessary or appropriate. He never did take me up on my offers, but I felt certain that he knew who I was and how I had been involved with Iran, although he never openly expressed same.

I took my responsibility as an official representative of the Islamic Republic very seriously. It is obvious that it was an unusual circumstance for an American to be able to be a spokesperson (at least symbolically) for the Islamic People's republic of Iran. Whether it was the influence of Hamid, or a "leap of faith" from someone in the Iranian Gymnastics Federation or Olympic Committee, I will always be profoundly grateful that I was given the opportunity to represent Iran in international competition.

"The greatness of man consists in saying what is true and in acting according to Nature."
Hericlitus

Chapter Five

MERRIE ENGLAND

A number of years ago the World Championships were held in Birmingham. As a general rule, countries competing can be divided into two groups. There are the rich countries, where the delegations house themselves in quality hotels and the "little" or "poor" countries who try to find the cheapest accommodation possible without sleeping on the street. We have always been among the latter.

At the 1993 Worlds, the Local Organizing Committee offered cheap housing at a dormitory at the University of Birmingham. Relatively spartan, but perfectly serviceable, the dorm had a couple of great features…first, the cafeteria was open late and served both pizza (never had a bacon and egg pizza before, and beer until midnight). This was fortunate because Birmingham, while a fairly large city, seems to roll it's sidewalks up around 9 pm….it was almost impossible to try to find food after evening training or competition. The other great thing about being at the University dorms was that all the little countries were present….at night, it was like a huge party every night…people from oh, 40 countries hanging out and chatting with one another….it's this kind of activity that is one part of going to international events so much fun.

A other aspect of the University of which we were unaware was their automatic wakeup system, albeit one which actually only works on the side of the dormitory facing a large pond. Which is, depending on one's lifestyle or the time one went to bed the previous evening, either a good or (as in our case) a not-so-good thing. Every morning, shortly before dawn, literally HUNDREDS of geese start quacking, honking, or whatever nerve-wracking, cacophonous, and sleep-depriving racket they indulge in (ummm, in which they indulge….no sleeping in for us in the 2 weeks we were there, that's for sure!

Aston Villa

Before heading over to England, I checked the Premier Football League schedule to see if Aston Villa, one of the countries legendary teams (the first one to win the League-Cup double way back in 1896) was going to be playing at home during our time in Birmingham. It turned out that some reporter from the Birmingham paper got hold of my story from whomever had received my inquiry at the organizing committee, and contacted me…this is the mid-1990s and email had not yet become the universal communication medium that it is today…how did an American (lots of Europeans seem to think we're still fighting the American Indians over here)…"how did a Yank come to be a big fan of "The Villa" he wondered. Well, actually "assumed" more than wondered, because, big soccer fan that I am, I don't really follow Aston Villa at all…I'm a Tottenham Hotspur supporter. In any event, going along with the whole thing, I wrote him back with a fictitious story of "back in the days" of the North American Soccer League, I used to watch Seattle Sounders games (this part is true…I had season tickets for a number of years)…in any event, I wrote this reporter that seated next to me at Sounders matches was an old Englishman (this is all completely made up) who was a passionate Villa fan who would regale me of tales from their glorious past….they won, for example the 1957 FA Cup and blab la bla …..well, I had actually more or less forgotten all this, but on the day we arrived in Birmingham and were in the process of checking in, THE SAME REPORTER who obviously was also covering the gymnastics event, had found out approximately what time we were arriving, and showed up to meet us while we're being credentialed! Now I had to answer questions face to face without the luxury of looking (or in my case, plausibly making) something up.

He asked a few relatively innocuous questions, and indicated that our "interview" would be part of a "color piece" that would appear in the paper the following week in conjunction with the competition, and took his leave. Well, I thought that that would be the end of it, but no….apparently, Mr. same reporter actually contacted the team, and I received a phone call from somebody in their publicity office….would I be free on the Sunday after next? If so, Aston Villa has arranged for a pre-match tour of the grounds and complimentary box seat tickets for two to watch the Aston Villa-Coventry Premier League match taking place on that day!

What the heck, of course, it sounds like it would be a blast…..as usual it seems, I managed to underestimate the whole cool craziness of it. Ummm, perhaps better, more accurately put, I underestimated the craziness of "them". Sports fans can range from relatively normal people to absolute wackos….when we got to the grounds, we were introduced to two of the more extreme nut-jobs I've ever met, and when I was a kid, I was a pretty fanatical (that's where the word "fan" derives from)…in the 19th century, base-ball fans were known as "cranks" which often seems appropriate too…

Oh, full disclosure here….the real reason I know about fandom and "cranks" is that I was (am a 'recovering'?) team fanatic of the ultimate order….when I was a kid, I was a maniacal Baltimore Colts football fan….never-mind the fact that I'd never been to Baltimore, just understand that at the time Seattle didn't have a team and that the San Francisco 49ers were 800+ miles away…nevertheless, I loved the Colts, and , obsessive that I can be, wanted to know everything (and I mean e-v-e-r-y-t-h-i-i-n-g about them….does the reader remember (of course you don't, no one does or should!) the "Nat Craddock Controversy"? Here's how nuts I was….I collected Colts media guides, and the ones from the early years of the franchise (1953-59 or so) I didn't have copies….in any event, I wrote the team, got photocopies of the statistics, and on a manual typewriter (for you young whippersnappers, there was a time before the Internet or Excel spreadsheets where all information needed to be entered an collated mechanically….), and one summer, during the evenings, typed up statistical cards in every single statistical category available. Thank goodness, a. professional football has nothing approaching the statistical compilation of major league baseball…..for example, there is a "box score" available for basically every major league game ever played (all hits, runs, putouts, strikeouts, et.al.) dating back to May 2, 1871 when the Ft. Wayne Kekiongas beat the Forest City Greys in the first game of the National Association 2-0. The history of baseball, if one were to attempt to record it on 3 x 5 typed cards would be oppressive to what was (then) this teenager….in any event, I dutifully (albcit cnthusiastically) recorded (or perhaps more accurately) recompiled the statistical data of the (then) 15 year history of the Baltimore Colts professional gridiron football franchise….then, to my astonishment, it appeared clear that there were inaccuracies in the record books.

Yes, with all due respect to the nutcases that ushered us around Villa Park, I confess to being a card-carrying member of the "lunatic fringe:….upon review of one of the media guides, I actually found several factual errors…at the time I was reviewing them (late 1960s), the Colts press-book recorded that Bert Rechichar

(1953-59) had the team record for the most punt return yardage (talk about obscure nonsense!) with 844 yards….it turned out, according to my (accurate) 3x5 cards that Alvin Haymond (1964-66) was the actual all-time team leader with 926 yards….now all that might strike the reader as stupifyingly boring and irrelevant nonsense (appropriately so!), but to delve a bit further, while there were two or three other issues which I was able to resolve, the real contribution I made to the recording of team history was the resolution of as mentioned above, the "Nat Craddock Controversy". In point of fact, there never was a controversy until I brought it to the attention of the team public relations director. The facts are as follows: all teams in all sports in all media guides a.k.a. pressbooks include an all-time team roster, in other words the names of all the individuals who have actually appeared in an official game….remember the film "Field of Dreams"? "Go the distance?" what's with the Archie Graham character? In any event, it turns out that at the time, the "all-time roster" of the Baltimore Colts did NOT include Nate Craddock.

What the heck? When reviewing the statistical records, I discovered that Mr. Craddock, who attended Parsons College (I do not know if he actually graduated because I didn't bother to research it to that level!), carried the ball one time in 1963 for a one yard gain. As I pointed out to the team's press relations department in a letter, if in fact, someone actually rushed the ball during an official league game, then axiomatically, that person was a member of the team and should appear on the all-time roster. The press department (no doubt shaking their collective heads and over lunch commenting "who the hell is this loony in Seattle and what's with the Nat Craddock nonsense…) graciously agreed to correct the mistake and encouraged (no doubt tongue in cheek) me to continue to "advise" them should I find any subsequent errors….now I admit, I'm still bitter….like the Brooklyn Dodger fans of old, I'm still pissed off that the Colts were stolen from Baltimore <29 March, 1984>.

One of the more surreal and wonderful sports experiences of my life was during the Thanksgiving weekend of 1998. Hannah's two sons Todd and Kris were both (separately but simultaneously) pursuing graduate degrees at George Washington University in Washington DC and Hannah and I traveled back east to spend the holiday weekend with them. By complete coincidence, Baltimore, which subsequently had taken over the "original" Cleveland Browns franchise and renamed the "Ravens" were hosting for the first time since they had left, the Colts who were now (and still are) based in Indianapolis. In any event, Kris knew about my Colts connection (and eternal enmity towards the Indy plunderers), and scored us tickets to the game up in Baltimore a mere 70 kilometers away…..it was an almost 'out of body' experience….we had seats adjacent to an old guy who had had Colts season tickets from 1955 (first game, Alan Ameche's debut, first carry, 79 yard touchdown run to set up an upset of the Chicago Bears!), through the 1983 and last Colt's season in the old Memorial Stadium….what a conversation….

To sum up, I have been to many venues in my life for sporting events, and I don't think I'll ever experience anything quite as weird as the folks from Baltimore booing (and yet yearning) for the royal blue and white uniforms with the horseshoes on the white helmets that the Indianapolis team brought into that stadium…..a see-saw game, the Ravens came from two touchdowns back in the 4th quarter, and the 'good-guys' prevailed….at the final gun, the then quarterback of the Baltimore team Jim Harbaugh took a knee to end the game, then picking up the ball sprinted about 80 yards to the Raven's 20 yard line, and handed the ball to the legendary Johnny Unitas…..the jumbo-tron captured the moment for all those who couldn't see it "up close and personal"….I have never heard a louder crowd roar than that….of course, the fact that I was at full-volume presumably should not surprise the reader either........point of story.....I know where these Aston Villa guys are coming from...

in any event, our tour guides were two men in their 20s who were lifelong, absolutely loyal and crazed Villa fans who had managed (apparently it was their dream job in life) to get jobs doing tours and other minor administrative things for the club. As we walk around the pitch, they give us a complete history of every part of the construction of the grounds. We were escorted into a long hallway with photos on both walls, and we're "treated" to an excruciating description of the date, location, meaning (and naming all the persons in the photo) of each one....stuff like, "oh here is a photo of Joe Blow's goal in the 1967 Youth (meaning their JV squad, not even a full Villa match) Cup quarter-final...and over there to the right is so and so who was traded to Portsmouth or somebody a year later....they went on for like half an hour for a walk which should have taken about 2 minutes. In the trophy room, we get a full historical description of each trophy and what it means and who did it and on and on and on....it was a strange combination of being tickled that the club had responded to my nonsense with such a nice gesture, boredom from listening to these two maniacs rave on about the most trivial trivia, and trying to keep from cracking up because the whole scenario was so damned funny.

The topper to the whole thing was us getting a chance to visit "the locker room". The two Stooges are acting like we're Howard Carter about to enter Pharaoh Tutankhamen's tomb in 1922...."Oh look, here's the lockers....oh look, here's the actual game jerseys they're going to put on....oh look, here's the....respectful silence...the loo......and over here, the baths......I'm biting my lip to try not to burst out laughing at the ridiculous over-the-topness of it all.....eventually, we thanked them....amazing....oh, the game was great too... Aston Villa 2 Coventry 0.

Russians

I alluded earlier to how great it is to stay in a place like the dormitory at the University where all the countries can intermingle...it really is wonderful....however, depending on a given set of circumstances, there can be some, well, let's call them "interesting" downsides....after the last night of competition, the FIG always has a closing banquet or party....these usually end at or before 11 pm, and naturally, many folks are still revved up and eager to continue the party. We needed to catch a 4:30 am bus which would take us (and many of the other delegations) from Birmingham down to Heathrow Airport in order to catch connections. For this particular event, we had actually flown Hannah's daughter Shaye, who was in high school at the time over to England and she stayed with us (and was actually credentialed as a "physiotherapist"!) at the event...as and/or slightly before she arrived, she was extremely nervous..."oh what will I do there, who will I be able to talk to?" she'd lament...."don't be silly, you'll make friends with some of the volunteers and gymnasts." "Oh no I won't no one will want to talk with me..." Well, it took maybe half-a day for that to all fall apart....Shaye became one of the 'darlings' of the various men's teams, and towards the end of the event, maybe knew, ONLY 50 or 60 volunteers...we're working, and she's walking with us, "hi Shaye, hi Shaye, good morning Shaye, it was ridiculous...and also it was wonderful to see how much fun she was having during her spring break....what'd you do during spring break? "Oh, sat around the house and watched tv." "Shaye, what did you do during break?" Oh, I flew by myself to England and was the physiotherapist for Bolivia at the World Gymnastics Championships." Oh.

In any event, she indeed had become a popular young lady amongst the male gymnasts. At the time, Dmitri Karbenenko (subsequently he changed his nationality and was the number one gymnast on the French team for many years) was a young Russian gymnast...18 years old at the time, Dmitri was physically the biggest, strongest guy in the competition. Now, I don't want to make too broad of a national stereotype, but Russians, especially Russian males hanging around at a party are known to drink. And Russians don't drink pink squirrels or rusty nails, or even margaritas....Russians drink vodka. They drink it straight. And they drink a lot of it. Karbenenko might be big (for a gymnast) and he's young, but....drink enough vodka, and, sure enough, you're going to be drunk.

Moving slightly backwards, after the banquet, we'd had a long day, and Hannah and I went up to pack, and get to bed for what was going to be a short night, 'cause we needed to be downstairs and ready to get on that bus which was leaving at 4:30. Shaye wanted to stay up awhile and maybe party a little bit and say goodbye to all her newfound friends. It had been such a great experience for her, we certainly weren't going to object to an hour or so, told her that, reminded her of how early we needed to get going (Shaye never was and to this day is NOT an early riser), and took our leave of her.

Snnnorrrre....at 03:30 we get up, dress, and get our things together. At 3:45 or so, heck, we even beat the geese up this morning!...Hannah goes to wake up Shaye, and she's not in her room! Well, that's an unpleasant surprise, so we head downstairs, and yes, there is still the remnants of a party going on, those late, everybody's beat, but the last few stragglers aren't quite yet ready to call it quits moment, and lo and behold, here she of course is, sitting on Dmitri Karbenenko's lap. Hannah approaches her, more relieved than upset, "Shaye, it's time to go, now go upstairs and get your things together, we need to get on the bus." A very very drunken Dmitri slurs, "No!" Hannah and I both look at him....turning her head back to Shaye, Hannah says "I mean it, we need to go now." Dmitri repeats his slurred "NO!".....Now Hannah is angry..."Shaye, get up off his lap and let's go...Now!"

Dmitri sort of wavers side to side, turns his head up and looks directly at Hannah for what's probably the first time and says: "SHUT UP! Sheee's nuuuuht goooin annnnyware!" Hannah takes a step towards him, I take two steps that manages to get me between them, and here I am, 4 am, and my job is to find a way to keep my banty-rooster of a wife to keep from assaulting a large and very inebriated world-class athlete, which as far as I could anticipate would precipitate a sequence of (to my mind) extremely unpleasant consequences......great.

Shaye, seeing the murderous look in her mother's eyes manages to extricate herself from Dmitri's somewhat uncoordinated grasp, and with a "I'll talk to you later Dmitri", gets up, going, and simultaneously grabbing ahold of my spouse's arm (firmly I might add), I separate the imminent combatant s from each other and beat a hasty retreat upstairs to our room and luggage. Amazingly, we actually did make it onto the Heathrow 4:30 am express.

There's a bit more to come regarding the bus, but I want to make this clear: We understand that Mr. Karbenenko had had a little too much of the joy juice that evening, and no harm was done...it's a true story, but just a story. We've never brought it up to him in the 15 years that we've seen him around at events. He's a fabulous gymnast and is a wonderful man and father. Mr. Karbenenko is one of the class acts that we've known in the sport.

Well, there are bus-rides and then there are bus-rides. The three and a half hours from Birmingham down to Heathrow were three of the longest, strangest hours ever in a bus....when I was in high school, my mom put me and my brother on a bus and sent us (unsupervised, those were the days!) from Tacoma to my grandmother's house in Renovo Pennsylvania on a Greyhound bus....the fat lady who got on the bus in the middle of the night at some North Dakota whistle-stop who woke me up and prattled on...endlessly...about her two kids (oh yes, I got to see pictures and everything!) comes to excruciatingly painful mind....in any event, the bus is full of tired gymnasts, coaches, and officials, most of whom just want to try to get some catnap type sleep before they get off to find their flights.

We were sitting in the back of the bus, and I had just closed my eyes when (and remember, this is right on the heels of the Dmitri incident), I hear a clink...a clink of glass hitting glass on what turns out to be bottle on bottle...bottle as in bottle of vodka, or more precisely, bottles of vodka...yes, there are a group of, you guessed it, Russian coaches seated in the final row of the bus, opening up and mainlining bottles of vodka....which in and of itself would be fine, perhaps they'll drink themselves to sleep, but oh no, we're far too late into the evening for anything as civilized as that to occur...these gentlemen have been slamming the stuff for god only knows how long, and...again, perhaps I shouldn't venture into 'national generalizations;, but man, Russians can really drink a lot before they pass out, or in this case quiet down....well, the volume of the conversation gradually increases, and then becomes a cacophonous group sing-along....and we are not talking choir or barbershop quartet quality here either....more like several bull elephants (or perhaps more accurately bull harbor seals or walruses!) racketing it up. Well, to the good, since it's still pitch black outside, when one's eyes are closed, one is at least, not being assaulted by excruciatingly bright light... ears? Oh, I'm getting a headache from the din....did I mention that at least back then, a lot of Europeans smoke?

Ummm, would it be fair to generalize that many Eastern Europeans smoke? How 'bout Russians, do Russians smoke? Do they smoke those awful, nasty Eastern bloc cigarettes, and do they smoke them like a pack or two chimney-style at a time? You're damned right they do, and if you are with a group of drunken Russian gymnastics coaches caterwauling and fuming like industrial smokestacks in a small enclosed space like a fully packed bus for 3 ½ hours you will have a reasonably clear picture of what Dante's 3rd level of hell is like! I've never been more relieved to get to an airport in my life.....I think it took 3 days (and several showers) to shake the smell....my lungs maybe have never yet completely recovered.

Old Packhorse

One trait I know I bring as a traveler is one of boundless interest and curiosity about the peoples and places I encounter. I've told many many people, that I have never, in all the times I've been to New York City, ever had a bad, or even rude encounter with anybody there. I understand of course that living in the Big Apple can be incredibly stressful, trying to make it there is maybe tougher than making it anywhere...but as an outsider, I come in with a sense of wonder, enthusiasm, and excitement that I know is palpable to people who encounter me.

The same seems to hold true universally regarding any new place....we put Shaye on the plane at Heathrow after the competition, and we were going to spend the next week exploring and enjoying London; had never been there before this competition....so, the first day we're in London, we go and find the nice B&B that we'd reserved in the Cheswick district, just a little ways outside the main part of the city...there's a wonderful old pub right down the block called "The Old Packhorse" (what a great name!), and we go in to have a little lunch. What would you like to drink?" What beer do you have on tap?" The barmaid names several of which I've heard and says, "and also London Pride". "What's London Pride?"

I inquire....an heretofore unnoticed particularly grizzled old guy is sitting on a barstool just to my left....he leans to his right and nudges me in the ribs with his right forefinger…"Here ya are, gov'ner…try a bit a this." And with that, he slides his mug, which is about ¾ full 'cause he's had a few gulps of it himself already, of London Pride over to me to sample. Well, what the heck? So I take his beer, have a sip or gulp or two myself, and respond, "Well, thank you very much sir, it's excellent." Handing the mug back to him, I turn and tell the waitress, "I think I'll have a pint of that London Pride to go with my shepherd's pie, thank you very much." What a blast….I'm in a bar in London, and some complete stranger passes me his beer to drink from!

One of the contrasts that I find so fascinating between Europe and America, is how relatively "new" America is as a physical place, and how much history in Europe is piled on top of itself. The layers are thick in so many places in the Old World, and on occasion, can be graphically displayed. We embraced the whole traditional tourist thing (well, not exactly…I explore on my own, don't do groups, didn't do that double-decker open bus thing, but you know, National Gallery, Westminster Abbey, that kind of thing….Hannah and I were just emerging from the Tower of London, and crossing the street when in front of an adjacent church, there was a big wooden sign: "John Quincy Adams was married here in 1798."

What the heck? Now, it turns out of course to be true, but I'm wondering why this is some weird advertising come-on to visit the place…I mean, how many Brits, or Frenchmen, or whomever…even Americans would go out of their way in a place like London, to see such a minor 'landmark'.

In the foyer of the church is an elderly gentleman, impeccably dressed in a simple, yet elegant gray suit. "Excuse me sir, I saw the sign outside indicating that John Quincy Adams was married here." "You're Americans." he responds. Oh really. How could you possibly tell. No, I wasn't sarcastic with him…I simply said, "Yes sir, we are." He responds, "He was one of your Presidents you know."

No s---. And the sky is blue when it's not cloudy or raining. "Uhh, yes sir I know, but that isn't really…" "Yes," interrupts me, "he was a member of your diplomatic mission during the negotiations that your then Secretary of State John Jay negotiated with the crown, and he and his bride were married in this very church."

"You don't say…you know, this is our first time to London, and I find there's so much history here."

"Oh yes, and as a matter of fact, our little church has some rather intriguing features …we're not St. Paul's or Westminster Abbey, but, well, come let me show you." We walk behind him and he takes us into the main part of the sanctuary. "The church has been here for many years…it was partially damaged in the War, and had had a fire in the mid-19th century, but, here' you can see" he walks us to one of the pillars supporting the ceiling…"here is one of the finest examples of a stone Saxon arch in all of England." Saxon, I ask?

Yes, he says, "this pillar is part of the original foundation of the church and dates from the 9th century." That's incredible, I say…and it's still part of the structure today…"Oh yes. Come, I'll take you downstairs…there's something here I think you'll be interested in."

We follow him to what I assume is the basement….He walks us to a lectern with a very old book placed on top of it. He points: "Do you know that name?" In script, dated sometime in October 1644, the name William Penn has been inked into the book. "Umm, yes I do indeed." "William Penn was the founder of your colony Pennsylvania. This is our record of baptisms. William Penn was baptized in this church, and over here," we walk a few feet to the right "is his baptismal font." Ahah!! I know this is incorrect. "Sir, I believe you are in error. If I am not mistaken, William Penn's baptismal font is in Philadelphia and I say that because I have seen it myself on a trip there a number of years ago." "I see sir," he replied, "that you are a student of history….as a matter of fact, it is the top of the baptismal font that is in Philadelphia…the base of the Philadelphia font is a replica." Amazing.

"Now, since you have such a keen sense of history, let me take you to our subbasement…I think you'll find it of interest also." At this point, I'm completely captivated, and we descend another set of stairs and come into a dark place with a low ceiling. Our guide turns on the lights…behind a roped off area is about a 10 foot by 10 foot floor composed of small brick-colored tiles. "Our church was not the first building on this spot… what you are looking at are the tiles of the courtyard of the Roman villa that existed here in the 2nd century A.D." Incredible.

As we ascend to the main part of the church, I cannot help but noticing the distinctive stained glass on one wall of the vestibule. I ask, "I see this is fairly modern…"

"Oh yes," says the guide, "we sustained some damaged glass in the bombing in the War."

"I see," I note…"I'm curious…I think I'm reasonably knowledgeable about the history of World War Two, but I'm amazed that there is so many wonderful places here in London that survived the blitz…I don't recall anything specific, but did the Germans try to avoid hitting the most important landmarks?"

"Oh no…you may recall that much of the bombing was concentrated on the industrial center of the city which is more to the East, but I can assure you that Mr. Hitler did everything in his power to obliterate our London."

"You know, you're church and this city are so rich in history…but we come from a city that has a long history too."

"Really?" he responds with polite interest.

"Yessir, I come from Seattle, a city on the west coast of the United States."

"Yes, I've heard of your Seattle…it apparently rains a lot. "

"Yessir, along with the old architecture, it has that in common with London too. As I was saying, we've got quite a history…there's a building in Seattle that goes all the way back to 1888!"

He gets the joke and we smile together as co-conspirators.

I look back at the stained glass window…it was created after the war (or at least after 1940), and is a miniature depiction of The Battle of Britain, with planes, British fields, and fliers depicted wearing lined leather jackets and skullcaps….

"Excuse me sir, but isn't this The Battle of Britain."

"Oh yes,", he closes his eyes and smiles oh so gently….

"If you don't mind my asking….what were you doing during the battle?"

The response: "I flew Spitfires for the RAF."

Holy cripes! Amazing.

Decima

A couple more quick anecdotes…we were headed to Egypt for a competition, and had a full day layover in England….this was several years after the Birmingham World Championships, and I've never worried too much about itineraries…meaning, of course that I'll never miss a plane, but once on the ground, I don't feel compelled to have every single detail organized in advance. It's quite a contrast to my Aussie mate Trevor Dowdell who has to have everything on every trip itinerized, organized, and reserved in advance. Whenever he comes to Seattle, we get this lengthy trip-tych covering virtually every aspect….but I digress….we land at Heathrow, and are going to spend 30 hours or so in England….we get on the tube, and sure enough, head to the Cheswick stop, and remembering our great time in the City a few years earlier, walk the two blocks, suitcases rolling along behind us to Decima McQuiston's b&b…naww, no reason to bother calling ahead, we're in the neighborhood, just drop in….so we do….ringgggggg….ringggggggg…..she's not there…a neighbor pops her head out the front door, "Are ya lookin' for Decima, dearie?" "Yes, maam, do you have any idea when she'll be back?" "I think she's at the hairdressers…you should try again after 12." "Thank you very much!"

Soooo, we wander around the neighborhood, and up by the shops adjacent to "The Old Packhorse", and finally back to the McQuiston B&B….ringggggg….Ms. McQuiston (her hair looks great) answers the door…..takes a long look at us, squints then drops her left ear slightly towards her shoulder…."You're….you're the American gymnastics people, are you not?" It had been 4 years since we had actually been here, and yup, that's who we are…this lady has a great memory…."Ummm, we're in town overnight and were wondering if it would be possible to get a room for the evening." "Of course, how nice to see you!", she ushers us in, and we're ready to go hit the town…..

Charing-Cross

Many people may remember the film, "84 Charing Cross Road". Well, I'm a rather serious (albeit on a limited budget) bibliophile, and since we're in London, thought it would be great to walk down the two-block section of bookstores known as the Charing Cross…

(a slight digression…)

I've got a modest collection of antiquarian books and am particularly interested in incunables. I love book hunting, and when time and budget allow, am always sniffing around old bookstores for treasures. The internet has made this both easier, and in some ways a bit less fun, because there is less, well, sleuthing than there used to be because it's so much easier (the sloth in me!) to find what one wants, there's almost less of an incentive to stumble across unexpected treasures…well, for those that aren't book collectors, believe me, book hunting is very similar (or so I believe) to hunting or fishing…..the emotional flux goes from periods of tedium as one thumbs through row after row of trash (one man's trash, another's treasure of course) looking for that exceptional gem….for many years I loved to go up to Vancouver Canada and prowl around…the city had/has many nice old bookstores. It was a summer day when my gymnastics friend Hardy Fink (who now runs the FIG Academies, more on this later) and I walked into McLoud's bookstore off Pender Street. A rather officious gentleman comes up to us, and asks, "May I help you?" in a rather condescending tone….we were wearing jeans and t-shirts and apparently didn't look like the Leonard Pinth Garnell character so memorably portrayed by Dan Ackroyd. I pipe up with "Yes, we're looking for some incredibly rare books at some absurdly low prices." He sniffed a bit, then responded, "well, we don't have any of those here….maybe you should try that paperback store down the street." Such dismissiveness. Oh, the slings and slights we bookmen must bear. In any event, we wander around the store, and I finally ask him to open up a glass case that looks like it has some interesting things in it….rather reluctantly, he does so….I carefully look at a couple of the items, and seizing on a nicely bound 1752 copy of Twining's "Aristotle: Nicomachean Ethics", I pull out U.$300.00 in front of the guy from my wallet and ask casually: "Do you take cash and would American dollars be acceptable?" Well, you can surmise that his tone changed immediately…..

my favorite book story….more digression, but we'll get back to Charing-Cross eventually…)

previous year, Bond's bookstore, also in Vancouver…Hardy and I are wandering through the stacks, they've got a lot of really interesting antiquarian things in the shop, he's looking for old gym books, I'm poking around, looking for just about anything interesting, and I'm starting to get upset….there's this shelf, probably 3 rows full of 18th and (at the latest) very early 19th century books related to Greek and Roman literature, and the things are just tossed about on the shelves as if they were throwaways....suddenly, an epiphany.....in THIS bookstore, if THESE books are being treated like junk, it's because they are considered junk....ergo, the "really good stuff" is someplace else...and in every bookstore in the world, the really good stuff is on the bookshelves behind the counter....at Bonds, there is a long tall wall of books on one's left as you walk through the front door...the counter is about 20 feet inside the door, just in front of this left wall...just to the left of it, facing the main floor (and away from the wall) is a freestanding wooden glassed bookcase....I walk up beside the bookcase, and, as Holmes so memorably (and presumably so often) said to Watson, "the game's afoot". I can feel the blood pulsing in the veins above my cheekbones....my breathing is labored....if you are not a book collector, you may not understand, but there are occasions, where one knows, one KNOWS with absolute certainty, that there is "big game" afoot, and if only I can calm my mind, the books will call out to me...as absurd as this sounds, it is, as all collectors understand, indubitably true.....I try to control my breathing...I work to relax my muscles as I stand facing the wall...my heart is pounding, but I breathe deeply and try to let my mind be clear....let my mind clear, and the books will call....clear, calm, and.....right there, over to the left, second row from the bottom, second book from the divider...if one let's one's mind clear, the books will call out to you....second row, second book in, I turn and look....the book's binding, white, thick, torn on the bottom so a part of the interior stitching shows....

I walk over to the shelf, and pick the book up...it's old, obviously very old...I open it gingerly....rag paper....old Germanic script....no title page...a wonderful, aged, woody scent....a wonderful old book....a small note card slips out from the tome..."Viterbensius Commentaria" Johannes Annius Rome, 1498. If I don't gasp, I should have....I am holding in my hands, an incunable, a book from the 15th century...

There is only one category of books that is collectable simply because of age and that is books from the 15th century. Incunable is the singular of the Latin "incunabula", literally translated, "swaddling clothes", books (since the Gutenberg Bible was the first book printed with movable type <in Europe at least, there is some evidence that China had a technology that predated this> and it was printed no later than August 1456), ergo all books printed prior to 1501 are classified as incunables.

I approach the proprietor Mr. Wells (I'd been in the bookstore before) with the Annius. "Sir, can you tell me something about this book?" "It's interesting you noticed it," he responds..."I only acquired it last week...it's the oldest book in the store." "Yes, I'm interested in incunables, although I don't own any....what can you tell me about this book?" Well, booksellers have resources about their wares that the general public generally does not....well, according to Mr. Wells, this book was considered "incredibly rare" according to whatever reference source he was consulting from....do you believe this?...1856!!

It gets better...apparently Johannus Annius (whose real name was Giovanni Nanni) was (it turns out subsequently to be proven as) a notorious forger. This particular book, one copy of which exists in the British Museum, is an "alleged" history of the world through 1498. It turns out, that Nanni's "history" is completely bogus, and is derivative of the works of Joachim of Fiore (1135-1202), who to this day, is considered a controversial figure in the history of Western thought (and particularly the Catholic Church). Abbot Joachim, apparently spent most of his life straddling the line between papal approval and heresy...his most significant intellectual contribution was a theory of history that divided "history" into 3 groupings of 3 chronologically, and which ultimately implied that the Church as an institution would in the long-run of history be shed of its' authority and would be superceded with a form of millenarian socialism....Joachim, in fact, prefigures the broad socialist and populist thrusts of the 19th century, and remains a profoundly enigmatic and troublingly (to some!) subversive element to the establishment of social order to this day....Umberto Eco's "The Name of the Rose" refers to Joachim twice in the text, and for film fans, Sean Connery alludes to him at one point in the script....you gotta be kiddin' me....medieval heresy? A prefiguring of radical-anarchy? Forgery? An incredibly rare incunable? "How much do you want for it?" I didn't really ask this because the price is always penciled in on the first page inside the first board....U$1500. and this was in the late 80s.....oh, the agonies of trying to make a decision....."Could I do this on a payment plan""

"Of course" says Mr. Wells. "Here's U$200.00....I'll get the rest to you just as soon as I can....".......6 weeks later, I'm at the border crossing in Blaine...

"what was the purpose of your visit to Canada?" "Just visiting friends" "Where do your friends live?" "Up in Pt. Alberni...I spent the weekend and am just now taking the ferry back." "Do you have anything to declare?" "Nossir." "Welcome back to the USA." I drive through...two thirds of my responses are complete fabrications.....and I've brought another subversive text back to the spiritual and intellectual home of dissent, radicalism, craziness, subversion, and cool rockin' stuff! Joachim is the Chuck Berry of the 12th century! "Roll Over Pope Urban, and tell Augustine the news!!!!!"

But I digress....back at Charing Cross we attempt to cross the street....we are halted by a "do not cross/crime scene" tape and a couple of rather tall imposing, "Bobbies". I'm excited to go to the bookstores, and....another

digression....do you know the phrase, the saying "There's no such thing as a dumb question?" Do you believe it to be true? If you're answer is yes, then my response is, "You gotta be kiddin' me..." And, I (don't get me started on Salvadore Dali's great quote "the only difference between me and a madman is that I...an not mad") I've got two examples, me being the first to prove it....I wanna go to the bookstores, so when the light turns green (I look to the right to see the traffic 'cause we're in England of course where they drive on the "other" side of the street of course) I try, after looking, dip under the tape where a very large Bobbie with a very large helmet/hat bids me..."halloo,,,where'dya think you are goning?" "I want to go over to Charing Cross, to the bookstores."
"It's not allowed, ya cain't go that there now, ya." I try to cross again, he stops me and puts a (rather firm) hand on my shoulder.... "You are NOT permitted." He stares at me a bit more closely..."You're American." A statement of fact.
"Yes officer".
"Well", with maybe a Liverpudlian intonation, "ya caan't go there....it's orders."
"Well, with all due respect officer, why not? We're here briefly on holiday, and I'd like to go look at the bookstores." "Yeah, so would I" he says not unkindly, but obviously facetiously since it's apparent he's not huge big-literatiii, but that said, it seems clear that he's bent on not letting me go...once again, I appeal to his "better nature"..."Officer, I'm just looking to go visit a few of the bookstores down that road"...."Well, sir, you cannot. In point of fact, we have had a bomb scare."
Bomb scare? Well, how very interesting...what the hell does that have to do with me getting to go visit the bookstores/getting to do what I want when I want to do it? "Officer, surely one person walking across the street won't be a problem".
He looks down his long aquiline nose at me with a (do I perceive it incorrectly?) certain measured, if not contempt, condescension...."I will state it more clearly sir...we have had a bomb threat...the Irish Republican Army has contacted M5 and we have secured this area...all stores are closed and all personnel have been evacuated." Now the payoff, and I'm the unwitting (and clueless) straight man in this Abbot-Costello dialog...."Well, when will I be permitted to cross your street and go visit the bookstores?".......the poor man is now beyond contempt....it's clear that Britain should have held firm against the colonialists, since we are so obviously of inferior stock and mentally (if not morally) deficient to boot....he looks at me witheringly, and in measured tones replies..."Well sir, as a matter of policy, the IRA is NOT in the business of giving us the precise location and time of detonation of their explosive devises."
Oh.

Now, for the reader who might think that that is the single dumbest question ever posed, ("there's no such thing as a dumb question"....hey dummy, if the previous example hasn't convinced you, read on!)....I've got one that (with full understanding that those who might question my ranking based on the fact that the previous one was asked by me) if not tops it, certainly ranks "right up there".

A few years back, during a beautiful summer in the Pacific Northwest, my cousin Sharon who is a pharmacist born, bred, and living in Williamsport Pennsylvania came out to visit ...Sharon (as is true with most of my "east coast, mother's side of the family" relatives had never been west of Cleveland, Ohio Anyway, she came out to visit, and as with all guests, we do the typical mid-summer tourist spots, Pike Place Market, Space Needle, Seattle Underground, et.al. but as always, the best for people that don't live in the Northwest or on either of the coasts, is to as we did, take them on a ferry boat ride....it's a perfect late July day, and we board the Bainbridge Island ferry on our way to Scenic View State Park over on the Kitsap Peninsula just west of Seabeck (Seabeck basically is a grocery store cum post office, with a gas pump in front of it)....anyway, the ferry has pulled away from the dock and is chugging across Elliot Bay, a couple small cirrus clouds in the sky are the only things marring a perfect combination of blue sky and sea....there are seagulls languidly trolling the air, the updraft from the heat emanating from the result of the summer sun's rays on the water, keeping company, and boldly snatching the crackers the tourists toss into the air in order to see them, well, snatch the crackers tossed into the air....

We stand together at the bow of the boat (actually a fairly large ship although we call them ferry boats out of habit), forearms resting on the bulky green rail as the bow churns powerfully through the water...Bainbridge looms, oh 20 minutes away....Sharon is on my right...."So" she inquires out of the clear (not sky, not water) blue...."is Seattle at sea level or what?"
!!!!!?????

The words, the question slowly sinks into my consciousness.....whaaaa?
I ponder a moment....it feels like a long moment....I slowly, oh so slowly, turn my head, and look at her....I consciously make eye contact....Sharon's eyes meet mine in a long, inquiring (why is he looking at me in that way) look....my head, chin lifted, pivots back towards the west....I scan the horizon...then slowly, oh so but significantly slowly, I lower my head and my eyes peer directly at the water rushing under the bow of the boat....the waters of Puget Sound as the "Klamath"
forges ahead.....to my right, a small(er) voice: "Ummmm....I guess that was kind of a dumb question, huh?"
Here's your sign.

Brains

Back in the UK, one of the great recent traditions of the pubs,is "trivial pursuit"…it's become a Sunday early evening tradition in the UK for folks to gather together in pubs to play trivial pursuit in groups….many of the groups are quasi-formal teams who meet each week to compete for (relatively) insignificant prizes, and to enjoy a pint and bit of food while engaged in the spirit of, well, trivial competition….it's fun…. teams are often formed "on the spot" when for example, folks at the same table sit down and decide that they can take on the world…trivially of course speaking….

We had finished the day wandering around London….oh, shortly after the Charing Cross incident, I mentioned my interest in (it's now early Sunday afternoon) catching the Tottenham Hotspur-Chelsea match at Stamford Bridge, Chelsea's home pitch at 3 pm that afternoon….Spurs of course is my team in England, first and only non-league team to win the FA Cup (1901), and the first in the 20th century to win the "double" (League Championship and FA Cup 1961, the Danny Blanchflower team), and I've never actually seen them in person….

What's Hannah's response? "You've seen a football game (actually it's "match")

In England before (Aston Villa as rccounted above)…there's no reason to waste a Sunday afternoon seeing another one…" Crikey….so what does she insist we do (as a version of Chinese water torture)…you guessed it, we went friggin' shopping, but not only did we go shopping, but we went shopping in what part of London?

CHELSEA!!!!

There's an antique mall that we (read: SHE) got to prowl, and best (really I mean worst!) of all, we were one tube stop from the Chelsea grounds, and were on the train with masses of Spurs supporters wearing the white and blue cockerel scarves…..ridiculous….

In any event, back at "The Old Packhorse" after shopping, we are having a pint and a meal and are drafted into a trivia team….Hannah had picked up a button in one of the shops in Chelsea…a round button with an American flag background, it was captioned "Americans Have Smaller Brains." Well, in the full sense of truer truisms were never thought to be more valid (i.e. TRUE!), as soon as one of our teammates saw the button, of course our team was unanimously (actually there were two abstaining votes!) nominated and named, you guessed it, "Americans Have Smaller Brains." Sad to relate, we didn't win the contest, but a good time was had by all, and my teammates were happy to have a Yank in charge of answering all the North American questions.

Mid-day repast

A couple years later, we were in transit through Heathrow and were going to be on the ground for a total of 4 ½ hours. Some dear gymnastics friends, Mike and Tanya (more on her in the Namibia chapter) Swallow own a gym school not too far from the airport....brief though it might be, we were going to take this opportunity to touch base and catch up....the year before, I was coming out of the Olympic Museum in Lausanne Switzerland, and unbeknownst to us, Mike and Tanya were there for the competition. As I walk out, this attractive woman comes up the steps, and without hesitating a moment, walks directly up to me and gives me a great big hug and kiss....she was practically puckered up and ready to smooch before I realized who it was; naturally, it was Ms. Swallow....well, hello there, nice to see you, hey, gimme another peck right here on the lips. We clung to each other as old friends might, great big smiles on our faces, and about 2 minutes later, Mike who had been trailing at the bottom of the steps comes up and after a minute or two of scrutinizing us (remember, I've got my arms around the <narrow and shapely> waist of his wife and she has her arms around my neck says in his dry, English (actually I'm not entirely sure of Mike's provenance or sympathies since he was the coach of an Irish girl at the 1983 Worlds)....in any event, Mike walks up to us, and without batting an eye, taking in the scene, says dryly (and hilariously!)....I figured my wife was greeting a long-lost old friend....everything else being equal of course, I would wish that she would not indulge herself so....enthusiastically."....well, of course the three of us cracked up, I gave her a huge kiss full on the mouth, bent her over in a "tango dip step" and with a flourish let her up and let her go...."How are ya Mike, great to see you" as I followed up with a simultaneous "mano a mano" hug.... "It is great to see you, how's it goin'?"

In any event, back at Heathrow, we are being processed through customs...the customs agent takes my passport, (we can see Mike and Tanya standing beyond the glass partition about 10 meters away)....the Passport control agent fingers my passport....examining the various stamps from the breadth of the countries I've traveled....he takes his stamp and punches my entry into the UK officially...he looks up at me, and with a smile makes eye contact...."and how long will you be in England, sir?" he inquires.....I wait a beat...badda boom, badda bing.............."lunch."

The expression on his face makes it clear that he is happy that this colonial was kicked out of the Commonwealth on or about 1776.

"There are certain sections of New York, Major, that I wouldn't advise you to try and invade."
Humphrey Bogart (Casablanca, 1942)

Chapter Six

NIGERIA

The West African Country of Nigeria has a deserved reputation as one of the most unpleasant places in the world. While currently not particularly dangerous in the conventional sense, Nigeria has long been at the head of the line in terms of general chaos, disorganization, and a pervasive corruption that permeates most aspects of Nigerian life and culture.

Students of African history will recall the humanitarian catastrophe that was the attempted secession of the Ebo or Eastern part of Nigeria in the late 1960s as hundreds of thousands Nigerians perished in the still-birth of the nation of Biafra.....

An "artificial" country in that (as usual) it's borders were drawn by the outgoing colonial power (Great Britain) without respect to the history or interests of the 100 plus tribal groups within it's geographical limits, since its' independence in 1960, the country has been riven by ethnic strife, and in 40 of its' 48 years ruled by various military despots.

In short, who in their right mind would want to go there? Exactly! Just my 'cup of tea', so when offered the opportunity to go and spend several weeks working in Nigeria to develop a long-term strategic plan for their gymnastics Federation, jumped at the chance!

I'm partial to the "Lonely Planet" travel guides. In preparation for the trip to Nigeria, I was amused and chastened by the admonition (closely paraphrasing): "If you're headed to Nigeria, under no circumstances should one fly into Muhammed Murtala airport at night!" So? Naturally, our flight was booked to get into Murtala at approximately 10 pm. On a Saturday night. After about a 36 hour trip, Seattle, to London, to Brussels, to Lagos, we disembark the plane.

Although we had been acquainted with officials, coaches, and gymnasts from the Nigerian Olympic Committee and Gymnastics Federation for 2 years (and had served as credentialed assistant coaches at the Commonwealth Games), as we passed through (3 barriers) of Customs, we got our first real taste of what passes for Nigerian "hospitality"...."What have you got for me?" says the first Customs official, smiling as he waits to receive something before stamping our passport for entry. I pull out a gymnastics pin from my briefcase and hand it over to him. "Enjoy your stay in Nigeria", he responds, and passes me on to checkpoints numbers two and three where the same, more or less, "transaction" takes place.

We walked to the baggage claim area which is very informal and loosely supervised and looked for Mr. Elias Gora of the NOC who had informed us that he would be at the airport to meet us, and take us to our hotel. We searched extensively around the airport....no Mr. Gora. The luggages started to arrive through the carousel; we waited and watched as every single passenger over the course of 90 minutes or so received their luggage. Ours were not on the carousel.....we go to the baggage claim office....it's closed. It's now approaching one am on Sunday morning, and I'm starting to get a little worried. For the first and only time in a life of traveling around the world, I managed to have packed my overnight bag in my regular luggage. All I had on my person was my briefcase; all Hannah had was a small traveling bag. And, there was no one from the Olympic Committee (or any other organization here to pick us up).

We walked out onto the concourse....I've been in lots of "Third World" countries, but man, these guys are all armed to the teeth. As far as I can figure it out, there are at least 3 different groups of uniformed men armed with automatic weapons. I'm going to guess that the guys in the camouflaged khakis are the Nigerian army, the guys in the dark blue uniforms are either the State Police or local police, and the guys in the regular green are either local cops (armed with Kalishnikovs!), or the airport police...in any event, there are a LOT of guns at this airport as we're approaching 2 am....and still no Gora, dammit. Well, having no idea where anything is, I go back into the airport and find out from an ad, that there's a Hilton hotel about 5 miles from the airport, which is where the Sabena airline people are billeted. As I come out, a crowd has gathered around Hannah...apparently, there are about 25 cabdrivers who want to take us "for a ride" and being the only two non-natives (read: white people!) in the place, we stand out reasonably prominently. Well, I start to try to talk and get some separation from these folk, when the gendarmes come over, and two of them, not necessarily with malicious intent (and no, I'm not under sniper fire in Bosnia!), listening in on all the cross-babble, lower their weapons in the general direction of my torso.....I'm confident that they were not attempting to be threatening, but I can tell you that having a (presumably loaded) weapon pointed at me in a foreign country at night is damned scary! I sort of sidled sideways to get out of the line of fire of those muzzles I can tell you!

About this time, Hannah, who sometimes gets weary of my efforts at diplomacy, and who had been up about 2 days, lost it. She starts snarling, "I'm tired, I'm hungry, and I want to get out of this place...NOW! The cabbies start to back away....if I were them, I'd be wary of this crazy white woman yelling at me too! "YOU!! She points at one of the drivers...."Where's your cab?"...he points to the left...."let's go, and let's go NOW!" She storms towards the cab, the driver scampering after her, and me after him, pulling away from the several hands and arms that have me around the shoulders.

We got into the cab..."Take us to the nearest hotel." Hannah says...I instruct, "The Hyatt near the airport" please. Without hesitation, the cabbie drives us to the hotel. Now came the next "fun" part....he provides some ridiculous figure for the fare....at the hotel, they managed to have a room available, so thank goodness we were going to be able to check in....while we had some traveler's checks in American dollars (and a couple hundred U$ currency), there was no way I was going to change money in the hotel at the "official" exchange rate of 3 Nigerian naira to one US dollar...the real (i.e. black market rate) was, at the time, more like 55-60:1...yes, I'll wait and exchange the money in the morning when I can find something a little more reasonable.....meanwhile, our cabbie is standing by patiently waiting for (what he thinks will be) his 'windfall'. Well, I have to give him something....and the only money I have in my briefcase is large group of US coins that I was going to use as simple souvenirs...I dig into the briefcase, and come up with $6.24 in quarters, dimes, nickels, and pennies.....the cabbie looks at me like I'm both nuts and robbing HIM!!! I hand him the coins, bid him a quick goodnite and heartfelt thanks for getting us here, and boom, we step into the elevator, get to our room, and start to settle in.

Before dropping off to what was a fitful and worried sleep, we assessed our situation. Tomorrow/today was Sunday; no one in Nigeria knew where we were; we didn't have any luggage (i.e. change of clothes) and had been wearing the same clothes for two travel days. About the only thing Hannah had in her overnight bag was a change of underwear (hers), and a couple t-shirts and shorts (that we were going to use as souvenirs). A quick shower, and off to bed.

The next morning, (oops, I forgot to mention, Hannah had handwashed the shirts, socks, etc. we had had on the trip, and set them to dry over the lamps in the room.)....we got up late, close to noon...it had been a long trip and very late night...Nigeria is humid....v-e-r-y humid...and this Hilton does not have particularly good air conditioning....our clothes are still damp.

Taking inventory, I look like hell....my shaving kit is with our luggage which could be anywhere in the world but isn't here....I've got a 3 day-beard, rumpled and damp sweatpants, and about the only thing I can actually wear at this point is a t-shirt (which doesn't fit me) and some ugly green shorts....sheesh, need to get on the phone....Sabena airlines....the next flight from Brussels will be in tonite at 10 pm (22:00 hrs)....presumably our luggage will be there (which, of course, will necessitate another trip to the airport and back because they "don't deliver" in Lagos...we call the Olympic Committee....no answer, it's Sunday and they are closed....we call the Gymnastics Federation....ditto. Mrs. Wophill's number, Mr. Gora's number are not in the phone book, nor can anyone at the telephone exchange provide any information. Hmmmmmm. The main coach of the gymnastics team is Koicho Zlatev...perhaps the Bulgarian Embassy can help us. They answer their phone!

And while they express great sympathy, they do not know of Mr. Zlatev's precise domicile, but the nice lady on the other end of the phone says to check back tomorrow, she'll phone around and do what she can....I mean, how many international Bulgarian coaches (or even Bulgarians!) could their be in Lagos Nigeria at any given point in time?

Having exhausted, at least for the moment, the possible means for making contact, we decide (it's now early afternoon) that we're getting hungry....we wander downstairs to the lobby of the hotel....lots of folks milling around...we are acutely self-conscious....not because we are a minority of two in the place, but because due to our lack of luggage, we look like a couple of hoboes....meandering down a hallway, we're looking for a restaurant, and pass a door....there's a sign proclaiming "Lusty Pensa, here today!" There are some folks milling about what is obviously a reception room, man, these folks are 'dressed to the nines'....It looks like the fanciest wedding reception I've ever been to...Native Nigerian costumes consist of wonderful fabrics with great swaths of cloth draped around the women...lovely headdresses of all shapes, bright, shining silken gowns utilizing the entire color spectrum, (but shying away from blacks, grays, browns, and beige...) The men wear a diverse collection of tribal gowns, interspersed with what is obviously very expensive and tailored European suits. Grey charcoal pinstripe double vested seems to be the fashion of choice amongst the gentlemen who opt for the "Euro" look.

In any event, we are approached by a couple of the ladies who have come towards us down the hall, and one in a brilliant orange and red gown inquires politely and warmly, "Welcome...do you know Lusty Pensa?" "Well, ummm, no ma'am, we don't." Without a second glance at our rather (no, our obviously!) shabby attire, she explains, "Lusty Pensa is a musical group...they've just cut their first album, and we are having a party for them...they'll be playing a bit later...you are more than welcome to join us!"

Whatever pejoratives can be stated about Nigeria as a country and the way its' institutions (fail) to operate, the beauty of the country can be summed up in the attitudes of its' people....there are few if any people in the world more fun loving, open, and willing to share what they have with (in our case obvious!) strangers.

The two ladies, as I recall one of whom was an aunt of one of the band members, insisted that we join the party! Despite our demurrals (due to our embarrassment at looking like bums surrounded by all these elegant people!), they were emphatic and ultimately convincing as they ushered us into the room, and introduced us around as their new "American friends." We most definitely did get some inquiring, but not in any way negative or offensive looks. People couldn't have been nicer, inviting us to join the food and beverage table, asking us questions as to our reason for visiting Nigeria, etc.

Lusty Pensa was good! We had a blast at the party, and, although we never actually got to see any, we were prominently featured in a number of home videos as many of the folks attending the function were armed with video recorders. Perhaps the highlight of this rather surreal occasion was the rather flamboyant entrance of "Cholly Boy". A large man wearing a 3 piece Brooks Brothers suit, some serious diamond jewelry and sporting a stunning lady on his arm, Cholly Boy is/was one of Nigeria's more popular musicians and swept into the room like royalty, waving his left arm in a regal manner whilst bowing to people on the right. The crowd flocked to him, obviously excited by his presence.

It was an incredible scene, and the juxtaposition between the other guests' expensive and fashionable finery, and us, 2 swells right out of the Bowery could not have been more stark…and in a peculiar way, hilarious!

Fast forward to the following morning, we are about to embark on another round of phone calls, and I'm considering getting a taxi to take us directly to the Olympic Committee offices (wherever in Lagos) they might be, when our phone rings!

Oh, digression. I had to get a cab last night after the Lusty Pensa party and go out and attempt to retrieve our lost/late suitcases. While en route to the airport, I recall the true story of the Ugandan (?) soccer club which was about to leave Lagos via Murtala after an African Nations match, and looked out the windows to see their luggage being stolen by a group of robbers who had actually driven a truck out onto the airport tarmac, and literally "held up" the plane, while they unloaded luggage into the truck and fled...such are some of the more interesting "challenges" of life in this particular corner of the world....yes, got the luggage back finally, but, no big surprise here, someone (or someones!) along the way had made sure that we "had something for them". Yup, our luggage had been broken into, and a number of items removed! We was robbed in Nigeria!

The phone rings, and it is none other than Elias Gora on the phone...in his most conciliatory (and fake) voice, he goes on breathlessly, "Oh, I'm so happy we found you, I have no idea how you could have missed me at the airport," (Yeah, right.)

So Gora's going to come over and get us (covering his butt is what he's really up to, since he stood us up at the airport, and is probably terrified of us spilling the beans to some higher-up in the bureaucracy....), and we'll start our program later this afternoon.

It turns out (we eventually learned) that the nice lady from the Bulgarian Embassy had done some phoning around, and managed to locate a weightlifting coach who worked for the NOC. Serendipitously, Gora, NOC President Alhaji Adujumo NGF President Adamu Dyeri, Mrs. Wophill, Coaches Isiah Obanor, and Koicho Zlatev were having a meeting at the NOC office this morning, and Gora was explaining that the "American gymnastics people" didn't show up, so the coaches course would have to be canceled. At that exact moment, the weightlifting coach happens by the open door of the room in which they were holding their meeting, and overhearing the conversation, sticks his head in the door and contributes: "Oh, the American gymnastics coaches? They're out at the Hilton near the airport." THANK YOU Bulgarian Embassy!!

So, Gora comes flying over to the hotel, and is going to relocate us at one closer to the middle of downtown, and with Mrs. Wophill in tow, proceeds to take us to lunch at this pretty upscale restaurant. "Oh, I just don't understand how you could have missed me," he continues to press...."I waited for you for hours."

"Even though we have met on occasion before, I had a sign I held up and even paged you." Well, of course it was all nonsense, but what the heck...Mrs. Wophill doesn't need to know all this, and besides, never let them see you sweat. "Oh, these things happen", I respond casually, "it's not a problem, it all worked out."

"It must have been terrible for you," he pressed on doggedly, apparently secretly hoping (actually it was v-e-r-y transparent) that we had suffered on some level.

"Oh, no, really not a problem, we're pretty experienced travelers, and you know, these things happen..." Still, hoping to nail any loose ends shut, he lumbers on..."Well, didn't Madame Hannah say you had lost your luggage?"..."Oh yeah," I almost drawl, "but I went back out to the airport and got it back...there were some things missing but it's no big deal..." He still won't let it go, and I've been holding back my shovel hook..."Goodness, how terrible for you both, I'm so glad I was able to find you."

I have to suppress the urge to either laugh out loud or slap the guy...but I'm enjoying this too much to end it right now...."Awww what the hell….I change my mind…he's on the ropes and I'm Jack Dempsey, the Manassa Mauler and I unleash a killer uppercut that's lands flush on this palooka's kisser…..", naaaah," I play with the peas with my fork...."it's been pretty interesting really...you know yesterday, we met Cholly Boy..."

At which point Gora jerked forward in his chair...I thought he was going to spit out his fish! "CHOLLY BOY?" You met Cholly Boy???" he blurts out....he couldn't have been more shocked than if I actually had slapped him...

"Well, yeah" I respond, the perfect picture of casual innocence...."Cholly Boy the musician????"

This guy blew us off at the airport and jerked us around by neglecting us all week end....now this is fun...."Uhhhh, yeah....we were invited to this reception you see, and...", Mrs. Wophill has been sitting at the table quietly listening to this guy's spiel the whole time...I have no idea what she thinks about Mr. Gora or what their history might be, but she's listening very attentively to this exchange...."anyway, Hannah and I were at this very nice reception, and were introduced" (I'm embellishing a bit here, but that's ok...Gora's too stunned to notice or care) "to Cholly Boy....what a great guy, very personable!" With that, having twisted the shiv all the way into him, I figuratively step back to admire my handiwork as Gora completely deflates...."Cholly Boy", he says one more time, more to himself than to any of the rest of us at the table.....and thus, we begin our sojourn in Nigeria.

In 1993, and especially in 1994, when I saw the Nigerians at the Worlds, I made it a strong point to go over and speak with the team and their coaches. Hannah and I subsequently arranged that the Nigerians would be our guests at a training camp in Seattle prior to the 1994 Commonwealth Games, which were held in nearby Victoria, British Columbia. All went smoothly until we arrived in Canada. It seems that regardless of how straightforward something might presumably be, there always seems to be problems if it's at related to Nigeria. At the Commonwealth Games, the most significant was the refusal on the part of the Nigerian Olympic Committee to pay the monies that had been guaranteed to the athletes, and in particular to Athletics (i.e. the Track & Field). It turned out (or so the story went) that the officials in charge of the payments had no interest actually getting the funds to the athletes, but rather, were more focused on "ensuring" that the funds (i.e. embezzling) didn't go to any outlets other than their own pockets.

Nigeria has an amazing number of high level athletes who, if the country provided concentrated training, integrated support systems and any kind of long-range plan would be capable of being one of the dominant programs in international sport. Even with the almost complete lack of experience and little training, the gymnastics team at the 1994 Commonwealth Games was extremely competitive on the events upon which they concentrated. Cletus Okhpoh, Kingsley Eraghbe, Augustine Eraghbe, Smart Idahosa and Kenneth Obanor did a great job and the first two made event finals (Cletus on floor, and Kingsley on floor and vault).

I alluded in the "Miscellaneous nonsense" chapter about how being involved in major international events often entailed great experiences.....I believe I'm a competent coach technically, but know that my greatest strengths are in developing training plans for a given meet, (as a subset of same) and knowing how to "peak" the athletes for a given competition, and also feel that I'm effective in helping gymnasts achieve maximum performance "on the day", i.e. getting the maximum output on the competition floor.

As we marched into the venue at the Commonwealth Games, (a cramped, yet intimate converted hockey arena in Victoria, it was apparent that the guys on the Nigeria team were distracted and stressed. Coaches Zlatev and Obanor, who of course had been the primary trainers of the team apparently didn't see this particular issue in the same manner in which I did. It must be noted that Hannah and I hadn't actually been directly involved in the team's training for more than a couple weeks. As a result of our being at the Worlds earlier in the year and because of its proximity to Victoria, we had offered the Nigerians the opportunity to conduct their pre-competition training in Seattle which they gladly accepted. So, after a couple weeks of training, we had collectively traveled up to Victoria for the competition.

Nigeria was in the first session of competition. There was a full house as we completed the one touch warm-up on their first event, pommel horse....Koicho and Isiah were engaged in a conversation and weren't paying close attention to the guys...I noticed that a fairly prominent spectator had just entered the arena and was seated in the balcony just above and to our right. I called the team together..."Gentlemen, I know you're a little nervous just before competition...it's natural, but I want you to focus, and to put all this in perspective....just think, here we are, a beautiful summer day, you're about to represent your country at the Commonwealth Games....here we are, capacity crowd, 59 countries, worldwide television coverage, and..." I gestured towards the balcony and our prominent spectator no more than 10 meters away...."the Queen of England watching your performances.... Life simply can't get any better than this! Now let's go get 'em!" High fives all around, and we were ready to compete!!!

Perhaps the greatest, if not tragedy in the Homeric sense, misfortune of Nigerian life is, for many complex reasons, Nigeria is a country of unparalleled potential, that has yet to really coordinate its resources or develop strategic planning. While it's clearly true in the larger political sense, it's very specifically true in the narrower sense of sport.

From a sporting standpoint, there are few, if any countries in the world (the USA excepted) with the breadth and depth of potential athletic talent. Nigeria is the most populous country in Africa (120 million or more consisting of more than 100 different ethnic i.e. tribal backgrounds), and enjoys through its oil reserves, a potentially boundless source of wealth. That said, the level of success has not been proportional to its' potential. There are a number of interrelated reasons for this. First, there is a "kleptocracy" mentality amongst the elites of the sporting community. It is amazing to an outsider to watch financial agreements with athletes routinely violated by various officials.

During the Commonwealth Games, athletes were not provided meal money by Nigerian Team officials until the athletes actually had threatened to boycott the event. It should go without saying that this kind of stress and controversy is utterly counterproductive to the proper mental preparation for Elite (or any other kind) of competition. This behavior remains endemic within the Nigerian sporting community. Long respected for the world-class soccer football players the country has produced, regular readers of soccer periodicals will find continued conflict between the National Federation and its' star players.

Another problem that negatively affects Nigerian sport is a lack of long-term planning. It is unclear as to why this is so, but despite our best efforts, there was little interest paid in the development of a long-term comprehensive strategic plan. Another aspect that frankly astonished us is the "national perception" of where Nigeria might rank in the sporting community. Hannah and I had the opportunity to appear on two different nationally broadcast television shows while in Lagos. On both shows, we were asked the question: "Why can't Africans/black people do gymnastics?" I was absolutely floored! "Uhhh, do you mind if I ask why you ask that?" I responded. "Yes," said the first host...."when we watch the Olympics on television, we only see white people." What a perception!! I responded, "well, gymnastics is still a sport that needs to grow throughout Africa....and if you watch the Olympics, you'll notice that the Japanese and Chinese who are not white are very strong as well. But specifically to your point, you are misinformed. Blacks can be and are fabulous gymnasts. As a matter of fact, the current Gold Medalist in the All-Around for Women from the Commonwealth Games is Stella Umeh from Canada. It might be of interest for your viewers to know that Stella's parents are Nigerian; as a matter of fact, they met while students at Benin University here in this country, so as far as I'm concerned, while the Gold medal may physically be in Canada, it can also be claimed by Nigeria!"

Another aspect that limits sport in Nigeria is the long-held habit of "hoarding"....when we were conducting our coaches course, many of the coaches from around the country complained about a lack of equipment (as well as a lack of support from the Ministry of Sport or Gymnastics Federation). One day during lunchtime, Hannah and I started exploring Surulere Stadium, the National Stadium for the Football and Athletics programs. We were wandering around some dusty concourse, when we came around a corner and saw a number of storage containers and packages....remember at this time Nigeria was in its final preparation stages for the World Soccer Cup, and the country was going just about completely crazy....

We turned a corner, and I just about had a heart attack. The entire long (loooong) hallway is crammed with crated gymnastics equipment...there are 8 or 9 sets of parallel bars, at least 6 ring stands, 8 pommel horses, 7 or 8 horizontal bars, 9 or 10 balance beams and 12 (twelve!!!!) full sized-trampolines. They're just sitting here and have been here for at least a couple years. Unbelievable. When we go back to the meeting hall, stunned, we ask Mrs. Wophill about the equipment. "Oh yes, the Olympic Committee purchased all that several years ago. There's also two or 3 containers out in the harbor filled with landing mats and I believe at least 2 spring floors with carpet...I'm sure with the humidity here in Lagos, that the carpet may be ruined by now." "WHY hasn't the NOC distributed this equipment to the States or the gymnastics schools?" Mrs. Wophill shrugs..."Sometimes in Nigeria, things just work that way."

End of discussion. Unbelievable.

One of the most incredible ironies to me is that Nigeria, a country with over 120 million people consisting of over 100 tribes is one of the countries that most closely resembles the USA in terms of diversity. The athletic (and by any other metric) potential of the place is virtually unequalled and open-ended.....if, would it be possible to circumvent the political nonsense and corruption, Nigeria is one of three countries (the other two being Egypt and Mexico) that currently are not but I believe could be a super-power in international sport.

During our discussion on physical selection (which I'm philosophically opposed to using in terms of providing access to gymnastics instruction but is a reasonably reliable predictor of high-level gymnastics potential), I recounted one old DDR test for "courage where the coaches would ask a child to hang on a horizontal bar and ask the child to release and drop to the floor. In any event, after one day's training and lectures, we were relaxing by the pool by our hotel, and a native Nigerian dance group gave an outdoor performance on the deck. The culmination of dancing and tumbling resulted in a couple pyramid formations, the most difficult of which included a 12(?) year old boy climbing to the top of a three man pyramid, and from an approximate 10 foot meter kicked off the top (third) man's shoulder and executed a back salto to a STUCK LANDING ON CONCRETE!!! No mats, CONCRETE, pool decking!!!. We immediately went to the directors of the group and urged them to come to the Sports Complex the next day to be introduces to the gymnastics coaches and to Association officials. Conclusion: if you're planning on building a strong international program, exclude no one (one never knows who's going to be great administrators, coaches, judges, et.al. but....) everything else being equal, select fearless kids with strong tendons and ligaments!

"When a Leader's work is done, his aim fulfilled, his people will say: 'we did it ourselves.'"
Lao Tse

Chapter Seven

ZIMBABWE

Zimbabwe was in many ways a transformational experience for me; in the slightly less than 4 months I was there, I came to love the land and its' peoples, and to loathe the kleptocracy that permeates every aspect of Robert Mugabe's stranglehold on this battered country.

Having developed a modest reputation as a person who could run efficient and profitable gymnastics competitions, I had been contacted by long-time Zimbabwe Amateur Gymnastics Association (ZAGA) head Neil Nativel to coordinate the gymnastics competition for the All-African Games. Imagine my surprise when I get off the plane to find out that I was not only going to be the Competition Director for the Gymnastics Competition, but that they wanted me to be the coach of the Zimbabwe Men's team.

Well, what the heck....now, it turned out that there were a number of problems with this particular situation. It has always distressed me that (at least in our sport, although it's probably true throughout the human condition) that the fewer resources a group has, the more fiercely they seem to fight over 'control of the allocation of the resources", which, is, succinctly, the classic definition of "politics".

For reasons going back historically and beyond my interest, the Senior Men in the Zimbabwe program had been pitted against each other for years. The factionalism, and from the athletes perspective, perceived "favoritism" had resulted in a poisonous atmosphere where there was no concept of teamwork, no trust, and an actual dislike of each other on the part of several of the gymnasts. In Zimbabwe, as in much of Africa, tribal identity and loyalty still plays a profoundly important part in personal identity and how persons interact with those not from their own group.

For the record, the Senior Squad had one white (of Portuguese origin), one "colored" (a term and identity important in this part of the world), two Shonas (Mugabe's tribe), two Mtdebeles, and one Zulu.

My initial task was to set up a schedule, and to find some way that these guys could work together without rancor. After two days, I pulled the group together and explained that we were charged with preparing for the All-African Games. We were starting with a blank slate. I told them that whatever anyone else said to them, it didn't matter to me what their motivations were for participating, but that they had a simple choice. They could agree to participate in the team preparations, or they could choose to not be involved. I didn't care about team spirit, "school spirit", patriotism, love of country, "rah-rah", or any of the other things that people would be talking about in the leadup to the event. I was perfectly happy for them to be involved for their selfish motives.

As we went forward, I told them, they had 3 obligations: 1. come to practice unless they had cleared any exception with me beforehand. 2. be on time.
3. communicate with me regarding any gymnastics problems that they were having. Specifically, I wanted to know, a. anytime something was hurting or when they were in pain; b. I needed them to communicate to me anytime they were nervous about, or afraid of a skill. I reassured them that it was perfectly natural to have these feelings and that I would never tease or upbraid them about it and c. if they didn't understand what I was asking, to ask and get a clarification.
I told them that their sole responsibility was to do the gymnastics that we had mutually agreed that they were capable of performing. I would take care of everything else.

I further indicated that the final team makeup (5 competitors will be participating as the official team on the competition floor out of 7 squad members) would be determined by 3 weighted intersquad competitions. One of the historical drawbacks for gymnastics in Africa has been that due to the great distances required to travel for competition, few gymnasts have opportunities for more than the rare meet....it was important, not only to give the men some opportunities to "separate/select" themselves through a reasonably objective competitive process, but to give them some experiences of "hitting under pressure".

One of the most vital aspects of building a team is to not only keep the "rules" to a minimum (see above), but to make sure that the coach is completely consistent and accountable to the athletes for keeping up his end of the contract. When I told the athletes that they were required to be on time to practice, I also made it very clear that if practice was scheduled from 1800-2100 hours, that that not only meant that they needed to be in the training gym AT 1800 not 1801 or 2 or whatever, but that I was responsible for ensuring that practice would never go overtime. In fact, I explained to the gymnasts, that if, a practice hit the deadline of scheduled ending time that they had the right to walk out right then, even if I was in mid-sentence. This was tested early on, when, after our first workout or two together (I don't like unscheduled breaks in training), Lucky Mutare started to walk out of the gym...."Where are you going?"...."I've got to call my girlfriend" Lucky responded. "Oh. And why is that?" "I need to call her to tell her what time to come pick me up." "Lucky, I'm not sure if you understood me correctly, and I'll let you phone this one time, but....if I say practice is over at 9 o'clock, then if she's here at 9, she'll be right on time, because that's when practice will end. There may be a day here and there when we cut it short for some reason or another, but I promise you, we'll never go overtime." And we didn't, and the guys quickly came to understand that my word was gold regarding respecting the schedule.

I was confident that over time, by concentrating on "just gymnastics", that we would be able to reduce, if not completely eliminate the tensions that had been endemic amongst the group.. A couple weeks into our training, we had a moment which, paradoxically, turned out to be a real breakthrough. During our workouts, we would train two events at a time, and I was in the habit of randomly grouping the guys....on this particular morning, I said, "Khumbulani, you, Rick, Stan, and Wes" go to p-bars, the rest of you head over to the high bar." Then, we'd switch. Well, Rick Batista was having none of this. I had no idea what the problem was, but it was clear that Rick was sulking and upset. "Rick, what's the matter?" "Nothin'." Sulking and not quite stomping around, but again, obvious there was something eating at him....several inquiries and a half an hour later, he had gotten nothing done, and it was clear he was getting more frustrated as the morning went on...I finally pulled him aside and said: "Rick, I know your upset about something...if you tell me what it is, maybe I can fix it...if you don't talk to me, there's nothing I can do because I don't know what the problem is." He finally looks dully into my chest and says, gesturing towards the other 3 in his group, "I really don't like those guys." Now, Rick was fast friends with Warren Blumears, but I hadn't a clue....For the record, Rick was the white guy, Warren "colored, Khum the Zulu, and Wes and Stan, Shona.

In and of themselves, the ethnic identities would be of secondary importance, but as I indicated, they'd been exacerbated in previous seasons. Well, when Ricky confessed, "I don't like those guys.", I got a big smile on my face and responded, "Geez, Rick, well why didn't you just come out and say so? NO PROBLEM....you go over to high bar and join Warren's group....hey Wesley, c'mon over here and be on p-bars." And not only did that solve the problem for the day, but became a means by which we were able to bring the group closer together. How? I made a quiet joke out of it. The next practice, I (more or less randomly as always), broke the guys into two groups. "Lucky, you, Erasmus, Stan, and Khumbulani go to floor; Wes, you and "the twins" are on pommel horse. For the rest of our time together, I referred (and soon the rest of the team was enthusiastically chiming in)....Rick and Warren became permanently labeled "the twins"....a couple weeks later, Ricky came up to me, and confided: "Jim, we don't always have to be in the same rotation together, you know."

Creating bonds within a team is not an exact science or process, but rather an incremental progression of building one positive incident upon another. One should be alert for opportunities when they might present themselves. We were practicing one early July morning, when a small group of people walked into the gym. Ricky, who is a major film-buff, did a double-take. "Hey," he whispered,

"you know who that is?", pointing clandestinely..."Uhhh, looks vaguely familiar, but, no." "That's Mario VanPeebles! You know, the actor? Heartbreak Ridge with Clint Eastwood." Sure enough, it was Van Peebles, who, it turns out, was visiting Zimbabwe on vacation and was headed for one of the game reserves up by Victoria Falls. I approached him and yes, he confirmed that he's Mario Van Peebles, and said that he's always liked and admired gymnastics, but that he'd never really had the opportunity to try it. VanPeebles, if you've seen him in the movies, is on screen, one seriously "buff" dude...in person, he's about 5' 6" and built almost exactly like a gymnast. Powerful, but compact and certainly not oversized biceps or shoulders....wonderful gymnastics physique. "Hey, well as long as your here, would you like to try the trampoline?" "Oh, yeah, that'd be great" he replies. "Well, you've come to the right place...." "hey guys, c'mon over here...." my gymnasts approach...."Mario, I'd like to introduce you to the Zimbabwe National Men's Gymnastics team...we're in preparation for the upcoming All-African Games." And I introduce the guys one by one to Mario..."Hey, it's really nice to meet you guys...good luck at the Games...Gymnastics is probably my favorite sport to watch during the Olympics."

"Hey Rick," I say..."Mario would like to learn some skills on the trampoline...do you think you could help him?" "Uhh...sure" he says with a shy smile....I know his heart is thumping, and he is very pumped about the whole thing.

I leave him alone with Mario, and we go about workout for the next half-hour or so...but there's a little coda to this all....before he's ready to leave, I go into the small room that's my office, and get some paper and a marking pen. I then write on one of the sheets with the marker..."To Mario Van Peebles...Best of Luck, Always" and gather the guys into a group. "Gentlemen, I want you to each sign this paper....we're then going to give Mario VanPeebles your autographs!" Oh man, did they think that was the coolest idea....members of the "National Team" of Zimbabwe were not going to ask a Hollywood star for his autograph, but rather, they were going to give THEIR AUTOGRAPHS TO HIM!!! Whatta great turnaround idea!!! So, we got 7 signatures on the paper, and at the bottom, I wrote "Zimbabwe Men's Gymnastics Team", dated it, and had the guys go over and present it to Mario before he left the gym!

Working with these men was one of the two most enjoyable coaching experiences of my life; I'm enormously proud of them as individuals, and while I have no idea of what influence I might have had on each of them, it pleases me greatly that over a decade later, 6 of the 7 are still involved in gymnastics. Rick coaches a girls team at the Belvedere College Gym in Harare; Erasmus works with youth in the high density townships. Stan coaches at a club in Indianapolis Indiana, Khum the same in Roseburg Oregon. Warren coaches and teaches gym class at a club just north of Los Angeles, and Wesley coaches in Saskatoon Saskatchewan Canada.

Less enjoyable, however, was the wrenching, albiet intermittantly hilarious, experience of trying to coordinate a major gymnastics competition in the environment that is the "kleptocracy" of Zimbabwe. Let me share a few impressions and experiences.

The All-African Games is a multi-sport event held every 4 years and involves 52 of the 53 countries in Africa (Morocco does not attend for reasons which are not germane to this essay). After the Olympics and Commonwealth Games (59 nations), it is the largest multi-sport competition in the world. Zimbabwe, as the host nation, had of course, an enormous logistical and financial commitment in conducting the Games. I was, of course, not privy to much of the background information pertaining to the organization of the Games, but a number of particulars were "unusual" in my experience....the "Big Three" of the Zimbabwe Olympic Committee were President Tommy Sithole (who subsequently was voted onto the IOC as a Member), Secretary Edgar Rodgers, and Treasurer Mark Magnolius. Shortly after my arrival in Harare, Neil Nativel and I had meetings with first Mr. Rodgers, then Mr. Sithole. We were given a budget, and told that there would be supplies available for office-type expenses. One of the primary issues that needed to be resolved was the expansion of the Belvedere College Gymnasium which was the gymnastics venue for the Games. In essence, the East wall of the gym had been knocked out, and the facility was being extended by about 20 meters. There were approximately 100 days until the start of the event and the construction had just begun.

Attendance at any multi-sport is always a significant source of revenue...with 19 different sports involving over 50 countries spread over a two week period throughout Zimbabwe, one could anticipate easily a million plus tickets sold.

The manner in which this was handled at the Zimbabwe All-African Games was particularly stunning in its' brazenness. Mark Magnolius owns a chain of sporting goods stores throughout the country. The only location that event tickets could be purchased was "in person" at one of Magnolius's stores. While that might put a damper on ticket sales in that not all the population has easy access to the cities (which may be problematic since most of the folks living out in rural areas would presumably not be able to afford tickets or easy access to venues anyway), a unique feature of this particular system of ticket distribution was that tickets could only be purchased in...CASH!

In and of itself, this would not necessarily be a bad thing, but as it turned out, there never were supplies of any kind made available to our sub-organizing group. Moreover, the modest "budget" with which we had been provided proved to be a chimera. At no time did ZAGA receive any funding at all from COJA (the overall organizing committee for the Games.) As it turned out, with capacity crowds filling many of the venues, and with the Games considered an overall success by the participating nations, the Zimbabwe Olympic Committee stated that they had lost a great deal of money on the event. It might possibly be true, but interestingly and intriguingly, no final P&L was ever presented. Moreover, there was never any announcement of any kind pertaining to tickets sold or revenue derived therefrom. In fact, it was generally suspected, given the absence of any documentation (or financial controls) that Magnolius took the cash, stashed it, and either/or pocketed a significant portion of it, and/or divided the loot amongst his cronies.

Many (most?) of the higher ups in Mugabe's ZANU-PF cabal had their hands in the till during this event. One of the most stressful ongoing issues as the clock ticked down towards the Opening Ceremony was the state of the Belvedere gym. Daily I trekked down there with growing apprehension....while I'm no engineer or architect, it was apparent to me that we were behind schedule.

Although we were aware of a contractor who had several cement mixers available, they were not being utilized in the remodel and were sitting idle outside his office building in downtown Harare. How was Belvedere College Indoor Athletic Facility being reconstructed? Taking a page right out of the Middle Ages, the builders were mixing cement by hand. There were approximately 250 workers on site on any given day...several individuals were mixing concrete by hand in wheelbarrows...a bucket brigade would then dip 5 gallon buckets into the wheelbarrows, and pass them along to a 4-level scaffolding, where the bucket of concrete would be passed, hand over hand, up four stories, and a worker on the top level would pour 3-4 gallons of concrete into a wooden frame that served as the outline of the support pillar that would eventually emerge. It was an unbelievably frustrating scene, repeated day after day, with for me, increasing anxiety as the beginning of the Games drew nearer.

It came to a head one early afternoon.....I had been looking for answers in terms of a specific time estimate, and had 3 on-site subcontractors essentially pass the buck, not provide anything concrete (yes, that's a pun!), and subsequently referred me to “the other guy”. Subcontractor number 3 concluded his vague response by saying that he didn’t have a firm “end date” and that the foreman, the man sitting over in the pickup truck would be better positioned to give me an answer. So I wandered over to this mid-50ish gentleman, sitting on the side panel of his pickup truck; clad in overalls, he had just opened a black lunch pail and was pulling out a sandwich.

While attempting to engage him in conversation, I grew so frustrated by the lack of information and apparent unwillingness or inability of anyone present to provide me with direct answers to my questions, I was quite oblivious to the fact that I was interrupting his lunch! After enduring a few of my questions (and responding with noncommittal grunts), he unwrapped the wax paper from his second sandwich looked me up and down then summarily dismissed me by gesturing vaguely towards a cluster of workers standing around a pile of lumber..."You need to go talk to that black man over there."

That black man??? Uhhh, I’m the only white person on the jobsite, and there are somewhere between 250-300 “black men” milling around....I didn’t, of course, get an answer to my question, but surely, that’s one of the all-time great putdowns!!!

“That black man over there.....amazing!”

With time running out, it became necessary to confront the “big contractor” close up. Leo Mugabe is the nephew of Zimbabwe President Robert Mugabe, and known to be one of his closest cronies. At the time of these events, Leo was President of the Zimbabwe Soccer Association, and owned the largest construction firm in the country. He had 6 cement mixers sitting idle outside his spacious Harare offices; on the afternoon Neil and I met him, we were ushered into his plush penthouse office, where Mugabe held court brandishing a foot-long Cuban cigar. His position was simple: “When COJA pays for the service, COJA will get my equipment.” As an outsider, I had no say in the matter; somehow, Neil, who was not particularly popular within the ZOC establishment eventually managed to persuade Tommy Sithole to cough up the bribe.

Coda:

In 2003, Mugabe was fired as ZSA President after he was caught embezzling U$61,000 from a FIFA grant to the Federation. It is alleged that Leo had to be "looked after" by foreign companies seeking to do business in Zimbabwe. When a French company was awarded the contract for a new airport in the capital, Harare, the government overruled the decision and instead appointed a Saudi company that had chosen Leo Mugabe to be its local agent. One financial paper described the coup as "Zimbabwe's most notorious act of cronyism."

I actually had the opportunity to meet Robert Mugabe personally. Shortly before the Opening Ceremonies, COJA held a reception at the National Stadium in which Mugabe gave a speech exhorting the athletes to perform their best and to win the majority of medals (an impossibility given the strengths of Nigeria, Egypt, and South Africa) at the Games. After the speech, there was some general milling around, and the Tae Kwon Do coach, who shared a space with us in our training hall, volunteered to take me over and introduce me. “Mr. President, my name is Jim Holt and I’m the Competition Director for Gymnastics and coaching the Men’s National team.” “Gymnastics,” he responded...."I hope we’ll do well in gymnastics....are you American?” “Yes Mr. President,” I responded..."very happy to be here, and if you’ll permit me”, (I reached on the lapel of my blazer on which I had placed a US Gymnastics Federation pin, I unpinned the pin, and his Secret Service/Police be damned, gently took hold of the lapel of his pinstriped suit, and pinned it on his jacket.“Umm, thank you.” He said distractedly as he started to walk away.

Mugabe is a surprisingly small and thin man....he has large hands, with long, very bony fingers that he uses constantly as gestures during his speeches. I don’t know if it’s possible to call Mugabe a “tragic” figure....certainly the devastation and death he has brought to his country in recent times will damn him in the court of history....I suppose the tragedy is that it could have turned out so differently. Mugabe, the heroic liberator of Rhodesia, triumphed in the late 70s in the war for independence which became reality in 1980. Once considered the breadbasket of and shining hope of Africa, Zimbabwe could have been the model for liberalism and a free functioning state that could have inspired so many others. Mugabe could have been Mandela before Mandela. Instead, he’s ended up as just another tin-pot African dictator....he had immortality within his grasp....and chose infamy.

One other sad anecdote… Prior to the opening of the Games, Belvedere College and the Ministry of Health had conceived of a nation-wide blood drive. This was highly publicized in the weeks leading up to the All-African Games, and its purported purpose was to build a nation-wide Blood Bank which could extend to humanitarian aid outside Zimbabwe should a calamity befall a neighboring country. A few days before the Opening Ceremony, although it was not disclosed to the public, the blood drive was quietly but abruptly canceled. A very few of us in the Organizing groups had learned that approximately 30% of early donors’ blood had tested positive for HIV. This remains a ticking time bomb that might yet ravage the subcontinent.

Notwithstanding the problems with the organization of the competition, and the corruption and frustration when dealing with government officials, being in Zimbabwe was a delightful experience. It’s people, like all I’ve encountered in my travels around the world, are bright, playful, warm, giving, and have a wonderfully sardonic sense of the idiosyncrasies of the culture in which they live.

During most of my time in the country, I was staying in a room at Neil Nativel's house. Our training gym was "The Gym Centre", a facility owned by Neil (although his "real life" job is in insurance). Neil had, at one time, been a teacher, had taught most of the gymnasts in the National program during their formative years, and is the person singularly most responsible for the establishment (in 1984) of ZAGA and its subsequent membership in the FIG.

The Centre was located several blocks from Neil's home, and to walk there, one had to cross a large field, with a couple jacaranda trees prominent in the middle.

Over a two-week period or so, as I walked back and forth through the field to the Gym Centre, I noticed that there was a fairly regular gathering of folks who sat under the trees...most of the time I could hear a small radio playing....one Friday evening after practice, as the sun was starting to cast long shadows, I was walking across the field, and several people gathered around the trees gestured to me "C'mon over, c'mon over here"....I walked over to them, and one fella says,

"You're the American gymnastics coach." Well, yes I am, and in a neighborhood like Borrowdale (honest, that's the name!), news and gossip about 'outsiders' apparently travels quickly...I had apparently been the topic of some speculation, and these folks wanted to check me out face to face....without further ado, a second gent hands me a "scud". "Why thank you very much", I reply and take a deep long draught of the beer. The native, 'home brewed', although one can buy it commercially as well, is "chibuku", which is a beer made out of fermented rice or barley....it's not bad, and actually has rice grains in the "brew" as one drinks....nicknamed "scud" because of the distinctive shape of the brown plastic container (resembles the "scud" missile from the first Gulf War), its cheap and therefore is the hootch of choice for the (generally impoverished) locals. In any event, I was delighted to be informally initiated into membership in the neighborhood. The dozen or so of us spent a happy hour watching the sun go down, the Southern Cross rise in the sky....it's true, or at least it was my impression, that even in the city, it gets dark quickly in Africa....we engaged in a general "bull session"...it turns out that all were intensely interested in "life in America", and for most (all?) of them, I was the first American they had ever met.

In turn, I wanted to know a little of their lives and thoughts on various aspects of life. Yes, Mugabe and Zanu-PF were prominent among topics of conversation.

So, it became a little ritual...each Friday, I would catch up with the locals underneath the jacaranda trees on my way back from practice. About every other Friday, I'd stop at the little grocery between the Gym Centre and the field, and spring for beer (the 'regular' kind), or chibuku...no big deal, it was on my route home....it felt nice to be informally accepted as part of the neighborhood (and yes, for the record, I was the only white person....as a foreigner, I think it was easier for them to see me as separate from the Zimbabwean whites).

In turn, while I think I have a general grasp of the history of the white minority in Zimbabwe (formerly Rhodesia, Zim is 97% black), it was profoundly saddening to me to hear the whites with whom I was in contact consistently refer to the blacks surrounding them (and in many cases, washing their clothes, preparing their meals, cleaning their houses, and attending to their landscaping), as "kaffirs", an equivalent to a very taboo American epithet. It was a term I heard daily, albeit only when blacks were out of earshot.

With about 3 weeks to go until the games, my wife Hannah arrived in the country to help with the final preparations for the competition. Having a room at the Nativel's place had worked well for me when I was in Zim by myself, but with two of us, Neil arranged to have us move into a neighbor's small guest house a couple blocks down the street. One might presume "well, a guest house is a guest house", but one would be wrong! This particular place had 3 distinctive features. First, it had a thatched roof....yup, just like in the pictures, the roof (and from the inside, the ceiling) consisted of matted straw! Very distinctive. Second, although we didn't encounter many mosquitoes during our time in Zim, the bed was surrounded by a mosquito net, which came in handy, because for almost a week, there was one mosquito with a gigantic "buzzing" sound that got into the room and flew around all night for several nights....it was almost impossible to get any sleep. Third, the grounds were 'protected' by a Rhodesian Ridgeback dog, who we subsequently named "Mzelikase" (Muh-zil-ee-ka-ze) after one of the ancient Mtebele kings....Ridgebacks, if you're not familiar with the breed, are exactly like they sound....they're huge, about the size of Great Danes, and have a distinctive ridge of hair (like a modified mohawk) running down their backs. This particular dog, apparently was used to sleeping in our little hut. The place had only one door, and it could be bolted, but damned if that dog couldn't manage to somehow worry that bolt open in the middle of the night.

So, thus, our odd interspecies ritual came about....just before turning out the lights at night, I'd close and bolt the door. When we'd wake up in the morning, that resourceful dog would be lying on the throw rug next to the dinette table, waiting for her morning dog biscuit. I have no idea how that animal managed to get the door open every night, but she did! Hilarious.

In any event, the All African Games opened in September, and the facility at Belvedere College indeed got finished....albeit at the very last possible moment.

The day before the competition started, the floor plates were cemented into the floor, and we were concerned up through the first day of the meet as to whether they'd actually be strong enough to maintain hold. To our relief, no plates came out, no equipment collapsed.

In addition to serving as Competition Director, and Head Men's Coach, Hannah and I were asked to be television "color" commentators. The All-African Games were broadcast throughout the continent via tape delay. So we were able to run the competition (and in my case, be on the floor with the team during our sessions), then, shortly later, go to the television production booth and do voice-overs for the hour or so of the edited competition that would be broadcast. I'd had a couple previous experiences doing commentary for televised gymnastics events and was quite comfortable with the job. Hannah was a great second, and overall it went quite smoothly, save for the following exchange....we're in the booth, watching the replays, and one gymnast, camera located directly behind the vaulting horse landing mats (i.e. the athlete is running directly at the camera and therefore our point of view), hits the board, reaches to the horse, and performs a round-off, back salto dismount....at least that's what I thought I saw....so I comment (remember, this is going out to millions of viewers) "So and so just performed a nice Tsukuhara vault which has a Start Value of 9.7...let's see what the judges think." A pause from my co-anchor....then Hannah says (in a tone that makes it clear she thinks I'm an idiot, "That wasn't a Tsukuhara, Jim." I stop....turn away from the monitor and look at her....(what the hell? You're ripping me in public???) "Ummm, what kind of vault was it Hannah?"

Now, to be fair, she was right...I missed the vault....it turns out, it was a round-off entry to the board vault known as a Yurchenko, named after Natalia Yurchenko the gymnast who first performed it in international competition. Note that Yurchenko starts with the letter "Y".

"What kind of vault was it Hannah?" Not expecting to be put on the spot, she rifles through the rolodex of gymnastics skills in her mind and blurts out, "It was a....Yamashita!" The audiotape is rolling, the producer is looking at us like we're crazy, and I look at Hannah like she's lost her mind which she may very well just have done....

"Yamashita? Yamashita?" I repeat, trying to make sense of her nonsensical response...."Yes, Yamashita, as I'm sure many of our viewers know, was the 1964 Olympic Gold Medalist on this event, and the pike-open front handspring vault, which he pioneered was therefore, named after him."

I pause....while the above comment is factually true, I of course do not believe that any viewer knows any of this, nor do I think they'll be able to follow the specifics of the comment....we're completely off the rails at this point, and it's crazy fun to be doing it on an internationally broadcast event!

"As a matter of fact," I continue along my merry and utterly tangential tangent, "I was actually in a meet with Yamashita once. I was a freshman in college, he was doing a guest-professorship at the University of Alberta, and competed at the Pacific Northwest Championships." Now Hannah is looking at me like I'm the crazy one and the producer is doubled over in laughter, holding her hand over her mouth, and suppressing the noise so it doesn't picked up by the microphone.

"And," I conclude, "it's interesting that Mr. Yamashita is now legally known as Mr. Matsuda. When he got married, his wife was the last person in the family clan, and her family had been ancient samurai, so in order to keep the name alive, he took her last name."

"Now, our next vaulter....."

I've never made much money doing the work I love. In fact, the 4 day television gig in Zimbabwe was both the easiest and (for the amount of time invested, easily) the most lucrative. We were paid the equivalent of U$5500. for our commentary. There was only one small problem...we were paid in Zimbabwean currency, and it was illegal to change Zim money into hard currency and take it out of the country. What a dilemma. Fortunately, there is a thriving black market in Zimbabwe, and almost anything is "doable'. We had made some acquaintances of an English ExPat couple (real people from England, not Rhodesians who underwent an involuntary nationality change in 1980!) who happened to still have holdings in England, and were willing to trade our Zimbabwe currency (which they of course could use since they were living there) for a bank draft of British pounds which we'd be able to of course transfer into US dollars at any bank basically when we got out of Zimbabwe. So there is the very brief (and satisfying) anecdote of how we broke the laws of the country and "scammed" Robert Mugabe!

One last note....I'm comfortable wherever I am in the world, but had a moment that reminded me that I was most definitely in Africa. A little north of Harare there's a small (maybe a square mile) game preserve. It's surrounded by an 18-20 foot high chain length fence, and I believe the only animals that reside (or at least reside and stay alive for very long) is a pride of lions. People visit the reserve by getting into Reservation vans where they are guided with a slow drive around the complex...windows most definitely are required to be up! Well, one afternoon, Colleen Nativel's father (her parents live a short distance from the Nativels) and I were driving back from a trip out of town, and were going past the reserve...inquiring as to what it was, Colleen's dad told me, and I asked it it were possible to see any of the game from the road. He stopped the car and we crossed the dusty road (no blacktop once you get to the real outskirts of town!), stepped over a small ditch and walked over and stood close to the fence. "Can you see anything?" I asked...he says, "Come on over here...look". We moved about 20 feet to our left, and there, about 100 yards past the chain link was a large outcrop of rock and to its right and meandering towards us, a grove of small trees. On the top flat stone, an adult lioness lay with her back towards us, sunning herself. She raised her head and looked vaguely in our direction, perhaps sensing or hearing our presence. There was no perhaps....a moment later, she had disappeared behind the rock, and what seemed like a split second later, came bounding, no charging towards us, and with an almost ear-shattering roar, leapt at us and exploded, claws beared and fanged jaw open into the fence directly above us. CHRIST!!!! My heart hit my throat as I jumped back and tripped over the ditch....Jesus!!! The fence clanged and shook as the giant cat rebounded off and landed gracefully, doing a quick pirouette, glared back at us, and just to make sure we got her point.....snarled menacingly as if to say "get the hell off, and stay away from my property!" I have no idea how those hunters in the old days could wander around with these things in their midst.

That is in retrospect, perhaps the single most frightening moment of my life, and the kitty was behind the fence! "Charged by a lion in deepest Africa..." who's gonna believe that absolutely true story.....incredible.

Groucho: "Here is a viaduct leading over to the mainland.
Chico: "Why a duck?"
Groucho: "I'm all right, how are you? I say, here is a little peninsula, and here is a viaduct leading over to the mainland."
Chico: Alright, why a duck?"
Groucho: (pause)" I'm not playing "Ask Me Another', I say that's a viaduct."
Chico: "Alright! Why a duck? Why that...why a duck? Why a no chicken?"
Groucho: "Well, I don't know why a no chicken; I'm a stranger here myself. All I know is that it's a viaduct. You try to cross over there a chicken and you'll find out why a duck."
Chico: "When I go someplace I just..."
Groucho: (interrupts) "It's...deep water, that's why a duck. It's deep water."
Chico: "That's why a duck..."
Groucho: "Well, I'm sorry the matter ever came up. All I know is that it's a viaduct."
Chico: "Now look, alright, I catc ona why a horse, why a chicken, why a this, why a that...I no catch ona why a duck."
Groucho: "I was only fooling...I was only fooling. They're gonna build a tunnel there in the morning. Now is that clear to you?"
Chico: Yes, everything excepta why a duck."
Groucho and Chico Marx (Cocoanuts, 1929)

Chapter Eight

FUN WITH PASSPORTS

With all the other absurdities that I've had to deal with over the years, perhaps the most ludicrous (and on a certain level, I'm confident that few if any in gymnastics has had experiences like the two I'm about to share) has to do with "passports", those otherwise inviolable documents that, well, document one's existence and associate an individual human with a given nation-state. It must have been wonderful for Richard Burton, Henry Lawrenson, and Gertrude Bell to wander around the globe without the worry and "fuss" of having to provide/show documentation of where they were from at every turn....in our case....

During our stay in Bolivia, we had suggested that there was no reason that the country couldn't enter female athletes in international competition (along with Ignacio Morales or more)...Alejandro Gensollen, the then coach at Club 7 in Santa Cruz took us at our word and suggested that Cecelia Maas, one of his top athletes would be a great candidate to compete internationally and would we possibly consider working with her. Absolutely.

After speaking with her parents, we arranged for Cecelia to travel with us to the USA and live with us in order to prepare for the (4 months away) World Championships. Cece as a result of this collaboration achieved this goal and became the first Bolivian woman to compete at this level.

During our meeting with her parents, we were provided a photocopy of her birth certificate….for those not versed in the arcane regulations of international gymnastics, there is a minimum age that a gymnast must attain in order to be eligible to compete at international meets. While it remains a source of continuing policy discussion (and controversy, see 2008 Beijing Olympics), it is well understood that adolescent girls can perform (and win) at the highest levels of the sport. It has been deemed appropriate that children not be exposed at too young an age and the rules state simply that a gymnast must be 16 years of age in the year of the competition.

Cecelia's birth certificate made it clear that she was 16 years of age. She was born in 1978 and would be representing Bolivia at the 1994 World Championships. No problem.

She moved up to Seattle, and began training and living with us. All was proceeding smoothly, and I was quite pleased with how well her gymnastics was going, and especially how happily she seemed to be settling into our home. She loved our dog Max, got along great with Hannah's daughter Shaye, and even (ever the dutiful "step'-parent, I) dragged me off to Sunday (Spanish speaking) Mass each week.

About 2 months before the Worlds, I had to send passports to the Australian consulate in San Francisco in order to secure visas. This is always something I take very seriously and always with plenty of lead time in case there's some/any irregularities or problems (as we shall see in the "Nashwan Comes to America" chapter. I collect the passports and just before I put them in the mailer, I reviewed each one….my heart almost stopped when I looked at Cecelia's and then looked hard a second, and disbelieving, rubbed my eyes and stared at it for a third time…clearly marked, no mistake, the year of her birth was 1980!!! Which of course would make her ineligible to compete, and make all the time and investment on the part of multiple persons a waste….I hastily called a family conference?

"Cecelia, we've got a problem. It's a serious problem. Your passport has a different date than that which I saw on the photocopy of your birth certificate."

Silence and two large almond eyes staring back at me.

"If we can't get this worked out, you will not be able to compete at the Worlds."

The teargates open, and the flood (accompanied by sobs!) opens up….

Through tears, Cecelia tells the story...."someone" (she really didn't know who) at Club 7 in Santa Cruz really wanted to win some junior competition and in order to make it happen, they entered some "over-age" gymnasts(including Cecelia!) into the competition, and were able to get it verified by either (it never was made entirely clear) getting a passport issued from the Bolivian government while providing false information (i.e. the wrong birth date), or by altering (very convincingly if in fact altered!) her valid passport.

Christ, it's always something....just once I'd love to have an international project go smoothly and according to schedule.

Fortunately, Bolivia has a consul in Seattle, and Sr. Ricardo Antezana is a pretty good guy with whom I've worked previously (for Ignacio). So I called him up, made an appointment, and he ushered us into his office.

"What can I do for you?" he inquired.

I explained the situation as best I understood it in detail.

"That's not possible." He responded.

"Sr. Antezana, it is possible and it has happened."

"Mr. Holt, you are mistaken; it is not possible."

"Sr., I understand it is highly unlikely, is definitely improper, and presumably illegal, but I assure you it has happened. This girl was born in 1978."

He turned to Cecelia and asks a couple questions in rapid fire Spanish....

Like a little church mouse, she timidly replied.

He turned again to me, and said, "I've been the consul for 35 years and have never heard of such a thing."

I reached into my briefcase, pulled out the copy of Cece's birth certificate (1978!)

Laying it on Sr. Antezana's desk, and pointing to that date, then the 1980 on the open passport...."See for yourself."

He leaned forward, his head, almost like a majestic pigeon, bobs back and forth about 3 times.....leaning farther forward, he pulled his glasses about halfway down his nose and took one more long look.

"Mr. Holt, you will excuse me for a few minutes. He had a private room off his main "reception" office, and left us sitting, facing his now empty desk. As he stood and walked into the privacy of the inner office, he scooped up both birth certificate and passport. We waited.....we could hear muffled tones behind the door as he was speaking to someone on the phone...I can only surmise that he was speaking with someone in Bolivia...perhaps the passport control people in Santa Cruz?

Suddenly the volume increases as Sr. Antezana was well, basically shouting at whomever is on the other end of the line.....it was clear that he was convinced that we were telling the truth and equally clear that somebody in

South America was quaking in their shoes at that moment because we've got one extremely agitated consul in the next room yelling at them!

Subsequent to a few moments of this, the private room falls silent.....6-7 minutes go by, nothing.....we wait....finally, the door swung open, and Sr. Antezana walked (rather serenely I think) back to his chair and sat down.

"Excuse me." he said, straightening his already perfectly aligned tie...."it was necessary for me to make a phone call in order to clarify this matter."

He extended across the desk to me a NEW Bolivian passport...actually, and I've never seen this before or since, it's a brand new passport with Cecelia's old one stapled securely to it.

"I think this will solve your problems." I look inside the passport. There's a freshly typed 1978 right where it should be in Cecelia's brand new document. He turned to Cecelia whose still sitting kind of all scrunched up. "Young lady, I know that this was not your doing, but you should not have permitted this to happen and you should have communicated the situation immediately. Do you understand?"

Meekly: "Yes, sir."

"Good. Now, I want to wish you all the best of luck in your competition."

"Mr. Holt, thank you for your efforts on behalf of my country."

"De nada Sr. Antezana....muchas gracias por su ayuda!"

"My pleasure."

As I sit here writing this, I can duplicate the sigh of relief that accompanied that moment....

When Robert Crumb's Mr. Natural asserts: "The entire universe is completely insane.", I suspect that he neglected two important words:"especially Nigeria!"

As recounted elsewhere in the book, Hannah and I had served as Assistant Coaches for Nigeria at the 1994 Commonwealth Games... ....moreover, as recounted previously, we had been in Nigeria for a couple weeks that Fall. As we'll describe in more detail in the Namibia chapter, Hannah and I were competition directors for the initial Junior African Championships which took place in early 1995. Apparently the Nigerians were unaware of our involvement, or at (most benevolently phrased...) they presumably did not understand the "comprehensive nature" of our involvement with the event.

"Comprehensive" to me means that one is intimately integrated with every aspect and detail, and wears "different hats" as required.

One of the hats that Hannah and I wore were registering the various delegations as they arrived at the venue in Walvis Bay by collecting entry fees and reviewing "proof" of citizenship/age as required by the statutes of the African Gymnastics Union.

Sooooo, we're sitting at a table in a small tent one afternoon, having just processed without incident the Algerian delegation, when we were told that

Nigeria has just arrived, and will be entering the tent shortly….a couple minutes later, gymnast Peter Ojo sticks his head in the door, with Coach Isiah Obanor one stride behind him…Peter, apparently passport in hand (and Isiah) look up, seeing Hannah and me…freeze….without even acknowledging our presence, or the fact (in Isiah's case!) that we had spent 5 weeks together on two continents over the last year!....they freeze for a couple long moments, then exit the tent….what the heck? We wait… oh probably a full 10 minutes elapse and then, the Nigerian athletes slip into the registration tent in a line, passports in hand….on one flank, Obanor stands with gym bag slung over his shoulder looking at us without comment or smile…on the other flank, Koicho Zlatev, the Bulgarian in charge of the national program is all false camaraderie and "hail fellow" phony (and loud) noise, presumably in an attempt to obfuscate the absurd nonsense that followed….with two people whom the Nigerians KNEW knew them sitting at the table awaiting registration, and with basically no other options, they gamely moved into the tent and attempted to register…)

Somewhat (was this just my opinion or was I reading something into this?) shamefacedly, Peter hands over his passport.

Arguably, the two most important particulars in a passport are, depending of course on the particular context, the national identification of the person, i.e. is this person legitimately a citizen of the country from which the passport is issued and secondly, as in the case of this particular event and it's requirement that there are age groups to take into account, the birth date(s) of the specific individuals…..

I opened Mr. Ojo's passport…..the birth date had apparently been altered….it was obvious that they had moments before erased whatever date had been visible in the document, and instead there was a date WRITTEN IN BALL-POINT PEN!...This date claimed that Peter was 4 or 5 years younger than we knew him to be…..I know that there are instances where this has happened over the years at many many sporting events, but I can honestly say there, in all probability has never been anything quite as blatant and dishonest as this….. take a grey (ink) eraser, grind out the date of birth originally inscribed onto the document and then modify it by erasing the original, and just write some bogus date in ink?? Even in Nigeria, the home of fraud, this seems brazenly "over the top."

The next 8 passports were all variations on the same thing….Beauty Idiaho, whom Hannah had worked with at length the preceding Autumn when we were in Lagos was an (at least) 24 year old woman who has a child….we knew that because we know HER. The notion that they could pass this fully developed woman and mother off as 15 just because they've erased a line in her passport and substituted an inked and penned date was ludicrous…

I commented, not to the gymnasts, but to the two coaches hovering anxiously, "You must be kidding…We're supposed to document the age-group, and you expect anybody to believe that your Senior national team is comprised of under 16 year olds?"

"Yes!" says coach Zlatev

"Koicho, have you forgotten, than Hannah and I worked with almost all of these athletes (note: after the Commonwealth Games when we did our IOC Solidarity Course (for 17 days!) in Nigeria, we were involved with these very same athletes on a daily basis) and know them personally?"

Zlatev: "So?"

Many years ago (although it does not feel that way) when I was coaching at university, the then coach of UCSanta Barbara Mircea Badalescu (former Romanian national team member and multiple times Olympic judge) told me, "Jim, international sport is 'world war' without bullets'." At the time, (naïve fool that I am) I thought it a rather curious and somewhat silly view of the world…it turns out that many many people think of it that way….it doesn't matter whether it's right or wrong, whatever one can "get away" with is ok….I have previously discussed, and we shall continue to explore the notion that "the ends justify the means."

Back to thc discussion at hand….me: "You've altered the dates on these passports and these are senior gymnasts…."

Koicho: "Our head of Delegation will deal with this matter."

Fine by me….I'm trying to coordinate a successful competition, and frankly, do NOT want to get caught up in the "sturm und drang" of African gymnastics politics….so I punt….I go to the President of the UAG, Algerian Mohammed Yamani…..Yamani is a most intriguing and interesting individual…Mohammed was a young man during the demise of the French colonial Empire and Algeria's struggle for independence. He first, was on the French National Team in the late 1950s and early 60s and in 1964 he became Algeria's first Olympian at the Tokyo Games….Mohammed, who's native languages are Arabic and French taught himself (a very grammatically correct and nuanced) English in the 1990's in his 50's, no mean feat….Yamani is a compromiser by his life experience and I postulate his personal temperament…..

When I brought the Nigerian passport issue to his attention, he responded in his usual measured fashion, "Ummmm, this is a problem…we shall have to investigate it thoroughly." Again, I point out that the ultimate resolution didn't matter to me one way or the other personally, but I was ethically bound to bring the issue to the "authorities" attention….Yamani apparently approached the Nigerians….they apparently (and appropriately given the circumstances) stalled and played for time….the training went forward…there was no resolution to the matter, although, even though I didn't broach the topic, it apparently became common knowledge throughout the various delegations present at the event....

Fast forward several days to the first day of competition....still no resolution, and in my capacity as Competition Director, I approached Mr. Yamani and mentioned to him that the African Gymnastics Union (of which he was/is President) Championships had regulations regarding eligibility based on age, and that the issue pertaining to the legitimacy of the Nigerian delegation has not yet been resolved.

Mohammed, who wants the best for the sport, took a deep breath, and it was clear that he was distressed to be "put on the spot" and required to make a decision. It was one hour until the beginning of the men's qualifying competition. He asked for the Nigerian Head of Delegation, NGF President Dyeri to meet with him and me outside the Walvis Bay competition venue....accompanying Dyeri are his (apparently ever present) coaches Obanor and Zlatev....

It's a beautiful, early autumn (we are on the southwestern coast of southern Africa on a sun swept March morning) day as we confer on a patio just outside the gym....Mohammed turns to Adejumo..."there has been a question raised as to the validity of the birthdates on your passports....I spoke to you about this a number of days prior when it was brought to my attention....can you clarify?"

Adejumo, in a masterpiece of obfuscation (more precisely, a "perfect" evasion) responded...."Mr. Yamani, Mr. President, we have done everything possible to provide concrete documentation that the birth dates on the passports are valid. Immediately after you raised this issue with me, I collected and subsequently sent all passports of all participating athletes to our Embassy in Swakopmund...I have been in daily contact with them by telephone asking that they resolve this issue, but have yet to receive a specific reply....as you perhaps know, today is a national holiday here in Namibia and all government offices are closed as is our embassy..." In the classic gesture of all Third World bureaucrats, Adejumo finishes with (it's not quite a flourish, but one might understand that it's a summarizing....) "helpless" shrug of the shoulders...and I loved the part where he put his arms to the side and turned his palms up....metaphorically, 'what can I do, what more can one ask of me?" Right.

Yamani has both played this game before, and understands the consequences(regardless of his personal opinion of these brigands) of "literally" applying the rules...of course he understands that this feeble and oh so transparent "excuse" is nonsense...but...he, and anybody who understands a bigger picture realizes that to disqualify these athletes, however shameful the actions of their Federation, places the future participation of Nigeria in jeopardy and significantly weakens the possibility that the (at least at that time) fragile coalition that is gymnastics in Africa….as unfair as it is to the countries and gymnasts who are here honestly and legitimately, Mr. Yamani, in an obviously compromised, but in my personal opinion, Solomanic decision, concludes (and I'm sure it just about KILLED him to do so given that he has to think these people are jokes!)…

"President Dyeri, I did not realize that you had gone to these lengths to document the legitimacy of your claims….although it is regrettable that we cannot have definitive documented proof….given the circumstances, and given the (crocodile tears here) unfortunate transposition of the national holiday with our competitive schedule….it seems prudent that your athletes should have the opportunity to participate."

Smiles and handshakes all around….everybody that's here is going to compete….I walk into the venue, it's now 30 minutes or so before the march-in….I share the resolution with Zimbabwe's President, Neil Nativel…his impromptu response, "You've got to be joking!"

South African Judge, the late J.C. Clouete: "That is absurd…I must speak with Yamani!..."

Moroccan President Mohammed al-Youbi: "Jim, you must do something to stop this!"

In any event, as we have seen previously, Nigeria's senior team did participate in the initial Junior African Championships through the mechanism (or perhaps better phrased "contrived" mechanics) of forged passports and garnered medals at same.

Coda:

We're in Zimbabwe for the All-African Championships in the training gym….this time, I'm not (nor did I want to be) responsible for the registration of delegations….the Nigerians appear at the door, and Hannah and I are rushed by the athletes…Peter Ojo gives Hannah a big hug and more or less the same for me…."Man, it is GREAT to see you" I say…"welcome to Zimbabwe…."

"Mr. Jim, it is so good to see you and Madam Hannah!"

Over to my right, Beauty and Hannah are hugging, then break and are arm in arm….it's all good….

A bit later on, the team is stretching and working out the kinks….Beauty puts on a pair of grips and heads over to the uneven bars just about the time that the Zimbabwe men's team is leaving the gym….I wander over….

"You look great!"

"Mr. Jim, it's good to be here and be with you and Hannah again."

"If you don't mind my asking, what was with the passports back in Namibia."

Beauty, who is a real beauty, cracked a huge, mygod she's got great teeth smile, and laughed from the gut….

"What did you expect? Of course, we're NIGERIANS!!!!"

Belly laughs all around, including mine!….."but of course…."

"Enthusiasm is the fulcrum that moves the world."
Abel Gance

Chapter Nine

NAMIBIA

I have bittersweet feelings about Namibia. During the 1994 Commonwealth Games (as described earlier in the vignette starring Rob Paridis) , Hannah and I were approached by Namibian Gym Federation President Valere-is Geldenhuys and asked to coordinate the first (and to date only) African Junior Championship which was to be held in March 1995.

We arrived in Namibia just less than 2 months prior to the start of the competition, and understood from the earliest date that coordinating the competition was going to be an interesting challenge.

We had three objectives for the event:

1. to ensure that the event was financially successful (i.e. made money in a part of the world where no one thought a gymnastics event could possibly come out in the black money-wise)
2. for all sessions of the meet to start on time, and
3. for the all aspects of the event to run smoothly and quickly, thereby providing both spectators and participants a quality experience and to be a model for future competitions on the continent.

My larger objective, of course, was to strengthen gymnastics on the continent generally, and to ensure that the Namibian Federation would, as a result of hosting the event, be perceived as a credible and competent organization capable of building the sport in that country.

My job as Competition Director was to set up a workable structure, define the job parameters, and to make suggestions to the department heads when I felt that I could enhance their decision-making process. At no time did I intervene in a decision that one of the department heads made. Our organizational model was based on a modified version of the 1991 Worlds manual and procedures. I stressed from the outset (and continued to do so throughout that once an individual had "signed-off" on the specific tasks within his/her organizational box, if that person made a decision pertaining to that aspect of the competition, I couldn't come in and overrule him/her. This was met with a bit of confusion at first, and a little bit later, a minor (very small actually) resistance from a few folks, but basically the staff was thrilled at the idea of independence and autonomy.

There was one critical function that I reserved for myself . I made it very clear to the Federation President that under no circumstances was she to spend money or write a check without my approval. . In other words, I made all financial decisions pertaining to the operation of the event and thereby was able to ensure a profit (ultimately of U.$.15,000. !!) in a part of the world that had never considered the possibility of actually generating a profit from gymnastics.

Namibia is an intriguing place. Independent (from South Africa) as recently as 1991, it originally (well, original in the European sense of the word) was settled by Afrikaners, and became German Southwest Africa in the late 19th century. Although the Boer War was primarily fought farther to the East, the Afrikaners and English settlers were at odds, with the Germanic influence retaining primacy. At the conclusion of the Great War (1914-18) German Southwest Africa was absorbed into the British Commonwealth as part of the Republic of South Africa.

Namibia has a population of approximately 1.5 million people, of whom over 90% are native Africans (i.e. black). It's more or less a democracy, and has a first world infrastructure. One of the most important things for people to understand is that Africa is BIG. Namibia is one of the most sparsely populated countries in the world.

Because of the country's German heritage, gymnastics enjoys an unusual visibility relative its' numbers of participants. Turnvereins played a major role in introducing sport to the country, and indeed one of the major landmarks in Windhoek is the original Turnhalle (dating from 1900); it is the site where the modern political independence movement began in the 1970s, thereby making it a significant landmark in Namibian history..

Several clubs throughout the country actually have (and still use for recreation classes) pre World War II (at least!) gymnastics equipment; in Swakopmund, I swung circles on a pommel horse with stitched leather handles, and rings with "wrought iron" adjustable buckles, and in two (!) other facilities encountered vaulting horses with lowered rear ends and (!!!!) carved hooves..

There were two significant organizational problems pertaining to the success of the event. First, many of the foreign delegations were unable to communicate their itinerary or the composition of their delegation to the Organizing Committee in a timely fashion in '95. This has traditionally been the situation with many. of the developing countries at whatever level of competition, regardless of the length of timeline allotted to/for them for same. Even though fax and email are now virtually universally accessible, the communications infrastructure in Africa still lags far behind the "First World".

It was simply not possible on many occasions to transmit communications because of the inadequate communication systems in many countries. This made accurately planning for size and composition of delegations, and concomitantly their housing arrangements very difficult for the Organizers. In addition, although it was clearly stated on the Inscription that the Delegations were responsible for coordinating their transportation to Walvis Bay only South Africa complied. The remaining delegations got as far as Windhoek (the major airline destination) 390 km from Walvis Bay. I made a conscious decision to strain our transport system to accommodate our guests. I felt (and still do) that accommodating their domestic transport needs was a major factor in the event's success. The Ministry of Youth and Sport donated busses and Avis Rent a Car donate 2 cars; these were utilized constantly during the 10 days our foreign guests were in Namibia.

One other problem in Africa is the dearth of qualified officials; combined with the extreme distances entailed in a continental competition, we were very concerned about the officiating as we approached the Championships. This subsequently turned out to be an unfounded worry. The various Federations were very conscientious in bringing judges as part of their delegations. Indeed, for all the men's and women's competitions our judges panels consisted of all FIG brevets.

Happily, Mr. Karl-Heinz Schocke was induced to come and preside as the Technical advisor of the Men's artistic competition. With his vast experience, his standing within the FIG and obvious interest in development in this part of the world, Mr. Schocke's presence provided additional legitimacy to this event and was a very positive statement about the efforts of the UAG. Karl Heinz did his usual outstanding job; in this instance, he gently, positively, but firmly insisted that the judging be fair and timely. For the women, Tanya Swallow (Great Britain) presided as the competition referee; her diplomatic skills and judging expertise enabled the women to resolve their disagreements with dispatch.. Because of the tight time frame in the competitive schedule, I repeatedly stressed at the various technical meetings, the need for the judges to arrive at their scores quickly. Annette Nel of South Africa did an incredible job getting her Rhythmic panels to quickly compute scores; working with these three great professionals was a personal highlight of the Championships for me.

Loos (not the battle)

One of the most intriguing and baffling aspects about Namibia for me is its extraordinary and arguably unique contrasts….this remote part of Southern African sports a first world infrastructure…in fact, one of the most peculiar albeit delightful aspects of the country is its…dare I say it…restrooms….now, if one hasn't actually been there, this will seem inconceivable, but, in the 2 months I was there, I traveled around most of the country, and at whatever truck-stop or whistle-stop that I might go into, the restrooms were absolutely immaculate....I am keenly aware of how bizarre (or obscure) this might be perceived by the armchair reader, but it's true....just about anywhere you go in Namibia, the folks there have some strange cultural impetus to make their toilets these "oases" in the middle of some traveler's journey. We stop for gas at some godforsaken Shell(or British Petroleum) or someone-pump station just outside Outchavarango....I need to use the loo so to speak....I get the key, and walk into this tiny corner of....what the hell....Switzerland.....immaculate....absolutely pristine....not just clean, but LINEN hand-towels....boutique bars of hand-soap....DOILIES draped over the arms of the "rest chair" opposite the toilet.....no, I do not recall a bidet in this particular "truck-stop in the middle of nowhere, but...." Perched on top of the lid of the toilet....candles, beautiful wax candles....oh, and the mirror, framed in gilt....lastly, spotless as the place was, and as oh so perfect as the bathroom tissue (discreetly placed next to one's right hand), the (hey, has anybody actually seen one of these since the crazy old ladies house in the 1940's black comedy film "Arsenic and Old Lace"?) draped (oh so tastefully) on the toilet was a friggin' ANTIMACASSAR!!!!! Dali meets Crumb meets Josephine Hull!!!! Like an out of body experience....with metaphorical crumpets....

Word to the wise....if you're traveling around Namibia, be sure to WASH YOUR HANDS before signing the guest book. Yup, Namibia has to be the only country I've been to or ever hear of where the restrooms at truck-stops have guest-books!!

Namibia has some unique geographic qualities as well. The country is located (as any globe or map will indicate) on the Atlantic Ocean which directly abuts the world's oldest desert...perhaps my all-time favorite road sign is the one on the road between Walvis Bay and Swakopmund....it is a triangular (warning) sign that says simply "SAND"....ummmm, yeah....as one travels on the highway going South, on your left is sand....and on the right (or West) side of the road there is the Atlantic Ocean....why not a sign indicating.....water, agua, H2O....because of the dust that the sands kick up over the course of a long day, the sunsets in Namibia are unsurpassed anywhere in the world....the reds, blues, oranges, and vivid purples are simply astounding....all that said, the simple (comedic) pleasure of a road-sign indicating "sand" which identifies one of the worlds' great deserts (and the only one contiguous with an ocean!) and it's corresponding absence of sign indicating "water" is a silly, but deeply satisfying pleasure.

Beaters

Hannah and I needed independent transportation in order to function. I'm not one to stand on ceremony certainly don't need anything fancy, and the organization was on a stringent (due to my penuriousness!) budget. In the spirit of running a "lean and mean" ship, the organizing committee managed to find us a vehicle which we could use in any way we chose..... when I was in college, Rea Anders one of our coaches told me that when he was in school, he got around as cheaply as possible by buying the cheapest and most beat-up piece of automotive junk that he could find, drive it around putting only gas, water, and maaaaybe a quart of oil once in awhile or so. When the car broke down after 4-5 months, he'd just leave it on the side of the road (never bothered to register the bill of sale with the State), then pony up another $50. somewhere and drive off with another "beater". I thought this a marvelously cool and cheap strategy and always imagined that Rae would carry a small revolver in the glove compartment, and when his chariot basically "gave up the ghost" that he'd put it out of it's misery by firing a couple slugs into it before walking away!

Anyway, the Namibians presented us with a vehicle oh so similar in spirit to the junk-heaps of my college years. They proudly handed us the keys to a dented blue and white 1963 Peugeot coupe. This might have been a decent car (in some French auto designers wildest ambitions while still on the drawing board), but the Peugeot of the early 60s was the French equivalent to the 1950s American Edsel. It was not particularly stylish, and it didn't run very well either.

Our particular little Peugeot of course had weathered over 3 decades of the bracing, but corrosive salt air of the Atlantic Ocean, and the perpetual "sandblasting" resulting from well, the friction of billions of grains of desert sand wafting across its path over the days and months and years. The driver's side door didn't open, so the driver (Hannah because it was a 4 speed and I'm not licensed to drive a stick) had to climb over the gearshift through the passenger side in order to get in....the driver's side window did not roll down.... you also had to pop the clutch to get the thing in gear more or less, because first gear was basically non-existent...apparently the teeth for that gear had been worn smooth over the years....even though I wasn't the driver, I was an active participant in at least all the times in which we needed to move from either parallel or diagonal parking. You see, there was no "reverse" gear left in the car either, so when we had to go in reverse, I'd get in front of the car, and push the front bumper or hood to get it moving backward....sort of manual, manual transmission so to speak!

Namibia is almost all desert....it rarely rains there....we had the car over a month, and didn't discover until one dark night as we were returning to Swakopmund from a very late evening getting the final touches on the competition venue together, that, an unusual squall had come up from the Atlantic, our little Peugeot's windshield wipers didn't work either. Oh, my passenger side window did manage to roll down, so I was able (what a refreshing facial it is to hang one's face out a side window on a windy oceanfront road in a rain squall at 1 am while one tries to keep the driver abreast of what's happening on the road)to transmit directions to my basically blind driver....naturally, given every other distinguishing feature of this vehicle, only one headlight worked, and that occasionally blinked off...

Most notably (or most embarrassingly actually), the car leaked oil....or, I should say gushed oil almost as if it had a big hole in the oil pan....which it either did, or the gasket sealing the pan to the engine had either disintegrated or been ruptured beyond any possible functional use....in the center of Swakopmund, there is an attractive core of buildings fronting red brick streets. After the first day we parked there, I pushed the Peugeot back out onto the road, and was nonplussed and embarrassed at the puddle of oil which now stained the otherwise pristine brick.

I immediately acquired a metal pan and put it in the back of the car. Whenever we subsequently went to park, I'd take the pan out, and put it under the engine block. When we returned to the vehicle, just before we'd push the car back out onto the street, I'd pop the hood, take the pan, and "recycle" the collected oil which had spilled/seeped from the block into the pan, and pour it back into the car......sheesh! Rae woulda been proud of me!

It really doesn't matter that Namibia branched off from South Africa in the early 1990s in order to become independent....at its' core, (at least in the part that has European influence), Namibia has much deeper roots with the land of the Hohenzollerns than it does with Albion. In Swakopmund, on the coast where we were primarily housed, Hannah and I had struck up a fast friendship with the (then) head girls coach Phil Barker of England...as a matter of fact, Phil had matriculated down to Namibia courtesy of Mike and Tanya Swallow (see above) where he had previously been employed at their Hillington School of Gymnastics just outside of Heathrow airport..

Oh....slight digression....if you browse the Lonely Planet guide to Namibia, and look up the section on Swakopmund, you will find a reference to the "Martin Luther tractor. Said tractor is a derelict and rusting old, well, tractor and rests on the south side of the road (possibly could be called a highway or thoroughfare) on the way from Windhoek to Swakopmund) ....it was brought down to the area around the time of World War One (some of us prefer the term "The Great War" which was what it was referred to contemporaneously), to do some farming or agriculture around the area...it turns out that the tractor was too heavy for the local soil that it was supposed to cultivate, or the natives didn't know how to replace the parts, or something reasonably nonsensical so that it became a boondoggle and ultimately was unworkable...hence, it has sit by the side of the road for more or less nine decades (and counting)….I know that Martin Luther was German, but I'm unclear as to the reason the tractor got named after him….if you're on your way to Kuki's tavern for beer (great Namibian-German beer by the way in Namibia!!!) and calamari on the road in from the capitol city, you'll pass the ML tractor….

I'm an enthusiastic traveler, and I love the part in "Pee-Wee's Big Adventure" where he travels to the Alamo and discovers to his dismay that "the Alamo doesn't have a basement"….in fact, I very much enjoy traveling around the United States and finding these weird and odd "travel destinations" that somehow are supposed to excite tourists into visiting various sites…..off the top of my head out on the West Coast where I reside, Gilmore California (the "Artichoke Capitol of the World"), Leavenworth Washington (a "fake" Bavarian town) located on the Eastern side of the Cascade mountains who adopted the whole neo (actually false) Oktoberfest theme in the 1960s, and of course, Las Vegas (where everything is gauche and fake) come immediately to mind….regardless, there is a certain charm in these peripheral (and ultimately pointless to anyone who doesn't actually reside there) "attractions"…compare and contrast, say, Paris, London, New York, Rome, Athens, Madrid, et.al. with (as cool as it might be) Sturgis South Dakota and it's biker heaven, or say Petaluma California (the "Arm Wrestling" Capitol of the World)…..and here in Namibia, the Lonely Planet guidebook considers an old, rusting tractor something of an attraction…go figure.

In any event, I was alluding to the Germanic influence… one evening Phil, Hannah, and I were hungry, and were eager to sample the wares of a place called "The Rathskeller" (Lonely Planet had recommended it!).

We were ushered into a booth, order our drinks (beer naturally!), and some food, and settle in for a bit of pub conviviality….Although we didn't really recognize it at first, we gradually became aware of tension in the room. There was a corresponding quiet….an unease…as our conversation fell to a whisper, we surreptitiously surveyed our surroundings, and it was obvious that virtually all the rest of the diners were either looking directly at us, or (obviously) discussing our presence….upon a short reflection, it dawned on us that we were the only booth in the place that were speaking English; every other table was speaking either German or Afrikaans. Well, we've got as much a right to be here as anybody else….I look around the room and see the glares…I look at Hannah…then, turning to Phil (an enthusiastic Liverpool football supporter if there ever was one), I editorialize in a low voice, "They're still pissed off that they lost World War Two!" Laughs all around….at least in our booth….

Perhaps an apocryphal story (but I hope is true)…..in 1990, the Soccer World Cup was held it Italy…. in the Semi-finals, Germany beat England 1-0.afterwards, so the story goes, the British Parliament was in session, this during the time of a downturn in the economy, and a Member of Parliament from the Labor Party was bemoaning the current circumstances and general condition of Mother England…"The economy is a disaster, our foreign policy is without direction, and my god, even in football….England is the founder of the world's game, and Germany, they've just started thinking about reunification, but Germany has beaten us at our National game!"

Margaret Thatcher, the (then) Prime Minister without missing a beat is supposed to have retorted, "Well, we've beaten them TWICE at THEIR national game in this century."

Don't recall if Phil, Hannah, and I discussed this, but drinks and laughs all around at the pro-German Rathskeller on that particular evening!

Phil was a great pal in the Australian sense…I had nothing to do with the training of his girls, but he was an invaluable contributor to the organization and eventual accomplishment of the championships. The venue at Walvish Bay was "b-a-r-e-l-y" large enough to fit a full set of apparatus. When I inspected the venue, I discovered that there were no floor plates for rings or horizontal bar (women's uneven bars used the high bar plates), and that the (unnecessary) floor plates for the men's pommel horse had been placed in the center of the gymnasium floor, and therefore unworkable.

While the Walvis Bay gymnasium is an excellent recreational facility, hosting an official international meet there was extremely challenging due to the very limited space. One morning, armed with the dimensions of the facility (and knowing that a section of the East end of the gym would be unavailable due to the implementation of spectator seating), the FIG apparatus specifications, a tape measure, and a surveyor's chalk-line, Phil and I went to work measuring, taping, and double-checking all the possible configurations of the apparatus….it became quickly apparent that we needed at least 3 more sets of floor plates and that the one set in the center of the event for the pommels was utterly useless….thank goodness Hans Techlenberg of Janssen-Fritchschen was able to "rush" an order down to us.

Phil and I were down on our knees, laboriously measuring and re-measuring, and laying out a chalk-line outlining the exact location of the plates. ….at one point, down on my knees, dripping in sweat (it was hot and humid this time of the year in Namibia), I looked up, and there was a custodian running a "wet" shop vacuum across our floor, ERASING all of the marks that Phil and I had painstakingly applied….I bolted up off the floor, very upset, and confronted the man…"What the heck do you think you're doing? We're trying to measure this facility for our upcoming meet!!?"

Placidly, apathetically, he responds, "Just doin' my job." Which in this case apparently meant cleaning the floor on a Monday afternoon, regardless of whatever other event might be going on…."just doin' my job"…god, how I HATE that phrase….in any event, after significant harassment (read: I lost my

composure…Phil actually had to step between us and ask me to lower my voice!)
his supervisor eventually showed up and after a short negotiation, the Super promised that his man would cease and desist, that we would have their full cooperation, and in exchange, I would supply him (personally) with a quart of Jim Beam whiskey.

Only the “see that black man over there” (see ZIM chapter) rivals the “Zamboni in Africa incident for comedic outrageousness!”

Dieter/Dongina

One of the great couples we’ve met through gymnastics is Dieter and Dongina Risser. Dongina is a Nationally rated judge in Namibia and is more or less President Geldenhuys’s assistant….she’s got a heart of gold, and she and Dieter (who is not directly involved with gymnastics per se) always supports her activities. One activity they have made into a fairly lucrative “sideline” business is guiding tours to the Etosha Pan National Game Reserve. Dieter has a great deal of experience in wildlife, and is an expert at “sniffing out” where the game might be. At the conclusion of the Championships, he and Dongina took Hannah, me, Phil Barker, one of the Namibian coaches from Russia named Yuri, and Tanya Swallow on a 4 day safari.

Etosha Pan is an astonishing place….in the space of 96 hours we were able to see just about every big game animal (sans lions!) that are indigenous to that part of Africa, including, but not limited to giraffes, warthogs, water buffalo, wildebeests, zebras, rhinoceroses, and several magnificent herds of elephants only yards from our convy.

Dieter’s running commentary was extraordinarily interesting and informative. In addition, he assiduously showed concern for the well-being and creature comforts of our little safari. We were up and about and hit the road early each morning. By 9:30 am, he stopped the convy for “break-time”, figuring that the effort of pursuing big game was making us all (including himself!) thirsty. He’d walk to the back of the convy and earnestly inquire “hey, how ‘bout a peer (beer)?” Regardless of the answer, which was invariably “Sure!”, in order that our safari leader remain hydrated, he’d pop the top on one(or more) for himself….what a trip!

When one visits one of the great Game Parks in Africa, it’s important to understand that the traveler is considered the outsider; the park belongs ultimately to the wildlife that live there. At night, visitors travel to compounds where at a set time the gates are locked and one is basically locked inside until morning….if a convy is late arriving at a compound, you are basically out of luck and are going to be spending the evening in your vehicle….it’s a very tidy way to ensure that all the folks in the “Pan” are more or less rounded up and all accounted for by a given time each evening. Once inside a compound, there are some most interesting sights to see....One evening, we were inside the wire fence, and looking out at a (modestly but clearly lit) watering hole, where a number of large animals appeared....we saw a rare white Rhino show up to get a drink shortly before retiring for the evening....it requires a bit of patience, but Etosha Pan is truly one of the world's most remarkable parks.

The various compounds host a range of accommodations and amenities. In one there was a rather stylish (albeit in a folksy/neo-American Southwest sort of way) restaurant. After a long day on the trail, famished, we sat down for an anticipated great meal. Seven of us were at the table and one of the local waiters came over after filling up our water glasses and getting us a round of drinks to take our order. Dongina, ever the "practical" and "take charge" one, decided she would order for the group. Pointing to Dieter on her left, she indicated that "No. 1 here would like a Wildebeest steak": Yuri, seated next to Dieter, "Yuri, No. 2 there would like a salad and a Buffalo roast." Tanya, "Number 3 here, would like whatever it was she had ordered". Dongina proceeded in the same manner to order for Phil, Hannah, and me, and herself respectively.

The waiter excused himself, and we reinitiated the conversation, and while waiting, had a little bread and butter along with the drinks. There were a number of other tables with small groups of tourists like us, holed up here for the evening.

We waited....and waited.....it seemed an almost interminable time until the food arrived. "What's keeping them?" was a question on everyone's mind and certainly asked aloud more than once....finally, a phalanx of waiters emerged from the kitchen. To our astonishment, and almost immediately afterwards our incredulous amusement, the first waiter brought one Wildebeest stake....the second, brought TWO buffalo roasts, the third brought THREE plates of what Tanya had ordered, and yes, you guessed it, Phil got 4 plates of whatever he had ordered, I don't remember what I had for dinner that night, but yup, FIVE plates of whatever it was were set next to me, Hannah of course had SIX plates of her whatever, and the topper, Dongina, the unwitting architect of this disastrous (at least for the bottom line of the restaurant and the unfortunate beasts that "contributed" to this overkill of an order(!!!), got, absolutely nowhere to put it anywhere on our or adjoining tables, SEVEN courses of her menu item! For those of you playing along at home, that's 28 dinners ordered for a total of 7 people!!!

Who knows what was going on in the minds of the folks in the kitchen, and to this day we haven't the foggiest idea as to why SOMEBODY didn't come back out and get a clarification, but no, our waiter apparently not only misunderstood Dongina completely, but he somehow managed to take her numbers literally. Well, the restaurant was able to fob some of the plates at least onto other hungry tables awaiting their meals while our "battalion" had been given priority in the chow line….it's been over a decade, and when we met up with Dongina in Stuttgart in 2007, the first thing out of her mouth was "do you remember the time we were in the restaurant in Etosha Pan?"

Nonsense at meet

The competition itself turned out to be as is always the case, an intensely emotional, incredibly hectic and stressful, and in the end, a rather (perhaps looking back through the rosy glow of nostalgia) pleasurable experience…. There were 11 delegations represented at the event, which to this day is still the greatest aggregation of African countries to ever gather at a single gymnastics event….

The competition itself went off rather smoothly, with one exception….on the day of Men's team competition, all the teams were warming up with the exception of Algeria, and 10 minutes before the start of competition the Algerians arrived and Ali Zaater, President of the Federation approached me and indicated that their bus had not started and then had subsequently "broken down"….was this true? I had no idea, but I'm a stickler for adhering to the schedule and my initial reaction was to insist the meet proceed according to schedule. If anyone remembers the 1972 Olympics, there were American sprinters who's coach misread the times for the qualifying heats, and sure enough, the athletes, watching on German television heard their names announced as missing as the rest of the competitors warmed up in the starting blocks…..needless to say, the heat was run, the athletes, to the extreme displeasure (putting it mildly!) of the USOC were disqualified, and the event continued…..

With that as a precedent, I was not entirely happy with siddiqy Zaater's pleadings, but eventually relented due to the pragmatic (and collegial) exhortations of my friend…Ali (pleadingly) pointed out, "Surely Mr. Jim, in my place you would request the same….surely in your place, you would assume that I would agree to such a reasonable request…."

Well heck, when you put it that way…..

The Algerians got into the gym and hastily warmed up on all the apparatus. It didn't really matter that we started a few minutes late….what was important, as Ali pointed out, was that the event was a success and that athletes who had come 3500 miles to compete were given the opportunity to do so…I never (really) would have barred them from competing, but I was unhappy that the timeline was violated…..

One other happy aspect of the event was the successful negotiation with Namibian State Television to televise the Junior Championships, and in turn, their agreement to give continental broadcast rights to South African State television. I will of course, leave it for the reader to decide, but suffice to say the 35K SA rand "rights fee" guaranteed our ability to finish in the black financially.

As recounted in the June/July 1995 International Gymnast magazine,

"The Junior Championships was a special occasion in which the gymnastics youth of the continent provided an exciting, oftentimes sophisticated display of gymnastics in all three disciplines. One element helping to create the special flavor of this event is the extensive mix of languages and peoples that make up Africa. Imagine (for example) sitting in a judges meeting where a German (Karl Heins) speaks Russian to a Bulgarian coaching Nigeria who translated to English so that the Namibians can convert to French so that the Moroccans can translate to Arabic!"

Nigeria

In Walvis Bay, Nigeria brought a new team of "juniors" (see "Fun with Passports") (3 boys, 2 women). Peter Ojo won vault with a soaring Kasamatsu, and Olaniyi Ibitoye took the silver.....

Biting the hand that feeds you dept. (or perhaps more specifically, the lack of graciousness or context award):

"Chief, cook, bottle-washer"...., in the developing world, one wears many hats....in addition to my other responsibilities, I was the meet announcer...I'm very comfortable with public speaking and feel confident that I can find a way to communicate the "essence" of a competition (not necessarily the 'literal' truth) in a way that keeps spectators involved and informed. When Peter won his medal and I was announcing awards, and while I knew something about Nigerian gymnastics (see previous chapters), I assumed, it turns out incorrectly, that this was the first international medal that this young Federation had ever garnered.

When we got to vault results, I announced (close paraphrase)..."And the gold medalist, the vault champion of the 1995 Jr. African Championships, winning Nigeria's first medal in international competition, Peter Ojo!" Well, instead of accepting the award without comment(and overlooking, at least "publicly" my faux paus regarding the recent gymnastics history of Nigeria, the Nigerian coaches Koicho Zlatev and Isiah Obanor took great exception...catcalling from a bench not too far from my microphone, they shoutingly, "informed" me (and the audience) that I was mistaken and that in fact, Nigerians had previously won medals at some (I don't remember the specific) international competition...backpedaling, keenly embarrassed at their noisy interruption at what I intended as a very complimentary moment for Nigeria, and upset that they were interfering and diminishing Peter's "place in the sun" I apologized for the misstatement and soldiered on with my announcing....these guys completely misread my intent...given that I had had some history with them dating back almost 2 years to the Birmingham and Brisbane Worlds and our Commonwealth Games collaboration, I was disappointed that they reacted in such a harsh and non empathetic manner.

Cape Verde:

Cape Verde proved to be one of the highlights of the event. As recalled in IG:

"Situated in the Atlantic Ocean well of the coast of Gambia, the Cape Verdans made the longest trek. This former French colony has the smallest (approx. 250,000) population of the countries present, and arrived as unknowns, but its rhythmic athletes quickly became crowd favorites. . Lizandra Varela was a refreshing presence. Possessing a womanly physique made her something of an anomaly in a rhythmic competition, but she danced and used apparatus most proficiently and made for event finals. Elfin teammate Thelma Ramos (who subsequently qualified to the Athens Olympics in 2004!!) was the crowd darling and no slouch herself. Cape Verde was a most welcome and intriguing presence here."

Another highlight was the participation of

Angola:

Anilson de Silva, Angola's sole entrant had a fine meet but was unable to win any medals. Nevertheless, the likeable Angolan generated great media interest. His country (Namibia's northern neighbor) had fought against Namibia during its recent successful struggle for independence (1990-91) and relations between the countries (at least at that time) could be categorized as strained… The local press gave prominent coverage to what they characterized as "this breakthrough" Of his part, de Silva played to the crowds who responded with warmth and generous (read: long and loud) applause.. Is sport instrumental in breaking down walls between peoples? This rapproachment was a special moment during the Junior African Championships.

Namibia

IG: "....improbably, and wonderfully, there were the achievements of the host country. This young Federation hosted what may have been the finest (in retrospect, most observers agree) competition on the continent to date. The venue, running of events and ceremonial aspects were first rate. Gymnastically, Namibia was respectable in both rhythmic and women's artistic, the latter finishing 4th as a team….Fozie Friez-Franks narrowly missed winning a medal on floor, and rhythmic gymnast Nicole Berg became her first ever international gymnastics medalist with a silver in ball.

Initially, it was something of a shock to the African gymnastics community that little Namibia had been awarded this competition. They were subsequently most surprised at the warmth, enthusiasm, and most importantly, professional and efficient manner that the first (and to date ONLY) Junior African Championships were conducted. It is now likely that international gymnastics will be a regular occurrence in Walvis Bay. In the words of one gymnast, "This meet was really neat!" In summary, all hail President Valereis Geldenhuys, the Namibian Federation, and our gymnastics friends and colleagues throughout amazing Africa!"

"be careful of what you wish for department…."

From the outset it was apparent to us that Valereis Geldenhuys had ambitions for Namibian Gymnastics. When we spoke initially in Victoria, I shared with her my vision of what was possible, and urged her to focus the long-term prospects of the Federation, i.e. to "reach for the stars" as opposed to (for example) be better than Botswana…..whether because of my counsel, or because it segued with her ambitions, Ms. Geldenhuys took me at my word and involved me and Hannah at the uniquely successful Jr. African Championships.

Subsequently, I suggested that Namibia work to participate in the World Championships. I do not know the specific circumstances, but Fozie Fries-Franks, Namibia's top ranked gymnast (see above) at the '95 Junior Championships somehow "fell by the wayside" and Valereis's daughter Gharde emerged as the "top" gymnast from Namibia. As far as I'm concerned, there was no reason that the both of them couldn't progress, but….in early 1997, Valereis approached Hannah and me with the idea of coordinating a comprehensive training plan for Gharde, which we did, and on one occasion, Hannah actually listened to floor music and choreographed an elite floor routine via cross-continental telephone communication!!

I explained to Valereis that if her daughter (or any other Namibian female gymnast competed at the Worlds in 1997, it would set them up to participate in the 1999 Worlds which would be the qualifier to the 2000 Sydney Olympics. I further informed Valereis that there would be a "wild card" assignment for the top African girl from the Worlds in 1999 and that the only two other countries that I thought would participate would be Egypt and South Africa. I made it clear that with the right set of circumstances, Namibia could procure that wildcard spot to the 2000 Olympic Games.

Valereis's daughter participated, as per my suggestion and our peripheral involvement at the 1997 Worlds. At the FIG Congress in 1998 Ms. Geldenhuys requested from Hannah and me that her daughter Gharde come to the USA and live and train with us in preparation for the 1999 Worlds in Tienjin to qualify for Sydney. After a lengthy discussion, we agreed to house and train her, and that Hannah would be Gharde's official coach.

Her daughter (and to our consternation on disconcertingly extensive amounts of time, Valereis herself) lived in our house for 7 months. In retrospect, I acted foolishly in attempting to coordinate a maximally efficient training situation. I went to one of the gyms in town to ask one of my former gymnasts (an individual who, perhaps coincidentally was one of only two gymnasts who ever quit the UW team twice) who had developed a number of level 10s and one Elite.

Fool that I am, I trusted that this would be a "win-win" situation all around; the coach would have the opportunity to work with someone who was going to compete internationally, Gharde would be able to train with gymnasts better than her, et. al. I blindly and foolishly underestimated the appetite of the senior Geldenhuys, and overestimated her integrity regarding adherence to commitments.

Hannah acted as surrogate mother (the girl was 16 at the time), coach, medical professional, and physiotherapist. The younger Geldenhuys was rather fragile physically, and we spent endless hours working to keep her able to participate through a series of strains, sprains, and overuse injuries (trying to keep up with more accomplished and fit girls…) To make a long story short, Miss Geldenhuys, coached by Hannah and the other coach competed successfully in Tienjin, achieved our (2 years in the planning) objective of ranking as the top gymnast from Africa and qualified to the Olympic Games.

Despite the fact that Valereis had asked Hannah to coach and me to plan, despite the fact that she and her daughter had lived in our home for several months, despite our successful collaboration at the '95 Junior Africans and the '97 World Championships, and despite the fact that every aspect of my two-year game plan had been accomplished on schedule and achieved as projected, Ms. Geldenhuys moved her daughter out of our home three days after returning from Tienjin. She subsequently asked the other coach to accompany her daughter to Sydney in place of Hannah. Gharde finished last in the Sydney Olympic Games over a full point behind the next lowest competitor.

We had achieved everything we had planned and set out to accomplish for this small Federation. My wife Hannah had earned the right to and deserved to be the Namibia coach on the floor in Sydney.

Hannah has her own thoughts, but in my 43 years in gymnastics, this remains the single most bitter and negative experience I've ever had.

Coda:

We were informed subsequently (from outside parties) that Gharde, prior to going to Sydney had been given a gymnastics scholarship to the University of Washington; the coach that accompanied her to the Games was an assistant with that program at the time.

In the early 1930's Noel Coward was attending a party in Hollywood. He was introduced to one of MGM's premier stars Jean Harlow, who managed over the course of the evening to repeatedly mispronounce his name…finally, Coward purred, "I'm sorry dear, but the 'e' in Noel is pronounced identically as the 't' in Harlow"……………

"Be ashamed to die until you have won some victory for humanity."
Thomas Mann

Chapter Ten

YEMEN: "el corazon de Arabia"

Yemen....land of the Arabian Nights, home of the Queen of Sheba...located at the foot of the Arabian Peninsula, Yemenis are a fiercely independent and proud, yet very gentle and good natured people. The country is in many ways, the complete antithesis of how Western generally stereotype Arabia. One of the last parts of the world to embark on a course of modernity, the Yemenis overthrew their monarchy in 1962. Since then, Yemen has worked to remove itself from (what was then) a medieval level of both education and technology.

It is important for the Western reader to understand something about the challenges that are facing the Islamic world. When we discuss or mention "conservative" Islam and it's struggles to cope and adapt to "modernity", many people with little knowledge of Islamic history, and particularly Islamic intellectual history, erroneously (or perhaps more accurately "simplistically") reduce the problem(s) to a:

a religious doctrine that is at odds with the "modern" world and its' values,

b. a revolt/response to the historical effects of colonialism, and/or

c. an adaptation to modern technology, particularly communication, and specifically in how the 21st century our pan-global instant-communication "Internet" interconnectedness and access creates tensions when "traditional" mores clash against more open societies.

In fact, all of the above, each in its' way pertains to a much more fundamental dilemma.....in the West, in Europe, as all students of history know, the Church, the Christian Church ruled absolutely for almost a millennia after the fall of Rome...the political history of the last 1000 years, in one sense can be reduced to the theme of the struggle between the Church (or more broadly, "religion"), and the forces of "modernity:....first, the Church struggled (11th-13th/14th century) with the reintroduction of Greek thought into the Western mind. As an outcropping of that conflict (and defeat/retreat of the power of the Church), came the Renaissance and all that it entailed….coming on late heels of the Renaissance, was the Protestant Reformation (to this day, Catholics refer to it as "the Protestant Revolt")…regardless of the time and particular passions of the day, each of these broad movements resulted in an erosion of authority on the part of the "governing body", Holy Mother Church. Along with the Scientific Revolution in the late 16th and 17th centuries, and compounded with the Age of Enlightenment in the 18th century (and the concomitant evolution of nation-states), by the time of Benedict XIII in the late 19th century, the Catholic Church was on the defensive. We might well argue in the new millennia,(21st century) the historical path in the West, particularly in Europe, has seen the "Holy Roman Empire" supplanted by the Renaissance, which evolved into the "Age of Reason", which in turn, has morphed into our current "Age of Secularism or even Skepticism".

As (an assessment, not a value judgment) the West established itself as the dominant world culture, Islam has struggled to adapt. Most Westerners are unaware that the struggle to harmonize modernity with the social and religious precepts of Islam, is not at its' root, a conflict between Christianity and Islam, or the West and Orient.

It rather, harkens back and directly relates to the (lost but to a vast majority of Muslims, a nostalgic and elegiac "Golden Age")central debate in the history of Islamic thought. At a time when the highest civilization in Europe was arguably the Vikings, Baghdad and Cairo were the artistic and intellectual centers of the world….. While Western history superficially claims that the works of the ancients were lost to the world for 1500 years, the truth is much different. There was never a time that the writings of Thales, Anaximander, Socrates, Plato, and Aristotle had been lost to mankind. They had been subsequently translated into Latin, then Coptic, and finally Arabic where there thoughts and ideas were eagerly assimilated and debated by Islamic scholars for generations. In a similar, although the specific circumstances were different, the Islamic world examined (and speculated upon) the cosmology of the world, the place of man in the universe, and the epistemology by which knowledge might be learned/validated centuries before the same historical processes occurred in the West.

As with the Christian medieval scholars who later followed, Islamic intellectuals pondered and debated the nature of the Almighty and the validity of faith versus reason as the means by which knowledge might be known. The Persian Ibn Sina (980-1037) is one of the towering figures in the history of Philosophy. Perhaps more renowned in the West for his medical achievements (codified and expounded/improved upon the work of Galen), his philosophical encyclopedia *Kitab al-Shifa*, was a monumental work embodying a vast field of knowledge from philosophy to science. He classified the entire field of knowledge including: theoretical knowledge: physics, mathematics and metaphysics; and practical knowledge: ethics, economics and politics. His philosophy was a synthesis of Aristotelian tradition, Neoplatonic influences and Muslim theology. Within the context of his time, he was the supreme rationalist.

Ibn-Sina's ideas engendered a ferocious counter-reaction, the champion of which is the great mystic, al-Ghazali (1058-1111). Al-Ghazali's greatest treatise, *The Incoherence of the Philosophers* marked a turning point in Islamic philosophy in its vehement rejections of Aristotelianism and rationalism. The book took aim at the falasifa, a loosely defined group of Islamic philosophers from the 8th through the 11th centuries (notable among them al-Kindi and Al-Farabi) who drew intellectually upon the Ancient Greeks. Ghazali bitterly denounced Aristotle, Socrates and other Greek writers as non-believers and labeled those who employed their methods and ideas as corrupters of the Islamic faith.

The subsequent counter-counter- reaction to Ghazali was championed by Ibn-Rushd (Averroes in Western text) (1126-1198). My all-time favorite book title is his most significant work. In response to al-Ghazhali's "faith-based" epistemological approach, Ibn-Rushd produced *The Incoherence of the Incoherence* in which he defended Aristotelian philosophy against al-Ghazali's claims. Al-Ghazali argued that Aristotelianism, especially as presented in the writings of Ibn-Sina, was self-contradictory and an affront to the teachings of Islam. Ibn-Rushd's rebuttal was two-pronged: he contended both that al-Ghazali's arguments were mistaken and that, in any case, the system of Ibn-Sina was a distortion of genuine Aristotelianism so that al-Ghazali was attacking a "straw man." Ultimately this almost 200 year long conflict ended in the triumph of conservatism and the embrace on the part of the Islamic World of al-Ghazali's "faith based" world view.

The reader should note that while the specific circumstances (and ultimate outcome) are very different, the almost exact same conflict played itself out in Europe (Albert the Great, Aquinas, et.al.) which resulted in the Renaissance. In fact, in late medieval Europe, Aristotle was popularly known as "The Philosopher", and Ibn Rushd was known as "The Commentator". He is also the only "heathen" mentioned in Dante's Divine Comedy.

As with the West, 600 years ago, Islam must ultimately reconcile (or at least find a way to "accommodate") the dichotomy of "belief vs. skepticism". And as we outsiders sit as witnesses, let us not be too quick to pass judgment. We in the West had deadly religious wars as recently as 350 years ago, and we, who perceive Western Culture as so much more sophisticated have in the last hundred years promulgated two international (but not Islamic-Arab) conflicts which destroyed 100 million lives, and more recently, in America, there remains controversy in much of the country over whether evolution should be taught in public high schools.... the Islamic World has many contradictions and challenges....can we conclude that they are SO far behind us? The sensitive observer always looks for the commonalities amongst peoples. I find the parallel intellectual battles a fascinating point of comparison and connection. On to Sana'a!

Yemen, what an incredible dichotomy....the most conservative Islamic country in the world(after Saudi Arabia), and the epitome of the "Wild West" of American myth an imagination...a land where women, of course, can't be seen outside without their burkas/chadors, and a place in which, well, for the men, guns are a mark of manhood and honor....a place where there are still rigid social mores, and a land where literally "anything goes. I love the place!

On the latter point, two small anecdotes....I'm in the country for a couple days, and we are headed via Mr. Abdul-Magid's car towards the National Stadium in which the (such as it is) gymnastics complex is connected.... Mr. Abdul-Magid pulls the car over in order to purchase his daily ration of qat (more on this in a minute), we all get out to walk around the tiny suq (market), stretch our legs, and get a glimpse of what's being sold...on the other side of the road is a small herd of goats being overseen by a slightly built man, fully bearded and (in retrospect) looking out like he was some freedom-fighter from the 80s, small checkered kaffiya on top of his head, full beard, overlapping white/black and white/red checkerboard shawls criss-crossing his shoulders....as he urged the sheep on with his walking-staff, a Westerner could not overlook the bandoleers criss-crossed along his shoulders and the familiar banana-clipped personal arsenal that was the AK-47 slung over his shoulder.

What is that?" I naively inquired. :"What's what?" my colleagues replied. "That, that, well, Kalishnikov..."...all laughed...."my American friend" our interpreter Yahyah al-Dahemi chided me patiently, "everyone in Yemen has this weapon." It was true!!! Shades of Gunfight at the OK Corral or Tombstone Territory or the Gadsden Flag's sentiment, "Don't Tread On Me", there is no place in the world where weaponry is more revered, more respected, and more easily available than little Yemen on the edge of the Arabian Peninsula.

Bart and Peggy from the early 50's film noir "Gun Crazy" would be in hog heaven here.....it turns out, that shortly after reunification of the country (from it's early 1990s Civil War), the Government made an attempt to have the citizenry register their weapons. This failed utterly in a cascade of derisive laughter by the populace. In the capitol city, Sana'a, efforts were reintroduced and a grudging compromise of sorts was reached....in modern day Sana'a, the police do have the option of giving a citizen a ticket if they are openly "packing heat". So, for many of the populace, they simply walk around with concealed weapons.

Our goat herder? He was at or slightly outside the city limits, so wearing a bandoleer of bullets and having an AK-47 slung over his shoulder was "no big deal"

Nashwan al-Harazi, of whom we will hear more later, related an interesting (to me) family story and shared a picture. He has an 11 year-old nephew who, last year, attending school got into a discussion with his father (Nashwan's brother), about upcoming testing, and the father broached the possibility of an award for high marks. "What would you like to receive son, if you get high marks?" The boy replied, "I would like a Kalishnikov of my own." Well, you can imagine how that might play out in suburban Lake Oswego or Westchester County. Here in Southwestern Arabia? The boy studied hard, got great marks and is the proud owner of his own automatic weapon, proudly displayed in a photo sent recently!

"When you call me that....smile..."

One morning after my first round of lectures, the coaches and I were scheduled for a half day off so that they could take me sightseeing….we got on a bus seating about 30, and headed off to the mountains, and to a small village located on top of an extremely steep mesa. Blessed with a natural spring, the summit extends to 1000 meters above the plain below, and was literally invulnerable to attack until the advent of the airplane. As our bus ground its' way up the winding road leading to the village, the grade became so steep that it becomes necessary for all of us passengers to get out and actually push it until the grade leveled slightly…taking no chances (since at one point the vehicle actually started to roll backwards necessitating the use of air brakes to stop it (yikes, who wants to meet Allah after rolling backwards off the side of a cliff in Yemen!??), we all got out and pushed, then hiked our way the approximate 3 kilometers up to the top and into the village….as we hiked, the coaches made a row across the road, held hands and started to sing Yemeni songs….not too far up ahead, I hear a "crack!", then the same sound again, almost like a car backfire, but "sharper, more nasal." "CRACK!" What the heck is that?

Let me digress slightly….our driver was a gentleman of the old school. Wearing the traditional galibeya (the white gown favored by many men dressing informally in the Arab world, a kaffiya (the red and white headdress), and ubiquitous sandals….while we were driving up from town, I hadn't noticed the olive-green blanket covering the lump on the floor next to the driver's seat between us. "CRACKKK-pingggg!"

We turn a sharp corner of the road, and a little bit up and ahead of us is our bus, parked, our driver, with his AK-47 set to single-round deployment, firing at some birds circling around the cliff looming above us. What the hell, I think to myself. Our driver, graying, grizzled man who had not smiled the hour we had spent together in the bus, motions for me to come over. I do so, followed by Yahyah Dahemi, my interpreter, and a gaggle of coaches (who <happily> seemed attached to me at the hip, so apparently eager were they for either a. my company, or perhaps b. in amusement at my "fish out of water" potential pratfalls. Our driver motions with the weapon, and smiling asks me something in Arabic I don't understand…I turn to Yahyah…"he wants to know if you've ever handled an AK-47; he knows it is NOT an American weapon.?" I turn back from Yahyah to our bearded driver. "Tell him, no, I haven't had the opportunity."

Yahyah translates : "He wants to know if you'd like to shoot with it?" The driver grins, nods, and extends the weapon an inch or two in my direction. I get a little kid's smile just like I was surprised on my 7th birthday on my face…."HELL YES!" as everybody in the group breaks out in laughter….no translation necessary here! I'm handed the weapon, and Yahyah translates, "It's currently set on single-shot….take your time, it tends to shoot high, aim at a point on the cliff, and squeeze the trigger." Man, this is something out of an Indiana Jones film…..I take aim…"CRACK!" Again…"CRACK!" Wow….the driver reaches under my trigger finger and points to an upraised lever on the stock just before the banana clip. "He says if you want to put it on automatic fire, just flip the lever down….make sure you adjust for the different recoil." Everybody watches, smiling…..I take a deep breath, find a boulder about 100 meters away (point blank, but still….) flip the lever, remember that it tends to fire high, look down that short barrel, and….squeeze:

PUKA, PUKA, PUKA, PUKA, PUKA, PUKA, PUKA….eeeennnnggggh! Whatta blast!!! That last sound is one of the rounds ricocheting of the rock I had been aiming for….I had actually hit it!! I'm not particularly into guns or weapons of any kind, but lemme tell you, firing off an AK-47 in the mountains of Arabia is a totally cool, mindblowing blast!!! One more short burst, just for the pure nonsensical joy of it ("Top of the World MA! Top of the World!" - Jimmy Cagney as the deranged Cody Jarrett at the end of White Heat comes to mind), and with a huge grin,
and a "shukrun, siddiqy, shukrun!!" (thank you my friend, thank you) I hand the weapon back to our (he's now grinning too) driver, and my Yemeni friends clap me on the back…..I've been initiated once again, in a small but touching way, (even if only as a guest) into their brotherhood..one of the cherished mementos of that particular trip is a picture of our group, taken from on top of the bus, with the valley in the distance, of the guys, our driver, Nashwan perched directly over my shoulder, and me with aviator (cool, but I know I ain't no "Top Gunl!) sunglasses, on one knee, with that Kalishnikov, butt on the ground, muzzle cradled in my right hand, looking up at the camera…..wow…..

Virtually everyone is aware that Yemen is an extremely conservative Islamic country. One of the striking things about travel to me is the almost constant juxtaposition of "what we know" about a new place contrasted with the reality of an encounter in a new and unfamiliar environment. The great empiricist, Roger Bacon(1214-1294) once noted memorably *"Do not assume that that which one 'knows' to be the truth, is in fact, the truth."* Always be aware of and delve into the contradictions.

In no small part, because I was from America (even now, to many people in the world despite the Baywatch reruns, it remains the mystical land of unimagined wealth and mystery…sort of like a modern-Samarkand if you think about it), I was an "exotic" in Yemeni eyes and in great demand on virtually every evening I was in the country….people wanted to interact and "hang-out" with me….early on in the coaches course, I was invited to a wedding reception. Two of the coaches taking the course were going to have a dual wedding, and (I guess to them) having a foreigner, especially an American as a guest, was a source of great distinction, if not pride.

I dressed back at the hotel, changed into jacket, tie, slacks, put a "jambiya pin" on my lapel, and was picked up and taken to the function around noon….now, things are changing in Yemen, but this particular function was "traditional".

Upon arrival, I was embraced by a number of coaches who had now become friends and colleagues. In Yemen, there are still "arranged marriages"….earlier that morning, in separate meetings, the bride and the groom had met with their respective fathers, and the fathers in essence had given their blessings/acted as functionaries over the bond created between the couple. This is done in private, and is a contract between the fathers and children. After the "ceremony", the bride goes to a party (in the West, "reception") with her female friends and and the groom goes to the same with his male family and friends. As parties go in the conservative Arabian peninsula goes (lack of female presence excepted), it was interesting, high energy, and fun. About 50 men and boys milled around honking horns and making noise generally for about an hour, then early in the afternoon, we sat down to a communally shared meal of sweet tea, goat, vegetables, bread, and the honey-laced dessert so prized in this part of the world…..a traditional Arab meal, no utensils, one reaches into the broad platter with one's right hand, and….well, enjoy….

After the afternoon meal, we collectively went into one of the ceremonial sitting rooms that are ubiquitous in Yemeni homes…located in the front part of the main floor, just (as one walks in) to the left of the front door, the room is rectangular or square, the floor is covered with rich Persian carpets….there are cushioned with cushioned back supports emanating from all walls…no furniture in the Western sense, in essence, the "sofas" are all connected to the walls with the bottom part of the sofa on the floor….many of us crammed into what with 5-10 people would be a spacious room, and the second phase of the day's celebration began.

Qat (or gatt) is a pervasive and seminal aspect of Yemeni culture… Ghat has been grown for use as a stimulant for centuries in the Horn of Africa and the Arabian Peninsula. Ghat's fresh leaves and tops are chewed in order to achieve mild euphoria. Presumably, the reader understands that (mainstream Western) drugs and alcohol of any kind are strictly forbidden in Yemen. There are severe religious and criminal penalties that apply to anyone caught with same. Ghat is so popular in Yemen that its cultivation consumes much of the country's agricultural resources. It is estimated that almost half (!) of the country's water supply goes towards irrigating it. One reason for cultivating ghat in Yemen so widely is the high income it provides for farmers.

That afternoon, I was introduced to as my friends so quaintly phrased it: "the chewing of ghat". Two broad perspectives….as a first-time ghat chewer, I had no idea what I was getting into….on one level, I was disappointed that there didn't seem to be more of a "kick" to it…..well, after about 3 hours of chewing, I had a mild, almost like 3 cups of coffee-like buzz….for a "newbie" like me (or at least me personally), the effects don't really kick in until later….at the end of the evening, around midnite, at least 8 hours after I'd stopped chewing, it really hit me…I wanted to go to asleep because I had a long day ahead of me, and man, was I ever WIRED….I felt like I'd drained 20 cups of espresso….I was wide awake until damned near daylight….I stayed up and made pages and pages of notes of things which I thought I could do and were necessary to accomplish….one of them actually happened (see chapter on "Nashwan").

After our group ghat session, the coaches/guests took to the street….Sana'a is a huge warren, a connection/collection of neighborhoods…the social 'unit' is that of the block, the neighborhood…our wedding couples had been acqainted with each other(s) from early childhood, living on the same block and …it seemed very natural in this culture that they would have the opportunity to "connect" as adults….as a Westerner, I have no particular empathy or confidence that this promotes a better condition for the principals, their families, or the broader culture, but intellectually, I can recognize the "comfort/stability" level of the certainty of the process….

There was a "communal" room just off the courtyard of the neighborhood…again, juices and teas, and a number of different kinds of meats, veggies, and sweets available….as before, up in the mountains, the music swelled up, men sang and danced together under a candlelit canopy….a few of the young boys in the 'hood came up and looked at me curiously….one young boy (8-9), a strikingly handsome youth, put his hand on my (pale) face….ethnically, Yemeni's for the most part are (Western orientation) "olive-skinned"…my 7/8 Irish/Northern European was presumably new in this young man's experience….he rubbed my check, just to make sure it was real…..some of the other boys crowded around me., looking at me curiously…..one of the great folk dances of Yemen is the "jambiya dance"….the jambiya is the ceremonial curved sword (think scimitar, but dagger-sized with an irovy-butt) worn full-frontal, sheathed in a wide belt at the midsection of the waist….in any event, the men take off their jambiyas, and holding them at the tip of the blade (or balancing the tip of the blade on their chins (!!!), they dance in a circle around chairs, each other, imaginary objects, etc. For the men lacking in the courage (or coordination) to do a circle dance with the knife-blade pointing directly at their carotid artery, there's always the option to "hug the walls" and be a spectator to the spectacle…which I of course, who can't even do proper "western"(including foxtrot, texas two-step, or even the stroll!!) dances can't do….

Regardless, the child-posse that was shadowing me, insisted I participate in the festivities…so, I (with a totally straight face!) take the jambiya pin off the corner of my lapel (it's about 1 1.4 inches in total length, twirl it over my head, and walk to the center of the floor, where I canter around in a circle, waving this tiny pin over my head….the group collapses in convulsive laughter …."hey Mr. Jim", come drink some tea and please partake in the "chewing of the ghat" with us……whatta bunch of cool guys….now, for those who might have the slightest interest, two final points of observation: first, I went to a wedding reception in Yemen, damned near 12 hours long, and never spoke to a woman (never saw a woman except the ones peeking out from the second floor windows behind the curtains when we were out the the block courtyard!), and never saw the bride….at the very end of the function, the groom (and select friends) drove to a hotel where the bride and her friends had been partying, the groom and bride got together, the rest of the guests, I'm not sure, the bride and groom went off together, and the rest….well, I was definitely invited, but bushed and needed to prepare for the next morning's lectures, so I went back to the hotel….and of course, got no sleep due to the ghat!

Dinner/street

Despite it's ancient history and traditions, Yemen is at the same time a marvelously informal place. Sana'a in many ways (although it of course is distinctive in many other ways) is a typical major city…there are many many suqs(markets), stores, and of course, restaurants so that busy people can find sustenance….like many things in Yemen, however, even the "restaurants" have a novel and (depending on one's perspective) wonderfully odd appeal….on this given evening, Mr. Abdul Magid, Mr. Dahemi, and Nashwan al-Harazi came across a block of storefront food vendors….we stopped, ordered our food, and waited on the adjacent sidewalk…I should point out that seating was not available in this particular establishment. As a matter of fact, there are many many restaurants/.food services in Sana'a where seating is unavailable. When one walks up to a store front, you basically order off a menu, printed on the wall, behind the cashier (who is often also the cook) is a small grill and stove …in any event, we ordered our food and waited….just before the food was delivered through the window, our cashier/cook/waiter reached behind the stove and pulled out several large sheets of cardboard….handing them to us, he indicated by hand signal, that our order would be ready in a minute….Abdul-Magid and Nashwan reached for the cardboard, and proceeded to step off the sidewalk and place our "placemats" onto the middle (no, that's not quite right, actually just off the sidewalk, but most definitely out on the street. The paper plates were handed to me, Yahyah received the containers of "aysh (bread), filaphel (garbanzo bean spread), and samek (broiled fish)…I was handed the plates, napkins, and glasses of juice)….the four of us sat down on top of the cardboard IN THE STEET to enjoy our meal….a few minutes into the repast, a giant diesel truck pulls up beside us, billowing smoky fumes….so what? I like lox, I like smoked salmon at home, so I have a little diesel-smoked samek in Arabia, so what???? Salvadore Dali would love Yemen….I love this place….

Weasel/python

The National Museum in Sana'a, is a fascinating pastiche of pre-Islamic (remember, this part of the Arabian peninsula has been inhabited for 3500 <at least> years) art, folk-art and political "icons" from the last century, et.al. The pre-Islamic art , particularly the sculptures are striking…vaguely reminiscent of Assyrian and Sumerian art-forms, they are a charming backdrop/foundation for much of what is skipped over the last 15 centuries (remember, Islamic culture is iconoclastic)….in any event, also featured are a number of beautiful and intricate tapestries, including a magnificent green and gold threaded (I believe prayer rug) in which the opening words of the Koran were depicted in traditional Arabic script. When I attempted, in all innocence to take a photograph, one of the trustees came screaming at me, and brandished a, well, an axe-handle minus the axe….no one had informed me that this particular piece was off-limits!

It is important to recognize that in conservative Islam, "khaffirs" or non-believers are not welcome in "holy" places…..regardless of one's assessment of Osama bin-Ladens' deeds, (while the Western press does not readily publicize this), his primary issues have been not that America or the West is corrupt and immoral, but rather that the armies of the "crusaders" (300+ years of history and 9 invasions from the Islamic perspective!!) occupy Saudi Arabia (the Islamic "Holy Land" and a place whose cities Medina and Mecca, the

Koran explicitly forbids non-believers to enter)…in any event, the Museum in Sana'a is a wonderful (albeit eclectic) mixture of pre-Islamic art, Islamic tapestries, and modern day "kitsch"''…the kitchen includes the limousine in which circa 1962 the king of Yemen survived an assassination attempt (bullet-holes puncturing a 4 inch window barrier for the backseat), and my personal favorite display, a stuffed-animal trophy featuring a python putting a killer grip and bite on a weasel…this particular item was a "gift" from Saddam Hussein to President Ali Abdul al-Saleh. in any event, it's a fascinating place featuring a range of precious items ranging from the sublime to the simply bizarre.

The allure of the burka

I suspect that persons who have never been to a conservative Middle Eastern country have (as I recall I did) certain preconceived notions, not only about how "things are", but how one might react when encountering something new(the caveat of our friend Bacon notwithstanding).

In any event, the central area of Sana'a is very compact and while there is nothing like "skyscrapers", there is a great deal of both traffic and foot traffic along it's bustling streets. One is keenly aware that the women are restricted to wearing burkas, almost all the shrouds are black (a few charcoal greys and even an occasional grayish blue can be seen, and of course shroud the females from head to foot (to the ground really), with only an eye slit and hands showing. Some women go to the extremes (as can often be seen in Afghanistan) of gloving their hands and veiling (sort of like a beekeeper) their eyes so that no skin at all can be seen.

Most cultural mores have complex histories and rationales and as people we tend to take the ones of our culture for granted, and either over-generalize or oversimplify our notions of what and why other cultures do what they do. I've heard Westerners assert many times that the reason for Islamic women having the public dress codes they do is because in the Islamic world, the men want to oppress the women. While there is an aspect of human rights that certainly factors into this, it is by no means exclusive or even necessarily the primary one. To conservative Islam, a woman's sexuality is so powerful, the desire she inspires so explosive, that in order for the society to remain stable, and also for males to not give in to temptation and therefore commit egregious sins, it is considered necessary to remove the temptation as much as possible.

Is this a successful tactic? Well, yes. And...no. I can attest to the latter with this brief anecdote... I must have been in Sana'a for about a week; during the entire 2 ½ weeks I was in the country, I never had the opportunity to speak with a woman, due to this strict segregation of the genders. In any event, I was walking down one of the main streets in Sana'a, not really paying close attention to anything, although aware of the black-garbed shapes all around me. Approaching a curb, I saw a black-burka clad woman step off the sidewalk as she began crossing the street....my heart leapt into my throat...As she stepped forward, in sharp (and unbelievable!) contrast to the black hem of the drab raiment concealing all the rest of her, a stunning (I was stunned!) woman's evening pump extended forward. The body of it was shining emerald green, cut deep on the side and curving upwards to a bright gold 4 inch heel. The toecap was also of that bright gold hue, and while I know males are not supposed to stare at women in Islamic countries, I confess that I watched that shoe (and it's complement on the other foot) and ankle walk all the way across the street and beyond until their wearer disappeared into the crowd on the opposite side. As absurd as this might sound, it was a thrilling, and extremely powerful sight. Oh, and whatever my other foibles, I'm not even a shoe fetishist! Taken in context, it was a profoundly erotic moment.

A few days later, I encountered an even more fascinating juxtaposition pertaining to the conservative Islamic perspective on the body, sexuality, and it's relation to religious values.

It was about 09:00 and I've been picked up at my hotel by Mr. Abdul-Magid, one of the coaches, and who turned out to be a great friend. In much of the Middle East it seems polite to not simply call people by their first names, but to put a "Mister" in front of it...ergo, I am always "Mr. Jim" regardless of how familiar the persons I'm with are with me....my friend Mr. Abdul Magid drove an old, but serviceable Datsun, and he had his favorite radio station and Arabic music on as we headed towards the center of town. We passed small shops, a milling group of goats, and one of the outlying mosques, with it's minaret pointing towards an almost cloudless blue sky....I saw a small flock of pigeons flying across from Mr. Abdul's side of the road towards mine, and a large billboard caught my eye. I jerked to a completely upright position, and if one were looking at me, I'm sure you'd have seen my eyes bugging out.

"WHAT THE HECK IS...THAT?" I blurt out, pointing at the billboard. Looming over us on the billboard is an attractive woman wearing a blue headscarf seated, *naked to the waist and sporting two very large bare breasts with nipples front and center!!!!!*

Am I seeing things? Am I hallucinating? Is this some peculiar wet-dream? What the hell??? I'm in the friggin' Middle East...the Arabian Peninsula for godssake....Y-e-m-e-n. In fairness, as I gawk and take a second, closer look....no, that's not accurate, no second look, just a loooong....I'm staring at that billboard as hard as I've ever stared at anything, but I'm trying to focus because it feels like I've just had some weird out of body experience.....oh...at her waist, our lovely gal is cradling an infant...below that there's some Arabic script that I of course don't understand.

Infant aside, those are some amazing knockers! Aaaaaand, I'm in Yemen. "Mr. Abdul-Magid, what on earth is that?" "What do you mean, Mr. Jim?". "THAT??" He looks at me puzzled...."That, that woman...., ummm, she's not wearing a blouse or shirt or dress." "Oh," he replied, "she's a mother; the government wants mothers to breastfeed naturally; that's an advertisement publicizing that policy." Oh....a-ma-zinnnnng.

So, at least as I understand it, even though completely bare breasts are still taboo in say, Las Vegas Nevada USA....it's ok to show-off your hooters on billboards in Yemen as long as it pertains to motherhood. I found this disconnect between motherhood and sexuality absolutely fascinating in no small part because of how starkly it showcases the inconsistency (or hypocrisy if you will) in the Western world's objectification of the female body. From the Islamic perspective then, the female body, when thought of or gazed upon by a male, is so provocative, she so strong and his will so weak, that it needs to be concealed. Removed, however, from the sexual sphere and placed into the context of "motherhood", the breast becomes, not an erotic object or a trigger for male lust, but rather a functional (and, policy of the Yemeni government, fundamental) component of child-rearing. Pasties required in Vegas, but bare boobs ok in Sana'a....who could possibly dream stuff like this up?

Periodization (circa 1914 or so)

I'm conducting an IOC Coaches Development Course in Yemen (when I met Nashwan); Yemen, as anyone with a globe can confirm is 11 time-zones from the Pacific Coast of the US, and therefore about as remote as one can get and still be on Earth... in any event, one of my favorite topics to lecture on is building/developing a long-term periodized training plan. When I do the full lecture, it takes about 2 1/2 hours....I find it fascinating, but I understand that it can be tough to follow, especially if you're in a sunlit room and it's oh, say 75-85 minutes into the lecture and lunch will be coming up in a bit....anyway, I'm explaining with my graphs and things, and tying it in to Islamic references (like how the fasting of Ramadan will cut into one's energy level, so you need to factor that in when your developing your plan....also mentioned and got a nice laugh that the reason that there are so few Muslims in Alaska is that when Ramadan is in summer, 'cause it's light up there all the time, good Muslims are in danger of starving to death....(as usual I digress)

Anyhow, I've been in the country about a week, maybe 9 days and the 30 coaches and I are starting to get pretty comfortable with each other....guys bond easily, especially if they're all involved in something they're mutually passionate about, doesn't matter about language or culture differences....anyway, I'm nattering on <but hopefully communicating clearly and enthusiastically> about periodization, and a hand goes up in the front row..."Bashir, yes?" I ask.

His question: "What are the nutritional requirements of the players?" Gymnasts (gumbaz in arabic) are known as "players" in Yemen because people play gymnastics.....I look at him, thinking to myself...what the h---? what, nutrition?

So I stop for a moment, put my head down, and look over at him. "Bashir, let me answer your question with a question for the group....mmmmm, who here knows something about the history of motion pictures in the decades of the 1910s?

30 Arab heads go down, pondering a response....a hand goes up in the back of the room...."Mohammed!", I acknowledge....he stands up, looks at me, and earnestly replies....are you ready? "Charlie Chaplin!"

Well, I'm grinning from ear to ear and the tears are just about to fall out of the corner of my eyes in remembered mirth as I'm typing this in October 2008, but honest to Allah, I damned near fell over right then and there! Un-be-leee-va-ble.

I shook my head and sort of choked on the first word or two,

"Uhhhh....right....yes...YES!...absolutely! 100% correct......Charlie Chaplin made his film debut in February 1914, his Little Tramp character appeared in his second film "Kid Auto Races at Venice" later that month and he made several of his classic shorts during the decade of the 1910s. Mohammed, that was a wonderful answer."

The group looks at me expectantly. "Now dear colleagues, let me ask you another question." They lean forward in anticipation...."My question is: what does any of that have to do with what we are talking about?" Thirty Yemeni heads go down...and about 1/2 second later, the room explodes in laugher and raucousness as 29 coaches pile on poor Bashir, ragging on him and teasing him...."Woah, woah, woah fellas..." We're all practically in tears..."Hey guys, Bashir asked a really good question and we'll get back to it, but if we can, let's try to refocus for the next 45 minutes or so on "training plans". So everybody has a good laugh and a quick stretch, Bashir grinning shyly, and me with an ear to ear grin that stayed on my face for most of the rest of that day.

What a moment....here I am, half-way across the world, pull out the most obscure and off-topic thing I can think of off the top of my head, and THERE IS A CONNECTION (or more accurately an interconnection of connections) that in one moment makes us a united group and tightens the bonds we are developing by being together in a shared endeavor even tighter.....absolutely transcendent....

It happens all the time. honest.

One more thing....one of the most perfect parts of this story is that the

REAL butt of the humor is NOT Bashir, but me!!!!! I'm some "expert" from way off, ask the most absurd thing in the world, and my students' already KNOW the answer!!!!!!! I don't know about you, but god I think that's hilarious....I love getting tagged on the chin like that.

"My nationalism is intense internationalism. I am sick of the strife between nations and religions."
Mohandas K. Ghandi

Chapter Eleven

EGYPT

Is perhaps the most amazing place on earth.....land of the Pharaohs, 51 centuries of continuous history, the sands of the African/Saharan desert, ...ancient, incredible .EGYPT.

Individuals who haven't been there truly have no conception....the ancient notion of the "sands of history" that wash over this ancient land, both illuminate and obscure the incredible present and the astonishing past that are all part and parcel of this place....the Egyptians are a proud, self-determinative, and strong people....regardless of the excesses of Abdul Nasser in the 50's and 60s, and the demoralizing defeats from dealing with the Israel four decades ago, the people of Egypt are defiant, unbowed, and have a fierce pride in their country's place in World History and regional prominence, if not, "pride of place."

Hannah and I were invited to Egypt to assist in coordinating the African Gymnastics Championships....the (former) head of the Egyptian Gymnastics Federation, Mohammed Mahmood ab-del-aal whom we had met at a couple of previous competitions, had asked us, if we would consent to be involved (albeit not as the competition directors) at the African Championships We were quite excited at the opportunity, and responded "gladly"; although there was not a specific funding mechanism in place, we were invited to get on an airplane and come to Egypt....

We found a way by submitting a proposal to International Gymnast magazine which is owned and run by Paul Ziert and Bart Connor...our deepest thanks to those two gentlemen whom we believe are two of the most important, committed, and dedicated persons ever to be involved in the sport....it is a curious and sad commentary on the gymnastics "establishment" both in the USA and Internationally that neither of these accomplished men have ever held "official" positions, nor, (do I believe) that they've ever been asked to do so.

In any event, we arrived after a very long flight, and were greeted by a couple of rhythmic gymnastics friends….we were informed upon arrival that the "African Championships" had been canceled and that the primary purpose for our coming to Egypt in the first place had been eliminated…..

That said, we of course moved on to plan "B" and found a way to make our 6 week stay in Egypt positive and functional…..

Cairo, as anyone who has ever gone there, is one of the most amazing places on earth….a city of anywhere between 15 and 25 million (25,000,000!!!!) people crammed into an intimate geographic spot more or less 20 kilometers from one end to another), the contrasts between rich and poor, new and old are simply staggering….simplest and most obvious commercial example….if one has only seen the pyramids and Sphinx from photos, one would have no serious/real concept of how significantly the "modern world intervenes or imposes on same….across the street from the Sphinx, more or less 200 meters away, is a Pizza Hut restaurant….nothing against the entrepreneurs of the PH franchise, but it is quite incongruous to have a 20th/21st century store adjacent to this most ancient of landmarks….

There is, quite frankly, no "undeveloped" country with more sporting potential than Egypt. Despite the fact that the country has this giant chasm between "rich and poor", the private resources available (to the "rich" at least) are unsurpassed in the world. In Egypt, gymnastics programs are (as far as my knowledge goes, excepting the National team program in the Maadi suburb of Cairo), almost exclusively activities offered to their memberships by the various large sporting clubs. The Egyptian Sporting Club model is based loosely on the European experience. Historically, the majority of the clubs were founded by the British, and by tradition have catered to a particular class and level of wealth' while the political and social events since the 1952 revolution have impacted this, it is safe to say that membership in the various clubs is still strongly skewed towards the wealthy and powerful in Egypt.

Gezira Club-Cairo

Gezira is the oldest and richest club in Egypt. Founded by the British, it is situated in the wealthiest part of Cairo and offers 29 sports to the 25,000 families that are members (an estimated 80,000 individuals)... The club is limited to this number by its' constitution. There is a lengthy waiting list, and we were informed that to purchase a membership costs approximately 100K EP….annual fees are of course, less…The gymnastics training hall is 12000 square feet and has full sets of equipment for MAG, WAG, and Rhythmic. There are 60 players that comprise the three teams…during the summer they estimate that another 300 children will take part in their summer skills program. *There are no other gymnasts using the facility* The annual budget for gymnastics is 750,000 EP. As in all the other programs in Egypt, no one has seriously considered the possibility of making gymnastics a revenue-producing activity for the clubs!

As I have suggested, the possibilities of generating revenue in a club such as this are staggering! I almost fainted when I was informed that although the club had its membership computerized, Gezira had never even put out a newsletter for its members! We told everyone we encountered that there simply is no program anywhere in the USA with this potential and that no gymnastics person in America would believe it if we described it.

Cairo Sporting Club

Membership is approximately 10,000 families, the initiation fee and annual membership are similar to (albeit somewhat less) than Gezira; according to the late Capt. Abdel Raouf Al Hagazi (more on him later), Cairo Sporting club has traditionally been the strongest program and produced the most national team members.

Shooting Club-Cairo

Had a membership of 20,000 and a membership fee of approximately 300K EP/year. The gym had a new set of Janssen-Fritschen equipment; any international team would be comfortable training here; there were approximately 100 children in the program. The evening we were present, there were 11 coaches, all Egyptian, working with 35 children. We were asked by one parent if her 12-year old daughter should quit gymnastics on the recommendation of a coach who told her that she was "too old":.. It is imperative that Egyptian coaches be given more encouragement, education, and training. It, frankly, irritates me that this archaic "Eastern European", pre-pubescent 'little kids jumping around' model continues to exist in an era which encompasses Nastasia Liukin's artistry, and Oksana Chusovitna's endurance....women's gymnastics is for WOMEN...it can be a wonderful sport for active, adult females. Carly Patterson and Shaun Johnson should not be the only role models for young girls!

Alexandria Sporting Club

Had a membership of 30,000 and a Gezira-like initiation and annual fees; this is significant to understand the amount of money available for sport and recreation in Egypt. Sporting Club has a truly impressive physical plant; the club has traditionally raised additional monies through horse racing (!); the betting/spectator paddock sits on one side of the club with the racetrack on the outside boarder of the club's facilities; Alexandria SC sports two (!!!!!) Olympic size (50m) swimming pools (plus diving wells) adjacent to each other. The gymnastics hall (adjacent to the polo field!!!!!) is 25000 square feet with long range plans to build another training venue. . Currently, the gymnastics program shares the facility concurrent with the men's and women's basketball teams... Despite the noise and apparent chaos, the gymnasts get some reasonable amounts of training accomplished. Mr. Maoub, the assistant (because he's Egyptian) women's coach was the first individual I encountered in the country who used a written training plan and was attempting to document his athlete's physical preparation and training loads through written records. I was very impressed with his organization and enthusiasm and the results of his junior athletes. Alexandria also has a team program of about 60 athletes as well as a (year round) preschool program of an additional 100-120 students; in the summer, they have up to 500 children take part in their summer gymnastics program.

Olympic Club-Alexandria

Had a membership of 20,000 with a 30K EP initiation fee. They have one of the strongest football teams in Egypt, and a large physical plant. Gymnastics is a young sport for this club; started by Magda Zaki (brevet judge and longtime chair of the Women's Technical Committee, the program has about 50 children in an upstairs (boxing and weightlifting are below) facility with a low ceiling and vault runway that starts on an outside balcony (which is "inconvenient, but certainly not an insurmountable problem….many might recall that the several-time National and perennial conference champions Cal-Berkeley used to have to run down the hallway and through a door in order to vault in (what was then) Harmon Gym (now Haas Court).

Notwithstanding these limitations, the gymnasts in Olympic club, were strong, flexible, and had the most organized training of the facilities we visited; the 11-12 year old boys may only be in the gym 12 hours a week, but during that time, they constantly worked circles and travels on the floor pommels, planches (3 of the 6 team members can hold) on the pbars, ext. Olympic is the only one of the 6 clubs that doesn't have a foam pit.

Smora Club (Alexandria)

60,000 families are members of Smora! It has a small gymnastics facility (1200 sq. feet) which includes a pit at one end with a large facility scheduled for construction. The club boasted the World Jr. Squash Champion and also has a racetrack. In summary, the circumstances of the Sports clubs in Egypt simply do not exist in the USA... We were approached by a number of cubs and asked if we could a. coordinate a coaches development program for the club, and/or b. coordinate their program for a period of time ranging from 4 months to a year, to a long-term contract... We feels strongly that this structure is an incredible asset to Egyptian gymnastics, and properly managed, could be a tremendous source of revenue, as well as offering the opportunity for large numbers of children to become involved in gymnastics.

I stated repeatedly to my somewhat skeptical Egyptian colleagues that I was astonished at the quality of the training halls, and the actual resources that were available in Egypt. It is estimated that there are more people in Cairo alone than Bulgaria, Norway, and Ireland COMBINED!!!!

The 65 Sporting clubs we visited have a combined membership approaching 150,000 of the most financially well-off families in Egypt!
Not counting the national training center, 3 of the clubs have internationally acceptable training halls.

Cabbie

As most savvy travelers understand, when one travels in a developing country (or really just about anyplace) the locals will attempt to take advantage of the visitors on the level of "pocketbooks"...this is a particularly honored practice in places where haggling or bargaining are traditionally accepted (like places other than North America or Europe!)....In chaotic Cairo (meant in the best sense), the cabbies are particularly astute and adept at separating funds from the wallets of their passengers....we learned early on that it's an elaborate game that, if one enters into the spirit of it properly, no one takes personally, no one has bad feelings at the end of the exchange, and ultimately, with a little bit of practice, neither party feels like they have been "ripped off".....we were staying at the Indiana Hotel just to the west of the Nile a little bit south of the Gezira neighborhood....there was a small fleet of the ubiquitous black cabs just across the street prepared to ferry hotel guests to anywhere in the city one might be interested in going.....fortunately, since we actually knew some Caironites, (Cairoeans?), we had had a little background information about what "reasonable" charges might be.

Here's the way the "dance" works in Cairo....all the taxis (it seems like there are zillions of them!) are these beat up old black sedans....virtually all of them have meters and I would guesstimate that 99% of the meters are "broken"....in other words, the price of the cab ride is more or less whatever one negotiates....if you are not Egyptian, you should expect to pay 3 or 4 times the "Egyptian" rate.....well, there's ways of course around that....the prototypical scenario: a foreign customer gets into a cab and states his/her destination....sometimes the cabbies pretend not to speak English (although there may be sometimes that they actually don't, one can broadly assume that, given that Egypt was colonized by the British for 150 years) that most do...in any event, a customer gets in a cab and either states his destination, or shows the driver on a map...assuming the customer is not geographically challenged (and can't tell when he's being run around in circles), the driver will more or less take a route of least resistance (not an easy task in mid-day downtown Cairo with unbelievably congested traffic consisting of limitless numbers of small cars, vans, trucks, flatbed trucks, carts being pulled by donkeys, and bicyclists (often with large trays of loaves of bread balanced on the rider's head whilst weaving in and out of the (usually stalled!) automotive traffic....accompanied of course by a cacophonous and staccato honking of (endless!) horns....at the destination, the driver will immediately turn to the back seat where his customer (in hustling terms the appropriate word would be "mark"), and immediately demand some figure (as previously suggested!) several hundred percent over what the locals pay....not knowing any better, the harried, hectored traveler will usually "cough up."

Well, not us! Hannah and I have been to this kind of dance before (and as said, we had some inside information....). Soooo, if a ride from the Indiana on the west side of the Nile to the Olympic Committee offices on the far eastern end of town would normally be 10 Egyptian dollars, (by the way, if you haven't been to Cairo, it is an amazingly compact town....I'd guesstimate that from the pyramids on the west to the Olympic Complex on the east of town is only about 10-12 miles total....of course there are some residential suburbs, but for one of the world's most populous cities, it is truly a very intimate, compact place.....well, there's two real secrets to not getting ripped off in Cairo cabs...first, if the driver asks you anything about yourself, it's important to tell him that you're working for somebody local, in other words that you're some ex-pat who is living and working in Cairo....I always tell the cabbies that "I'm working with the Olympic Committee." If they think you're actually living in the town they're much less likely to assume that you don't know anything about the "real" rates for cabs.

Second, Hannah and I developed a set routine....note earlier that all the meters in the cabs "don't work"....if you don't bring up the rate or charge at the beginning of the ride it's almost guaranteed that the cabbie won't either....ergo, he thinks he's going to be able to demand whatever it is he claims is justified when you get to your destination.

Our protocol: I'd get in the front seat (Egypt is a relatively liberal place, but after all, it's still a Muslim country and women are not considered "equal" in the sense that they are in Europe or North America. Hannah would get in the back seat, and I'd hand her my briefcase (which would have my wallet in it.). We'd ride to our destination, then she would get out first, leave the briefcase in the backseat, but leave the back door (if it was a four-door cab) open. I'd roll down the passenger side window, step out of the car, and reach for my briefcase...I'd then take my wallet (or oftentimes, if we knew exactly where we were going in terms of rough distance, would already have the amount we were willing (and thought fair) to pay in my jacket pocket). In either case, I would retrieve the briefcase, close the passenger door, and hand the driver the money through the passenger side window, say "shukrun" (thank you), turn and walk into whatever building we were entering. Usually the driver would accept the amount without protest, on a couple occasions we'd get a (not necessarily in English) "Hey, what are you doing?", sort of impassioned response....in any event we always gave the cabbie what we understood to be a fair price, a little above what an Egyptian would pay for the same service, but weren't interested in being "ripped off" either....so fair's fair and as reasonably knowledgeable travelers, we felt we paid what was appropriate. In the event that the cabbie objected, the key to the whole dance was once we handed the funds over and said "shukrun", to keep walking regardless of whatever noise or action the cabbie took.

Worked like a charm the entire time we were in the country.

One other cab-ride incident....we had one cabbie who took us for a few rides from the Indiana and who didn't seem to mind being paid "slightly" over the Egyptian fare as opposed to ripping us off outrageously. He apparently understood that we weren't the typical "greenhorns" they're used to shearing. On this particular morning, I had a meeting at Helwan Physical Education University past the zoo just tucked off Pyramid Road. I had not been to the school before, and it turns out neither (despite his protestations that he knew exactly where the campus was) did our cabbie...Well, when it became apparent that he simply did not know where our destination was, I asked him twice to stop the cab....he mumbled that it was really close and that he would get us there....now, mid-morning traffic in Cairo is almost as congested as on Calle Buenos Aires in La Paz, and therefore doesn't move very fast...after the second request and his refusal to comply, I simply opened the passenger door and started to get out of the (moving!) cab....our driver slammed on his brakes in an abrupt and shocked reaction...when the cab came to a stop I told Hannah to "get out", which she promptly did.....we walked behind the cab to the nearest sidewalk, and managed to get another ride to Helwan.

The next day, "our" cabbie, seeing us come out of the hotel gave us a big smile and wave....go figure!

Since I've mentioned it, like La Paz there is a curious "small town" feel to Cairo....later on in our stay, we moved to a hotel on Pyramid Road. After several late night discussions with the folks in the Federation, we were arriving back at the hotel around 2 in the morning. At some point in the evening, traffic thins on the road down to a trickle, and at 2 am it's mostly deserted....an occasional car or taxi passes by....incredibly, on 4 out of 5 evenings, getting back at around the 0200-0230 time, we see....the first time we laughed, the second time we rubbed our eyes in astonishment because we simply didn't believe it, and the third and fourth times we just accepted it as part of the schedule of the neighborhood....in Egypt, anything, any odd thing is possible, if not probable....

walking down the middle of Pyramid Road in the near-dead of night, this ribbon of asphalt which daily is witness and service to the noise and tumult of one of the world's most crowded cities, is a shepherd wearing the traditional long white gown and sandals (just like 2000 years ago), herding his flock of goats/sheep DOWN THE MIDDLE OF THE STREET! Incredibly, it happened night after night!

Pyramid Road Hotel

The Egyptian Olympic Committee in conjunction with the Federation had arranged to put us up in the Indiana Hotel for a week; later, as a result of being asked to submit a paper at a Helwan University Physical Education Conference on behalf of the (US based) International Student Games organization , we were transferred (care of the school) to the Pyramid Road Hotel and a modest, but scrupulously clean room on the top floor of which had a balcony from which we could see the Pyramids of Giza in the near distance.....

Brief digression: virtually everyone on Earth has seen photographs of the Giza Pyramids. Like many "known" landmarks, I can assure you from personal experience that photographs convey nothing of the size and scale....these are (Eiffel Tower possibly excepted), the single most amazing man-made things I've ever seen. The Great Pyramid (the tomb of Pharaoh Cheops) was finished around 2650 B.C. The thing is almost 47 CENTURIES old....to put in context, Cheops' pyramid was as distant in time to Alexander the Great as Alexander is to us! The base of the pyramid covers 13 acres, and the thing is almost 500 feet high...that's almost the height of the Space Needle in Seattle! And (I love this) it and its main companion, the pyramid of Kephre (Cheop's son), the one with part of the facing still on it....were the tallest man-made structures in the world until Gustaf Eiffel's tower in the 1880s. (AD!)

So we're ensconced in a room on the top floor of the Pyramid Hotel; I've got a presentation to make a conference at the University at 0830 the following morning....Hannah and I get settled in just before 2300h, and lay down on what might pass for a double bed if we were dwarves, but is basically a small single....we get into a spooning position and just as we're about to drop off to dreamland, a bleat of horns, some rather dissonant strings, and what sounds like a large (v-e-r-y large) drum set obviously being percussioned by an extremely enthusiastic (and heavy handed!) percussionist starts blaring away...from .where is this sound coming from? Directly over our heads! Apparently, although we weren't informed of it, the PR Hotel has a DISCO on the "real" top or penthouse floor...we are merely on the floor directly below (and in this particular room) directly below the bandstand!

Oh man....well, this is Egypt, and I guess their union (if they have them) rules for musicians is a lot laxer than in the USA, because this wasn't some 45 minutes set, nooooo, they went on for over two hours before they took a break. Now, I have nothing against Arab or Egyptian music per se, it's just that because it's so foreign to my ear (early rock n roll, rockabilly, & Chicago blues is the stuff I like the best), it sort of grates on me after awhile, and two hours, especially 'cause I'm already in bed for goodnessakes and it's right over my head and because their floor (our ceiling!) is pulsating from the crowd jumping up and down on it!

It seems a little much.....well, obviously I'm a pansy and can't take a little "discomfort" from my comfortable couch-potato routine....so, I/we chalk it up to "one of those things, and just as we start to drift off to sleep....yup, you guessed it, they start up again and if possible, even louder and shriller (or is that just my subjective take?) than ever....it goes on until, what? I'm getting a headache and I'm bleary now and this bed is really small and the tossy-turny in the same place with the sheets now all rumpled and hot is starting to make this really irritating....finally, somewhere after 3am, blissful silence....ahhhhhh, my body starts to relax...I feel myself beginning that oh so delicious descent into those fleeting moments before one falls asleep....BLEAT! Nope!!!!! Damned if the racket doesn't recommence right at that moment....they're starting up again!!!! After another hour of sleepless tossing, an increasing headache, and now an emotional buildup of frustration, well, this set is a bit shorter...or should I say two sets, they're starting to blend together in my mind now as one long (and loud) nightmare....it's now approaching 5:30 in the morning, and dear God, please Allah, let this be the end.....no...if He's up there (Heaven I mean, NOT the friggin' disco!), he's determined to make me live out my all-time favorite Calvin and Hobbes cartoon:

first panel:... Calvin and Hobbes are sitting back to back under a tree....Hobbes asks Calvin: "Do you think there's a God?"
second panel: Calvin ponders the ultimate cosmological question....
third panel: Calvin, eyebrows furrowed: "Well...SOMEONE"S out to get me!"

Exactly.

Of course the band doesn't stop at 5:30....we get, as the sun starts to peak up over the dunes of this ancient land, one last shrieking, stomping, noisy endless 90 minutes, and it not so mercifully, but finally just concludes as the clock on the small table next to the bed hits 0700 straight up....my wake-up call is scheduled for 7:10....and yes, the front desk phones us right on time..... The one positive? Not that I have any fear of public speaking, but I was too damned tired and working too damned hard simply to stay awake at 8:30 to be nervous about my presentation.....

In retrospect, even tho' I'm not a huge fan of the music, I wish if I'd known that we were going to be up all night anyway, that we'd have wrangled an invite to (what we later learned to be) a mid-week wedding reception! Man, can those Egyptians party!

Citadel

I recount in the England chapter how almost mesmerized I was at (the church where John Quincy Adams was married) how the layers of history are piled upon each other....coming from North America, we simply don't have anything equivalent to this kind of thing. It's daunting in a way to ponder the so very brief life spans that even the centenarians amongst us enjoy, and the overreaching arc of time....to think that in so many parts of the world (unlike the US West Coast where I live) there is this changing of course, but unbroken thread of history and civilization that goes back millennia...and certainly, Egypt is the queen of historical continuity....

The Citadel is located on the shores of the Mediterranean in Alexandria. It dates from the 14th century where it served as a Muslim fort for the Mamluke Empire...it was built from the stones that were the foundation of "The Lighthouse at Alexandria" one of the "Seven Wonders of the Ancient World". It's now a museum and has many fascinating exhibits; for me, one of the most interesting is some copper sheathing (and other bric-brac) from the French ship "L'Orient" which was sunk by Horiatio Nelson at the Battle of the Nile in 1801...at the end of a long bloody day, the climax of the battle at dusk was when the French flagship was unable to control fires raging throughout her wooden structure, and the powder magazines detonated effectively disintegrating the ship in a giant geyser of flame, wood, iron, men, and smoke.....the centuries stacked one upon the other again.....

The Library at Alexandria

My passion for books is a topic which appears at times throughout this narrative. Many readers will recall that the greatest library in the Ancient World was the Library of Alexandria. Founded in the 3rd century BC, it is estimated to have had anywhere from 500,000 to over a million (minority view) volumes (or in the case of books in antiquity, scrolls). The specific circumstances of the library's demise or destruction are a subject of historical controversy, but suffice to say, this edifice of human learning ceased to exist in any meaningful fashion by the 8th century AD. We were taken on a tour of the Egyptian Women's Physical Education College in Alexandria. Among the facilities that the Dean and Faculty Advisor were proud to show us was their library. These are profoundly committed and dedicated women working to make inroads in a non-traditional field for women in Egypt. I admire their efforts enormously and especially because of the limited means at their disposal. The college is modest; the ambitions of its Board and faculty members are truly inspiring. Their library is about the size of a small branch library as seen in just about any US city. I couldn't suppress a small private joke....as I walked around the shelves, I made the comment, more to myself than the ladies…"Hmmm….I thought the "library of Alexandria" would be bigger." They didn't get my small joke. I'm certain it's just as well.

Olympic Complex

Egypt, in addition to the infrastructure of its' sporting clubs has an amazing Olympic complex. The football stadium holds 80,000, and there are two indoor arenas, the smaller of which is, oh probably a 5,000 capacity and the larger enjoys a capacity approaching 20,000. One of the real treats for anyone who has the opportunity to visit is to see Dr. Thoeni's Olympic memorabilia museum on the second floor of the EOC offices. Thoeni was an Olympic wrestler for Egypt at the Berlin Games of 1936 and as an official and eventually President of the EOC attended every Olympic Games at least until the late 80s (into the 1990s?). He was a voracious collector of everything Olympic, pins, plates, caps, whatever the memorabilia, he acquired it. In addition, as part of the official "Olympic family" for decades, he knew virtually everyone in sport and exchanged letters/documents/accumulated material. The Egyptian Olympic Museum doesn't have the square footage of the IOC Museum in Lausanne, but for actual collectable contemporary "stuff" on display, I'm confident the EOC is the better and more impressive of the two.

Colleagues

I loved being in Egypt. I enjoyed every moment of my experience there and in particular the warmth, enthusiasm and generosity of the people. Hannah and I were invited into more homes than in any other country we have ever visited. Former Rhythmic gymnast and judge Eiman Hammam and her family who live in Cairo let us stay in their flat in Alexandria…we did not expect to open up a refrigerator to find it full of food….the provisions included a "takeout" dinner of "kosharee" sitting there because Eimann remembered I had a passion for the dish. Mr. Fathee the Junior Boys Coach and his wife had us to a memorable dinner where we discussed gymnastics, life, and world politics.

We were invited to lunch by Mr. Mohammed Fidali, Dean Emeritus of Helwan University (then-86 years old and still carrying a 12 hour a week class-load "just to keep my hand in it and make sure that our students are being exposed to the nobility of physical education"), long-time colleague of Dr. Thoeni (and Vice-President of the EOC). He was quite simply, a legend in the Egyptian sporting and education communities; during our visit at Helwan, we were continuously interrupted by a steady stream of admirers. Most of the Sports administrators in Egypt were at one time or another his students or colleagues. I don;t know if I can say this about anyone else Ive ever been around, but Dr. Fidali was "beloved: by the people that know him, and was known by virtualy everyone involved in sport in Egypt.! Dr. Fidali and his wife invited us to lunch in their elegant apartment and we (probably shamelessly overstayed our welcome except that they insisted!) were there until dinner-time….a perfect afternoon….

Poignantly, one of our best Egyptian friends, Capt. Raouf al-Hagrazi who passed away too young just two years ago and who had been involved with coaching and administration for over 40 years and his wife shared a sumptuous feast on a moonlit evening in their home….Raouf exposed me (intentionally like the over-age scamp he so memorably was!) to the (questionable) pleasures of the hookah pipe…as I recall, we smoked a cherry-flavored briquette (or whatever the thing that burns is called)….I hacked of course, he laughed hilariously, and after we got back to the hotel, I spent what amounted to another sleepless night since the silia in my lungs twitched and vibrated frantically all night from the heretofore unexperienced trauma….as the ladies retired to wherever ladies retire after our meal, Raouf reached into his cabinet, pulled out two tumblers, and a bottle of Johnny Walker Red. He poured two generous helpings, handed me a glass, clinked a toast "to friends wherever in the world they might be", and proceeded to quaff the beverage….."Capt. Raouf"….I started diplomatically….probably sounded tentative….if I understand it correctly, because of the strictures in the Koran, good Muslims are not supposed to drink alcohol?" He looked at me seriously for a moment, then with a wink, and a huge laugh, he responded, "Well...I am NOT a very good Muslim!" Mutual laughs. Whatta great guy.

Finally, but certainly not least was the warmth and friendship extended to us by Nefissa Aref, a mother of one of the girls in Gezira Club who shared meals in their very spacious apartment, and took us to a number of nice places and restaurants in Cairo. Nefissa's daughter, Nirvana Zaher came the next year and spent part of the summer living and training with us. She subsequently became the first (and to date only) Egyptian gymnast to receive a scholarship to compete for an American University. Vana competed for 4 years at Sacramento State…we saw a number of her meets, had her team over to our house for a memorable spaghetti feed, and and think of her as a surrogate daughter.

We know that we will be lifelong friends!

In the last decade, Egypt has made enormous strides in the administration of its' program and in its competitive results. The country has had gymnasts compete in the last 3 Olympic Games and has progressed to regularly participate in Cup and Invitational competitions throughout the Mediterranean. I would suggest (although Algeria and South Africa might dispute it) that Egypt has re-emerged after a decades long slump as the primary gymnastics program in Africa.

There is no other country in the world that has the potential to be the "next big thing" in world gymnastics. Egypt has, I think has the existing infrastructure and population base to "explode" into a serious world contender. I would love to see the country develop a serious and integrated Junior program with regular testing.

One significant change I would like to see in program philosophy is to work to keep their female athletes in the sport longer; Egypt in many ways is still focused on the 1980s Eastern bloc model of "little girls in pigtails" being the only one's who can perform elite gymnastics.

One of my biggest regrets is the Federation's neglect of Nirvana Zaher…Vana never got the opportunity to compete at a Worlds (Egypt has never fielded a woman's team although they have sent girls as individuals)….she was (is) a beautiful woman gymnast who exhibited power, grace, and style throughout her career in the US university program….she would have made a lovely, lasting impression had she been given the chance to show the World the kind of female gymnast Egypt can produce.

Egypt has the facilities, the communication structure, geographic proximity to Europe, and above all potential political and sponsorship support to be a world power….I'd love to see them host a World Championships in the quadrennium following the 2012 Olympics in London.

"All progress has resulted from people who took unpopular positions."
Adlai Stevenson

Chapter Twelve

THE GOLD MEDAL THAT WASN'T

At the USA Championships in 1993, I had a gymnast who achieved a small piece of gymnastics immortality. Mike Williams was a gymnast from the UW and qualified to 4 USA Championships He made the US Senior National Team, and is best remembered for being the **only** American in history to compete a triple-salto on FX which he achieved at the 1993 Nationals in Salt Lake City. This feat subsequently published in a sequence photo in International Gymnast magazine.

One evening during the competition, I was approached by Paul O'Neill, the great rings specialist from Houston Baptist and the University of New Mexico, who won 3 NCAA Championships, and in 1992, at the first ever specialist World Championships in Paris France, placed 4th on the event in his first international competition. Paul congratulated me on Mike's performance, and we got to talking about the Worlds the following year; he was hoping to qualify for a spot on the US team. "Hey, I'm going to work out tomorrow morning, why don't you come over and watch?" Well, I hardly ever travel anywhere without my grips, and I had a really exciting idea. "Would it be ok if I worked out with you?" Paul says, "Sure, I'd love the company" Man, I was so excited, I could hardly sleep. I competed collegiately and had been to a few nationals, but this guy was far and away the best American ring man since...well, maybe George Gulack (1932 Olympic Champion). He'd placed 4th *in the world.* No way I was going to miss an opportunity like that.

Next day, we're stretched out, and start to get up on the apparatus, and I have to say, it was...well, let me put it this way....my last competition had been 6 years previous, and although I'd continued to workout, I knew that my physical skills were gradually (and continually) declining due to age. Well, working out with a world class gymnast that day was something very very special. I can honestly say, I was so pumped up, I felt like I was strong enough to bend steel, and about as light (if you've ever done gymnastics, think of the best you ever felt and you'll understand exactly the feeling that I felt that day) as balsa wood. I'm convinced that it was probably the single best level of performance EVER had. I mean, man, my giants were effortless. In the handstand, fully extend my shoulders, a slight flex of the glutes, move my hands imperceptively forward, and arms perfectly parallel, whoosh, what a drop!!! Just ride that baby on the upside, shift my wrists, and LOCK OUT in handstand. Man, it's never felt this good.

O'Neill, while vastly superior to me, was very complimentary. He watched a few and said: "Man, I really like that....you bail like Li Ning!" Are you kiddin' me? Go to YouTube...check out Li Ning...what a compliment!!!! Oh, quick, albiet obvious disclaimer: I"m NO Li Ning!!!

Anyway, Paul is rockin the joint (as usual) and awhile later looks at me doing some strength work and comments: "Hey Jim...you've got a really nice planche. Have you ever tried this?" He hops up on the rings, kips up to a planche, then lowers to a maltese...pauses 2 seconds, then pushes back up to a planche, and repeats the exercise 3 or 4 times and drops off. He looks at me. "What's the matter?" I must look like I've just been hit in the head with an axe....I know my jaw dropped open...."Uhhh, where'd you learn that?" "Oh, nobody taught me, it's just something I thought up...you should try it, it's a good exercise...why?"

I stare at him..."Uhhh, Paul, I've been in gymnastics for almost 30 years (at the time)....I know most of the great ringmen and I'm confident I've seen most if not all of the skills ever done....I know that that skill has never been performed in competition, and I'm certain that if you are able to put it into a routine, and if you can get selected for the US team that goes to Australia next year, you can WIN the World Championships on rings!"

"Really?"

"Absolutely."

"Will you help me?"

"Absolutely"

So, Paul and I made a pact....we'd work together to find a way to refine his technique and upgrade his difficulty so that he could move up from the fourth place finish he achieved as an international neophyte in Paris in 1992, and win the whole darned thing in '94.

At the time Paul was coaching in North Dakota. Between international "gigs", I was living in Seattle. Although it's not the optimal situation, IF there is a coach who understands the event and IF the athlete is of a high international caliber, it's possible (albeit not desirable, but we were constrained by circumstances) to "coach"/collaborate/communicate to devlop a training plan and schedule.

Paul communicated regularly by telephone and by sending regular (twice a month) videos. This "world-class" rings specialist, as amazing as his skills were had 4 primary weaknesses that needed to be addressed.

1. Paul had seriously "bowed" legs which detracted from his body line and thereby detracted from the aesthetic aspect of his set.
2. he did not have a particularly good toe point which was also negatively impacted body line…
3. on the "bail" or drop forward from handstand into his front giant swing, he lost pressure with his right arm (slight arm bend and early rotation of the wrist) and thereby created some slack in the ring cables which resulted in an audible "snap" at the bottom of his swing (again, alerting the judges that there was a technical flaw in his execution).
4. Paul's handstands because of his huge barrel chest looked "arched" rather than straight; although his shoulder angle more or less achieved 180 degrees, unless we could disguise what resembled those "banana back" trophy handstands from the 1950s, we'd have problems.

We worked diligently to correct all of the above. I speak at length of these specifics, not to bore the reader, but for the reader to understand that there are profoundly different levels even at the level of international sport. Although my métier has been the development of the sport into the "3rd World", and while I feel reasonably confident of my technical expertise, there is a HUGE difference between exposing individuals (or teams) the opportunity to compete at the highest levels and the reality of preparing individuals to TRIUMPH at a Worlds or Olympic competition. While I'm grateful for all the experiences I've had to contribute internationally, working with Paul (and Nashwan who we'll discuss in a later chapter) has been my only opportunity to work with an athlete who actually had the potential to MEDAL or even WIN at the World level.

In any event, Paul and I proceeded to make two changes in his routine first, we most definitely wanted the World to see the "O'Neill II", the horizontal hold (Maltese) press to planche (from arms parallel to arms supporting!). (briefest digression): subsequent to the execution of this element, the Hungarian Federation undertook a biomechanic analysis of the skill and concluded that in order to elevate from a maltese cross to a planche, a gymnast would have to be able to (think of the challenges of fulcrum/leverage to press 120% of his bodyweight….an astonishing figure, and if we look at the broad spectrum of gymnastics today (as this is written almost 15 years later, there are <my guess> fewer than 25-40 gymnasts in the World that can perform this skill).

There was (and remains to this day) no question in my mind that if the "cards had fallen right" that Paul would have been 1994 World Rings Champion. That said, as always in sport, there's a little more to it than simply being the best in the world. First, the USAG selection committee needed to name him to the US team in order for him to compete. In order to do that, he needed to

a. WIN the rings competition at the 1994 "Winter Cup", the semi-annual (US Championships is the other) ranking competition for American men's gymnastics and

b. win by a large enough margin that the committee would select him as a specialist as opposed to an all-arounder who might be able to contribute to the US team's chances later on in the quadrennium.....most readers will be aware that a majority of the "tactical" decisions by any Olympic sports organization are based on either the potential payoff in the proximate Olympic Games, or the (shorter term) reward of achieving medals at less prestigious events."

There is regrettably (depending on one's point of view of course) a subjective element in "team selection" when it is not based on strictly objective criteria. One of the virtues (and weaknesses) of the Olympic team selection process in USA Athletics (Track and Field) is that at the Olympic trials, the top "x" (I believe it is 3) athletes in a given discipline at the event qualify to the Olympics. Everyone else does not. Famously, in 1992, Dan O'Brien, the World Record Holder and National Champion in the Decathlon failed to clear a height in the pole vault at the US Olympic trials. It didn't matter that Dan was the gold-medal favorite for Barcelona....he didn't place at Trials, so he didn't go to the Games.

In the last 15 years, gymnastics, due to the extraordinary modifications of its' competitive structure, has introduced variables which in turn have resulted in
(in order to maximize the likelihood of winning medals) a "flexibility" or number of critical paths or options which have politicized in part at least (in the USA) the process of the selection process. While the landscape has profoundly changed, for traditionalists, it's almost inconceivable that Jamie Natalie (5th AA in trials in 2000) or in 2008 David Durante (3rd AA) or Guillermo Alvarez (6th) would NOT be on the team.

While it is possible that there can be a (sliding scale) objective criteria that includes specialists, the unfortunate reality is that anytime in sport that there is subjectivity, the (potentially ugly) head of politics or influence raises its head.

Happily, he dominated the rings competition and qualified to the Worlds easily and we continued. Paul was going to Brisbane to compete for the USA at the Worlds and I was going to be there as the coach of Ignacio Morales of Bolivia. While I was keenly aware that as a "foreign" and therefore not the "personal" coach of a US athlete, I was happy that we would both be at the event, and hopeful that our work together would culminate in success.

Unfortunately, even though I was at the event, because of my outsider status "officially", I was unable to be directly involved in the coaching decisions of the US delegation.

Paul and I had made two structural changes to his exercise. We included the maltese to planche press (O'Neill II in the Code of Points), a skill that had never before been done in international competition. Second, and arguably more importantly (see "arched back' flaw listed above) we changed his required strength press to handstand from a "stiff-stiff" (straight arms, straight legs, bent body piked at the waist) to a "straight-straight" (straight arms, straight body). Although he didn't need it, the straight straight was valued one letter-grade higher than the piked press. That however was NOT the reason for the substitution. I've long felt in constructing optional exercises that "working to a gymnast's strengths" really means "walling off (or avoiding!) their weaknesses."

Because of Paul's handstand issues, I felt it imperative that we do everything possible, especially in the "movement" phase of the press, to "hide" his particular structural weakness, the arched back.

To my dismay, on competition day, Paul, although executing the rest of his exercise flawlessly...well, we never were quite able to take the slack out of his forward bail, but that particular flaw could not tactically be avoided since in the 1993-1996 Code it was a special requirement for the gymnast to swing to handstand going both overgrip and undergrip directions...he had improved his technique, but Paul lost a little slack on his forward drop...everything else in the exercise was done as well as he could possibly have done it....his maltese, press to planche, full two second hold drew gasps from the crowd.

When he rolled into his L-support (half-lever), I was watching in the stands and counting. A "small" flaw in the rhythm of his previous routines was his tendency to "rush" the press from the L-support. I drilled into him repeatedly the admonition that it was ok to take one's time. I explained that (as Abie Grossfeld, the legendary US Olympian, college coach, and coach of the 1984 US Men's team) once so cogently put it, "not all skills are the same, and an "L" is a rest position." I told him repeatedly that the real key to this exercise was for him to take four deep breaths in the L, then slowly press with straight arms and straight body to handstand before he dropped into his dismount. Notwithstanding, the slight break in the bail (due to that bent arm) in the forward giant, with a slow straight-straight press following the pause for breath in the L support, Paul would leave the judges with virtually nothing to deduct. There were no weak spots! In order to beat him, everyone else in the competition would have to not only be perfect, but to have a higher degree of difficulty.

Another edge we had was that of all the competitors (Hungary's Sylvester Csollany and his somewhat questionable "original front uprise forward drop" skill possibly excepted), there was no other competitor who had already had a skill in the Code of Points named after him (in 1992 Paul had pioneered the layout Guzoghy (double layout within the rings and swing through) which was subsequently named the O'Neill. Moreover, there was likely no one in the competition who was going to introduce AN ADDITIONAL new skill (like Paul was with his maltese press to planche)....we had engineered a unique set of circumstances, which, if he performed them to his ability, optimized his chances of winning the World Championship.

To my absolute distress, after perfectly executing the first ¾ of his routine, he rolled into the L, paused for a single breath, then pressed to an extremely arched back straddle (legs apart) stiff-stiff press to handstand.

The US coaches decided to substitute the straight-straight for a stiff-stiff in order to conserve energy. *Paul did NOT need to conserve energy*; he was the strongest gymnast in the competition and a straight-straight for him was essentially just leaning forward and lifting to handstand. Second, a stiff-stiff exposed his technically flawed arched back to the judging panel. Third, and perhaps most damaging, a straddle, legs apart position exposed Paul's flawed leg-line and hooked feet due to his bowed legs. In point of fact it was my wife Hannah who insisted that Paul wear black pants and socks in the competition because that color scheme would best conceal his flawed body line in the eyes of the judges. Because I was not part of the US delegation at the event, and could not vigorously explain the rationales behind the exact construction of his routine(the bowed legs), the modification was made and I'm certain that it was a mistake which detracted from what Paul was capable of achieving.

Paul did his best, and his best was damned good. But...in international competition, it's not always sufficient....up last was reigning World Champion (and eventual 1996 Olympic Champion) Yuri Chechi from Italy. The capacity crowd gasped as the defending Champ slightly overshot his felge to handstand (I caught my breath and thought, "if life is fair" the judges are going to do the right thing and give the challenger the title")....he managed to pull his handstand back under control, and Chechi too stuck his dismount....now the 'bout goes to the cards...and after this titanic rumble, in a narrow decision, the judges allow the Champ to, however narrowly and flawed, retain his title....bitter disappointment, not for Paul, who was awarded the Silver medal (at the WORLD CHAMPIONSHIPS for goodnessake!)....but it was a unique opportunity gone awry.....very sad.....

Other Peak Moments

I've been involved in competitive gymnastics for 40 years and have participated in countless competitions. As a coach, there are easily two that stand out

In 1994, the Individual World Championships in Brisbane Australia had a unique format. The qualifying round for both Men's and Women's competi-

tions were divided into halves. In every other Worlds (or major international) all 6 men's and all 4 women's events are competed in the same day.
In Brisbane, Men competed Floor, Pommel Horse, and Rings, on day one, and the other three events on the second day of competition. Also, the men's all around competition had a unique wrinkle. If a country only had one gymnast competing, that gymnast was drawn to the last competition round. Therefore, in our case, since Ignacio Morales was the only gymnast competing for Bolivia, he not only had the opportunity to compete 3 different days of the competition (the first and only time that has happened with athletes I've coached), he was in the last round of All-Around. By a fortuitous (or not depending on one's perspective) circumstance, he was drawn into the same rotation and same event as defending (6 Gold medals in Barcelona) Olympic and World (1993) All-Around Champion Vitaly Scherbo.

At Worlds and major competitions, the media is not permitted access to the training halls. What we knew from the week preceding the event and in training, but what had not been revealed to the media was that the great Scherbo was both out of shape (fairly prominent "love handles" around his mid-section), and injured, which was in part a result of not being able to train effectively due to a nagging shoulder injury. It seemed obvious as the week leading up to the competition wore on, that the champ would concede his throne with a whimper. Surely, if Vitaly didn't actually scratch the competition, there was no way he could actually bc competitive.

The evening of the All-Around competition arrived. As we lined up to march out onto the competition floor, our group which was headed to pommel horse first, lined up behind the young lady holding the placard. The previous subdivision marched out of the arena, and Ivan Ivankov, Scherbo's teammate and presumed successor as lynchpin to the Belarussian team came by and gave him a collegial hug. It turned out, as we looked at the scoreboard, that Ivankov had had the meet of his life, and was in a lead that only a fully-fit Vitaly could conceivably overtake.

Ignacio was fired-up. So was I. Here we were, All-Around finals, capacity crowd, Australian (and World-wide television feeds), and little Bolivia was about to bang antlers with the best that the sport had produced. The theme "Waltzing Mathilda" escorted us into a raucous arena, populated by a shouting, singing throng of Aussies.

On our first event pommel horse, Ignacio hit his set in his quiet, competent way. I remember nothing else of the rotation except that Scherbo planted himself on the podium with authority, and with defiant confidence, rocked his set, finishing with the second highest score on the event in the competition(after Pae Gil Su the legendary PRK World and Olympic Champion).

We rotated to rings. Again, Iggy completed his set; the damaged Scherbo gamely tried to muscle through his routine, and almost after almost falling out of a handstand, botched his inverted cross with an extremely high and very short hold position...he almost dropped out of this as well, and scored well down in the placings with an 8.85.

While this might have destroyed the resolve of weaker individuals, all it seemed to do as our small "island" of gymnasts and coaches rotated to vault was to wake the Tiger and call him to the hunt. Scherbo, as he waited to vault was like a man possessed.....talking to himself, he stalked back and forth in the small space in front of the event seating....obviously angry at his rings performance, as soon as Ignacio (who was up immediately before him) landed his vault, Scherbo jumped up onto the podium, waived his coach away, and set his own vault board. He then, almost angrily stomped down to the end of the runway and flipped the placard over to indicate the vault number he was going to compete. (While required by the regulations, it was hardly necessary...every gymnastics person on the planet knew that Sherbo, once he completed his approach to the vault was going to launch a roundoff entry, double twisting Yurchenko....he exploded off the board, reached blindly back to the horse, (head missing contact by about 2 inches from the apparatus!), and goes up, up and out, 720% rotation and perfect stuck landing. He wins vault easily.

We rotate to parallel bars...the Tiger is fully awakened at this point....again, stalking up and down like a caged beast....on the apparatus, he executes flawlessly, until....the handstand just before the dismount, he drops and swings into his piked double salto dismount, and the damaged shoulder cruelly betrays him...as the feet swing up and over his head, his arm buckles and he drops backwards, flipping awkwardly, somehow managing to pull himself all the way around but without the customary push off the bars, Scherbo overcompensates, over-rotates, and sits down his dismount. Another low low score,and two 'broken" sets out of 4.

High bar is next...Scherbo is conceding NOTHING....he continues to pace, muttering and gesturing to himself....he jumps up to the high bar when Superior Judge Sawao Kato (twice Olympic Champion and once Runner-up in the All-Around...one of the greatest names in the sport's history himself) signals "go!"
and Vitaly simply, magnificently rocks a dynamic, virtually perfect set for the highest score of the day on the event.

Five down, one to go....Scherbo is the defending World and Olympic Champion on floor and does not disappoint....mounting with a roundoff, flip flop, and his trademark layout double double salto to perfect (BOOM!) stuck landing, he more or less detonates this routine and finishes, again, with the highest event score of the day. A mesmerizing, magnetic performance by a damaged but oh so game and competitive champion. The result? Ivankov wins the All-Around and Vitaly is the runner-up by the narrowest of margins.

At the press conference, at least one member of the media corps had been "tipped-off" to Vitaly's secret, his damaged shoulder. And the runner-ups response to queries pertaining to same?
"I do not know where you heard of this. I am not injured and my shoulder is fine."
"How do you account for your uncharacteristic mistakes on the rings and parallel bars?"
"I am human. Even the best of us can make mistakes."
"How does it feel to have Ivankov be the Champion?"
"The better man won today. I congratulate him."

Vitaly Scherbo won the 1994 Silver Medal in the All-Around with limited training and a damaged and painful shoulder. To see this magnificent gymnast fight to achieve every possible tenth that his body could produce, and to witness and experience the passion and intensity and grim yet joyful sense of purpose that he brought to the task is to see sport and human performance at its finest. Was it Hugh Akston in Ayn Rand's Atlas Shrugged who opined that "the rarest emotion is admiration?"

Participating in this event and experiencing, even vicariously Schrebo's intensity was awe inspiring....to witness the class and graciousness with which he refused excuses for his performance, and denied, even while justified any possible reason for same, and to see him graciously congratulate and shift credit to his younger teammate was among the more inspiring things I've ever seen in the sport, and the few hours that Ignacio and I shared with him in the 1994 World All-Around Finals is one of the peak experiences of my gymnastics life.

As soon as the draw for the 2007 World Championships was announced, I was confident, and as events proved that the feeling was not misplaced, that I would enjoy a similar "peak" experience in Stuttgart. Competition One, the qualifying round for men was broken into 9 subdivisions. As will be recounted a bit later, I was coach of Nashwan al-Harazi of Yemen, who had been drawn into the 9th subdivision. That subdivision was going to be "loaded". We were with a mixed group with the Czech Republic, and teams involved were Spain (who we were confident would be Olympic qualifiers), South Korea (same, plus strong medal contenders, including the #2 AA (controversially) from the Athens Olympics, and the up and coming, featuring the #3 AA from the '06 Worlds, Fabien Hambuchen, Germany. Ohhhh baby, on Sept. 4, at 19:00 hours we are going to march into a packed arena in

Stuttgart Germany just in front of the German National team with a worldwide tv feed. It's gonna be nuts!

Nuts? Easily understated.....of course I understand that the crowd had no interest in my one gymnast from Yemen....but...was amazing, profoundly wonderful experience...in major internationals, on competition day, warmup is not in the competition venue, but rather in an auxiliary facility....Nashwan stretched and did a few vaults, a couple floor exercise passes, and some circles and flairs on the pommel horse....there is an interesting contrast between men's and women's gymnastics at this level...Hannah always suggests that the women are more serious about training and competition than the men...she bases this (erroneous) opinion on the fact that the fact that in the training halls, the women seem much more intense than the men....on the surface, they do more full routines and do less "hanging/laying around" than the males....the reality is that women's gymnastics is not as physically taxing as mens...women have 4 events, 3 of which are leg or running events, and the men have 6 events, four of which are "arm" or upper-body events....there is no comparison between the energy drain on men's rings (for example) compared to women's balance beam....moreover, women gymnasts, at the elite level, notwithstanding the changes in the competition format, are much much younger and smaller than the men....at the 2008 Olympics, for example, the oldest US Woman Olympian Alicia Sacramone, dubbed the "grandmother" of the US team was almost 3 years younger than the youngest (Sasha Artemev) male Olympian....none of this is really significant given the particulars of our discussion, but back to September 4 in Stuttgart....the men's warm up gym was v-e-r-y casual....in so many ways, it truly reflected a 'calm before the storm"....Laslik Blanik, the Polish gymnast (who eventually became World Champion and subsequently Olympic Champion) did a couple explosive (how could it be any other way!??) handspring timers for vault, and went over and sat by himself, eyes closed, waiting for the "call-up'...the South Koreans, lay about on the floor mat...the Spanish, coach was continually nattering exhortative phrases to his troops who conspicuously ignored him....the Germans, continually hopping up and down like horses ready to get into the starting gate and get this thing going....I wasn't physically going to compete, but I completely understood from where it was they were coming!....it's going to be an amazing evening....

Eventually, they call us all up to the line and we break into our various groups. Nashwan and I fall in behind the Czech guys in our black tracksuits with the red trim and "Yemen" stitched vertically in the back....after we're all in line, we get a 'good luck" and march Olympic order (floor group in front) out through the training gym, into and through the passage-way....the gymnasts of subdivision eight troop past us as the theme music goes up, and we are, suddenly directed into the arena....the moment that I've been anticipating since the day the draw was announced has arrived…..looking at the back of Nashwan's head, his gym-bag slung over my shoulder, we step into the arena, and experience a visceral wall of sound and emotion….The din is almost deafening….we could be Elvis at the MGM or Stardust…while I understand that the noise is directed at the Germans just 2 groups in front, the venue is literally shaking as virtually every German fan is stomping on the floor and creating a very real (and not a little unsettling) rocking of the floor….we could be Bruce Springsteen as a spontaneous "wall of sound" (maybe that should be a Phil Spector reference) washes over us….looking up, the crowd in a spontaneous "wave", is a sea of red, yellow, and black, the colors of the German Republic…..

Every single hit German set (which was just about all, if not all of them) was met with an explosion of delirious celebration….being on the floor, even though it wasn't directed to us personally, was an incredible energy rush as we experienced the crowds energy and intensity wash over us….we rotated through five events, and finally arrived at parallel bars…

The crowd was in an almost frenzy, the Germans had just finished high bar and the (eventual) world champion on the event Fabian Hambuchen has just totally rocked his set….the place was going crazy as the host country rotates to pommels it's last event…it was a transcendent experience…gymnastics, as we think of it, was born in Germany (see Frederich Jahn), and for the sport to return full circle to its' birthplacc on this day was profoundly memorable)…

. Back on PBars, an event Nashwan has never competed or been judged in competition is about to start. We are engaged in the "one-touch" warm up. Over the last 11 years and 32 weeks, I've never actually seen Nashwan do a double salt dismount at the end of a full routine….I know and have seen that he can do the trick, but haven't seen it (EVER!!) at the end of a set…and here we are, due to the dictates however unreasonable they might be, of the Yemen Olympic Committee insisting that he do All-Around…well just before he goes up, I confront him (on this skill at least, for what must be the 20th time)…."Nashwan, I expect you to go up there, no matter what and do the double salto dismount.

"Mr. Jim, that's what I'm going to do."

"No, I really mean it, you've GOT to execute it!"

"Mr. Jim, that's what I'm going to do"

"I'm serious dammit…I've been waiting to see this the whole time we've been together….you MUST do this skill….

"Mr. Jim, I'm going to perform the 720 dismount."

"You PROMISE??"

"Yes, of course."

I wait tensely as Nashwan goes through a pretty darn solid p-bar routine, including a lovely Moy (learned it two months earlier) swing handstand pirouette, Stutz, etc. The last part of his set includes a back-uprise, straddle cut to L-support, stiff stiff press handstand to.....Nashwan locks out the handstand and waits....rocks back and forth, shifting his weight onto his left arm, then his right, then...waits.....I hold my breath...will he?

Then, swooping down, he drives his knees up and over his head, with a huge, high, double salto which he "nails" , feet landing solidly on the floor and causing a minor eruption of chalk at the base of the landing mats.

I didn't think about it, but I was so relieved and excited that the moment Nashwan hit the floor, I must have jumped about 3 feet in the air and let out a "whoop!" that caused both the high bar and parallel bar judging panels to turn and look at me....

"Oh, sorry, sorry, " I intone.....sheesh, whatta dope!!!! Keep your cool, pretend that you've been in the end zone before. As I turn to walk back to the seating area, Leonid Arkaev who is sitting at the FIG VIP table gives me a covert "thumbs up" and a wink. God, I LOVE being here and doing this!

The last routine concluded, the noise continuing unabated, we posed for group photos with our newly found Czech buddies. Hugs and handshakes abound. It felt like all the noise, enthusiasm, and yes, love in the place was directed at the delegation from Yemen...directed at Nashwan and me....I'll never forget those few moments as long as I live......we were indoors of course, but experienced what felt like....the fireworks of the best Fourth of July ever and a PERFECT SUNSET!!!!

"I got to keep movinnnn', I got to keep movinnnn',
Blues fallin' down like hail, blues fallin' down like hail,
Mmmmm-mm-mm-mm, blues fallin' down like hail, blues fallin' down like hail,
And the day keeps on worring' me, there's a hell-hound on my trail,
Hell-hound on my trail, hell-hound on my trail."
Robert Johnson, 1937

Chapter Thirteen

DEFEATS, DISAPPOINTMENTS

I am proud of what I've contributed to the development of gymnastics worldwide. There are fewer than 100 coaches (about 90) in the history of the sport (dating back to the 1903) World Championships who have participated in 8 or more World Championships and/or Olympic Games. I have (to date) coached at 11 Worlds (for 6 different Federations which is generally acknowledged to be without precedent).

I do not wish to overstate it, but I am confident that there are few people in the history of the sport who have been more passionately committed to and actively worked for the development of gymnastics in what is broadly understood to be the Third World than I have.

While I am proud of what I've accomplished, I'm saddened by the
a. projects that didn't happen
b. opportunities that didn't work out,
and
c. most importantly, the life-changing possibilities that went awry…..

As mentioned earlier in the narrative, my mantra has always been that the secret to success is to "keep getting up off the canvas". I've been hit in the chin, knocked down, and seemingly defeated so many times….like Arnold Schwartznegger's "Terminator" (or perhaps, Voltaire's Dr. Pangloss), I somehow found the resolve to get back up and "keep on keepin' on"….it is psychically so draining to KNOW, absolutely know that one is doing good things and benefiting people and to be blocked and not permitted to move forward.

Disappointments:

Khum

I have written previously of Zimbabwe....my finest athlete in the Zimbabwe team was Khumbulani Moyo...as I wrote in my official report to the ZAGA committee after the 1995 All-African Games:

> Participating at the World level profoundly changes the way the sport is perceived within a country, and forever alters the way a Federation and its' program are viewed around the world. I could spend literally hours explaining why this is the single most important project that ZAGA could pursue over the next year, but I am hopeful that the 4 months we spent together have given me some credibility within the Zimbabwean gymnastics community and that if for no other reason, you adapt this goal/project as a matter of faith. I assure you that Kumbulani Moyo can make a respectable showing at the Puerto Rico (1996) Worlds, especially on floor and vault.
>
> Do not be misled by the scores or the competitive results of the All-African Games. While we did not have an opportunity to do anything about it (or time for me to analyze this with you in detail at the time, the politics and biases of the judging of the other medal-contending nations were the most extreme (if largely "behind the scenes" in nature) of any international event with which I have ever been involved.... Khumbulani and I have discussed this opportunity in great detail. I believe that he has a new and clear understanding of his responsibilities and potential role in the sport and ZAGA than before. I also urge you to send Stan Chinyerere to the Worlds as his coach, but funding not permitting, I will be involved and will contribute in any capacity that ZAGA would deep appropriate.
>
> Funding for project:
>
> I have always felt that money (or lack thereof) should never be a hindrance in doing what one wants to do (or perhaps more precisely, funding considerations should always be a secondary consideration in determining the desirability of a goal. If you agree that sending Mr. Moyo to the World Championships is a vital step in the growth of the sport in Zimbabwe, then there will be a way to coordinate the funding.'

Unfortunately, ZAGA and it's President Neil Nativel did nothing to support this project, and in fact, (albeit in a "passive" capacity) worked to thwart Khumbulani's aspirations....whether this was because of covert racism (my personal opinion) or a simple misunderstanding/misjudgment of how international competition (and concomitantly Zimbabwe's and Khum's personal standing) might be involved I do not know....regardless, Zimbabwe refused to register Khumbulani for the 1996 Worlds, and subsequently although I pleaded with the Federation they refused to inscribe him to subsequent WCs.

The opportunity passed Khum and the country by. In the October 1997 International Gymnast magazine, there was a (melancholy) follow-up to the story....

"Something Ventured, Nothing Gained?"

> The World Championships is a landmark event for every first time participant. For some, winning gold is the measure. For others, taking part is a remarkable victory... For one individual, simply being at the Lausanne Worlds was an extraordinary achievement.
>
> Khumbulani Moyo is a four-time national champion of Zimbabwe but could not compete in Lausanne because his Federation sent his entry application too late...
>
> Moyo's saga began more than two years ago: " I have been trying for two years to represent my country at the World Championships but it is my own Federation that is holding the progress of gymnastics in Zimbabwe hostage", he says.
>
> Moyo had also hoped to compete at the 1996 Puerto Rico Worlds. "I was told that I wasn't good enough to compete at that level by officials in ZAGA (Zimbabwe Amateur Gymnastics Association) he said.
>
> Moyo senses that racial bias might be influencing the decisions from ZAGA which is almost exclusively white. Zimbabwe is 97per cent black, as are most of the gymnasts on the senior men's team.
>
> ZAGA President Neil Nativel admits the application to Lausanne was late, but also believes there was little to gain by sending Moyo: "Really, it was of no use for him to go there and disgrace himself", he told the Zimbabwe Independent.
>
> Moyo went anyway with the slim hope of being accepted as a participant at the last minute. He arrived in Lausanne with only 27 Swiss francs in his pocket. However, the FIG still would not grant him permission for him to compete, but it sold him a credential for 200 Swiss francs (the money was donated by Paul Ziert the publisher of International Gymnast magazine). The credential allowed Moyo access to the training hall where he worked out with the worlds top gymnasts and to the competition venue. The Barbados delegation offered housing to Moyo.
>
> "I can't put into words what it meant for these people to want to help me, " Moyo said. "This has been a great experience that I will never forget. Now I will work even harder to prove that this trust has not been misplaced.
>
> Khumbulani Moyo is the descendant of Zulu warriors, and is a proud and determined man. "I know that with hard work and a little good

fortune, you can have your dreams come true' he said. "I will work very hard to represent my country at next year's Commonwealth Games, and most importantly at the 1999 World Championships in China.

Khumbulani never did have the opportunity to compete at the Commonwealth Games or the World Championships. Today, he is a successful club coach and proud husband and father in Roseburg Oregon in the United States.

Bolivia 2005

One of my greatest disappointments has been my inability to attain a permanent position as the coach or program director of a national team. I actually thought it had happened in 2004 for Bolivia, but alas, it didn't. I'm still not certain of the particulars. Here's the story:

One evening in the summer of 2004, I was contacted by (then) BGF President Enrique Velasquez. He wanted me to be the Bolivian National Coach for the 2006 "Odesur" Games (a quadrennial multi-sport Championships for the countries of South America to be held in 2006) in Bolivia. I was ecstatic, and totally excited about the possibility that this could actually happen.

In addition, Enrique, wanted me to travel to Bolivia in early September 2004 (shortly after the Athens Olympics in which female Bolivian gymnast Maria Jose Fuentes competed).... to attend the National Championships and to tour the main gyms in the country. Yesssssss!!!!!

A short, (but it felt v-e-r-y long!) few weeks later, I got on a plane and headed to La Paz (see Bolivia chapter regarding that particular flight!) and the morning upon my arrival, was sequestered with a number of officials from the Bolivian Olympic Committee. "We are interested in your views on our gymnastics program and our gymnasts....how do you see yourself coordinating the activities of the members of the National Team?"

"I'm extremely excited at this opportunity," I responded. "I perceive the National Coach as working intimately/closely with the Program Director of each discipline, and in the absence of such a position (Bolivia does not have that particular position in their "all-volunteer" Federation), is the "de-facto" Program director. We have so many opportunities, using the mechanism of 'Odesur' to profoundly restructure gymnastics in this country and to set a structure and set of mechanisms in place that will make it function effectively long after the '06 Odessur experience is history."

The question next posed, "What is the composition of the National Team? How will you know who is in the training squad?"

"At this moment," I answered, "I have no idea who is in the training squad, but

between now (Sept. 2004) and the Games (May 2006) i.e. 19 months, I will propose and we will develop a strategic training program that will:
a. articulate the goals
b. set the timeline
c. determine the objective criteria
I'll be able to better answer the question better after I attend the Championships."

"Who will be in the pool of athletes for the training squad?"

"Everybody in Bolivia is a candidate for the training squad; the team will be selected from there, and I'm not sure what the specific process will be yet, but will make a formal written proposal after this trip, and hopefully have it ratified by the Federation." At the time, I thought all of this was clear, logical, and made obvious sense. In retrospect, I'm not sure if it was all "over their heads" or that there were agendas favoring particular states or athletes of which I was unaware.

Subsequent to my flight to Cochabamba (which arguably has the finest training/competition gym in the country), I spent the next 5 days watching training, and observing the National Championships. While I love Bolivia, I was (privately) shocked at the low level of skills and the strength and conditioning level of even the best athletes. As I proposed (using all the positive phrasing and reinforcement that I could muster), there was great potential (probably a misstatement), and with careful planning and diligent effort, we could make a statement at the Odesur Games.

After a fortnight working with the coaches and gymnasts, I suggested to the Federation that we needed to implement:

- a tiered age-group competition program with 4 levels for the men
- a tiered age group competition program with 4 levels for the women.
- a physical testing program adapted from an old Soviet model to be implemented 2 times/annum for both the men (and a similar but different) one for the women
- a detailed organizational chart for the Federation identifying the various departments (i.e. program, membership, public relations/publicity, sponsorships, events, et.al.) and an iteration of specific job functions (and possible projects) that could be developed in each department.
- a 19 month detailed training plan including dates for National "physical tests" and competitions which would (presumably identify the teams for the Odesur Games (and the rest of the quadrennium through 2008."

I was and remain very unhappy with the current approach by the country which basically is to "dumb-down" or modify the existing rules for Odessur…it is not a progressive, but reactive approach, and does not support the development of the sport in the country.

The level of strength and flexibility in Bolivia was truly a shock to me. The gymnasts were simply weak and inflexible, and very much below what I would consider an international standard of gymnastics

I had never been more excited about an opportunity.....however....as the days dragged on, Enrique was unable to provide a written contract whereupon we could formalize our agreement and my responsibilities. As the days dwindled, I became increasingly restive, and despite his reassurances, "everything will be ok", I've been in South America long enough to know that manana doesn't always mean that every problem is going to be solved. To put it bluntly, the longer this went unresolved, the more troubled I became....I love Bolivia, and I was very very excited at the opportunity, but I've now spent two weeks here (all expenses paid), but with no salary, and frankly, however much I love gymnastics, I'm working my tail off and not exactly on vacation.....

Digression: one time when I was coaching University in the USA, I went to the NCAA Championships in Lincoln Nebraska in early April. On one balmy prairie early-Spring morning, I walked into the Devaney Center (the University's main indoor facility where the championships were being held) for meetings, and the temperature was 79F....12 hours later when I was out of the center, it was 25F with a 30 mile per hour wind slamming a combination of snow and sleet into our faces....my collared shirt did little to keep the wind-shill (and wet snow) out that evening!!! The point of this digression? I spend 3 days going to meetings and gym competitions in the windswept prairie town of Lincoln Nebraska, and when I get home, more than one person queried me with, "How was your vacation?" Sheesh.

The day before I was scheduled to leave Bolivia's BOC, FBG, YOC, and I finally got the contract signed and I returned to the USA to prepare all documents and to develop our long-term training program.

About a month later, when the first salary payment was due, I received no communication and no money. A month after that, about the time I was preparing to return to Bolivia and take over full responsibilities, Enrique informed me that the BFG was canceling the contract! No reason, just canceling....he told me that I hadn't done the job...what???

I responded to him via email:

Enrique, we have discussed in great detail the scope of my activities for the next 2 years. Due to our long term personal relationship, my history with Bolivia gymnastics, and my professional experience I have suggested that the 2006 South American Championships and my contract with the Sports Ministry is a unique opportunity for gymnastics in Bolivia to grow and develop to unprecedented heights.

During our (too brief!) time together in Cochabamba and Santa Cruz, I suggested that the Federation utilize me in a number of capacities beyond simply coordinating the men's and women's national tams for 2006.

I will certainly accept your direction or supervision if you suggest that I limit myself to specific activities, but in Santa Cruz I recall that I mentioned being involved, among other things:

1. levels competitive systems
.2. physical preparation tests
3. involvement in meet organization for 2006 Championships
4. involvement in possible procurement of sponsorship

If you and BFG decide that my role is limited to maximizing success for 2006 I will certainly do so, but with respect, I suggest that together we could achieve much more.

There are 5 things that Bolivian gymnastics desperately needs in order to be successful

1. technical leadership and organization
2. leadership and inspiration
3. belief that success is possible
4. access to adequate equipment/training venues.
5. additional funding

I know that I can provide appropriate technical information and organization. I am certain that my unique strength is in sharing a vision of success (leadership, inspiration and a passionate conviction that success is possible) with the coaches and gymnasts....This attribute enhances the authority and position of you and the Federation. When I suggest to a Boris Lara or Saul Maeta that he could possibly participate in a World event, it provides and unbelievable stimulus and excitement....isn't that what we want for our gymnasts, for them to believe that their dreams can actually happen?

Apparently, that was not part of Enrique's agenda. He and BFG terminated the contract (even though the agreement was formally between me as an individual and the Sports Ministry headed by Prof. Felix Sandoval.

After receiving no response to my several follow-up emails requesting an explanation and a revisiting of the issue, I contacted a legal firm in La Paz, explained the situation and provided relevant documents.

Abagado/Attorney Sergio Salazar responded with the following email:

Mr. Holt,

We have reviewed the documents you sent us and it is our understanding that:

1. The Bolivian Gymnastics Federation has terminated the contract signed with you by e-mail.

2. If this is correct, we inform you that emails and even faxes are not considered in Bolivia as a valid mechanism for the termination of contracts

3. The only manner in which the BGF can terminate the contract with you would be with a notarized letter and this can only be done within Bolivian territory and only if any events of default have occurred on your behalf, thus operating a unilateral termination of the contract.

4. Hence, we believe that you should continue executing the contract since the termination done by the BGF is not valid or legally binding, for us the contract is still valid and in full force.
5. However, you should answer the emails sent to you by the BGF rejecting the termination and stating that you will continue to execute the contract as established by it. Please note that if you do not answer the emails in this sense a tacit termination could operate.
Should you require assistance in responding to the emails sent by the BGF please let us know at the following email addresses.
Best Regards,
Sergio Salazar-Marchicado

My response to Sr. Salazar was as follows:

Sr. Salazar.
Thank you very much for your reply and support.
As you have seen from the documents I have previously sent as email attachments, I have:
a. responded aggressively (as per your suggestion to BFG, its' attorney Gonzalo Balderrama, and various BFG members by emphatically rejecting the "termination"
b. informed BFG, its' members, and the Sports Ministry that I have continued work as specified in the contract.

The problem I have is HOW to compel BFG and the Sports Ministry to recognize that they entered into a valid contract extending from Oct. 2004 through May 2006, AND to force them to fulfill their obligations in that contract.

As I wrote to you initially, the Sports Ministry currently owes me 4 months (Oct.-Jan.) payments and I have received nothing.

Sergio, at this point, it seems my only recourse is to take legal action through the Bolivian legal system with you and your firm as my representatives.

You should be aware that BFG has no financial resources independent of the personal assets of the President and officers and therefore, it is possible/probable that the threat of legal action and financial consequences that might fall upon them personally may be powerful incentive to reassess their position.

My objectives remain as follows:
1. to have our contract enforced as signed, confirming my right to lead Bolivia gymnastics through the South American Championships in May 2006 (and to be paid the sums agreed upon in the contract.
2. If, for any reason, #1 is not possible, to sue for maximum possible financial damages for any legal reasons and for the largest amounts that you and your firm might believe recoverable.
I would hope that in any case, BFG be made liable for any legal expenses resulting from its' unilateral breach of our agreement.

Please contact me at your earliest convenience. I am enclosing contact information for BFG, its attorney, and Sports Ministry in order for you to contact them directly on my behalf. (Please of course copy me on any communications.
Thank you again for your help.
Muy cordialmente,
Jim Holt

In the end, BFG simply refused to respond to my communications. No monies were ever paid, and given the lack of assets, there seemed to be no real point in pursuing what might have been an expensive lawsuit.

Bolivia ended up forfeiting the hosting of the 2006 Odesur Games due to financial problems caused in part by local political wrangling. Argentina took over as "last minute" hosts of the event.

Enrique was defeated in his bid for Presidential re-election in December 2006.

Hannah and I took a group of US high school female gymnasts to Bolivia for two weeks in the summer of 2005; we were all warmly received by our Bolivian colleagues, Enrique excepted.

Despite my continued pleas and exhortations, no Bolivian athlete, male or female was given the opportunity to represent the country on the world level during the 2004-2008 quaddrennium.

The failure of this project to materialize is one of my saddest disappointments.

I love Bolivia, and if there is a future opportunity for me to be involved, I'll be there.

"Power tends to corrupt, and absolute power corrupts absolutely."
Lord Acton

Chapter Fourteen

IT'S ACADEMIC, SORT OF: FIG DEVELOPMENT

My single biggest regret is that I have no involvement with the FIG Academies program, or more broadly phrased, International Development within the FIG. Despite having extensive experience in the international development of gymnastics, I've never been asked to contribute. This is particularly distressing because I originally proposed the concept to the (then) FIG President Yuri Titov in 1994 and subsequently submitted a formal written proposal in 1996. Titov was enthusiastic about the idea, and had indicated verbally that he wanted to pursue the matter after the quadrennial election. Unfortunately (for me at least....I guess Yuri too!) he was narrowly defeated by Bruno Grandi. At the time Bruno gave lip service to the idea, and I had sent him a written draft proposal as well.

I learned in Political Science 101 that politics could be defined as "the struggle for control over the allocation of resources". It was later suggested to me that there is an inverse relationship between the significance or importance of the resource to be controlled, and the intensity and ferocity with which the contenders will fight for control of same.

This has been (depressingly) for me, a recurring experience in gymnastics. It is widely understood (and sometimes mocked) that coaches and judges will endure almost any kind of petty manipulation or debasement in order to be awarded the prestige of "a trip".

Perhaps the single most difficult aspect of the interpersonal dynamics within the sport for me are that in large part, people in gymnastics take disagreements over policy personally. People with limited perspectives tend to link disagreements over policy with evaluations of personality (i.e. they demonize individuals with whom they disagree), The idea that two attorneys could fight passionately on opposite sides for their respective clients, and once stepping out of the courtroom, lay down their cudgels and go have dinner or drinks together has always appealed to me. There was a time (and may be again) in American politics where bitter foes, Democrat and Republican could shout at each other from opposite viewpoints and upon passing through the Congressional cloakroom, would revert to friends and respected colleagues. In the world of gymnastics that I inhabit, the "petty" grudges and long-held grievances over policy differences have always struck me as childish and absurd. It most definitely holds the sport back from a certain level of professionalism, and I believe on a personal level has contributed at times to my lack of support.

Lamentably, FIG President Grandi is a person who takes disagreement very personally. I have been told by FIG employees that President Grandi "dislikes" me. In retrospect, it seems he began to formulate this feeling because I had (respectfully) disagreed with him on a particular matter of FIG policy. I was opposed to the elimination of Technical Assemblies and Grandi was for it….I made it known that I'm philosophically opposed to the centralization of authority and therefore axiomatically do not like consolidation of decision-making and therefore opposed the measure….my side lost. A more magnanimous person, or perhaps someone with a broader perspective might be able to distinguish between policy and personality… Bruno Grandi is not that person.

One can argue that the Academy program in its' current format performs such a limited service that the real value or merit can be seriously debated. The Academies program, in fairness, focuses on disseminating "technical" information (i.e. technique, biomechanics, et.al.) throughout the international community. My profound objection is that, given what the FIG is, its' responsibility, and its' potential to affect the growth of thc sport world-wide, how is it that "teaching kips or Kovacs" takes precedence over other more significant issues? Moreover, given limited resources, why on earth are the USA, France, and Russia recipients of Academy programs???

The FIG describes itself as the "governing" body of the sport. What it should be is the "servicing" body of the sport and serving (as well as working to expand) its' membership!

The FIG has no long-term strategic plan for the gymnastics. Want evidence? For the last decade and a half, the FIG has continuously "tinkered" with the its' competitive format and rule book. In Artistic Gymnastics, prior to 1992, the competitive format was compulsory-optional, 6 individuals per team, 5 scores to count….in 1992 (not necessarily a bad thing by the way) the FIG introduced specialist World Championships….in 1994, the sport introduced 7-6-5 for team competition, and before it was ever actually utilized a single time (Dortmund Worlds), the FIG again modified the competition format to 6-5-4….in 1996, the organization voted to eliminate compulsories, and in 2001 went to a team finals format of 6-3-3. After the judging fiasco in Athens in 2004, the FIG scrapped its' more than half-century old scoring format (and the 10.0) and adopted an open-ended scoring system. Just prior to the 2008 Beijing Olympics, it was decided that future team preliminary qualifications would limit team size to 5 individuals instead of 6. Contrasted to this, soccer football's last significant rule change was 1927 when the offside rule was modified, and baseball's last significant modification (designated hitter<1973>excepted) was moving the pitcher's mound back to 60'6"....in 1893! FIG has consistently been reactive rather than proactive, and an observer might ask the question, "what is the long-range plan and impact of these decisions?"

The answers? There is no long-term plan....no one knows the impact of the decisions because there has never been a control or test model.

How does the FIG serve its' constituent members? How does gymnastics compete with other sports (and concomitantly how does sport compete with all other recreational or entertainment activities)? The FIG has often been deficient in addressing these issues and in particular in the philosophy and manner in which it has approached the development of the sport world-wide.

The administrative conservatism (this is a body which refers to the persons holding positions in the organization as "authorities") and strategic myopia of the FIG are arguably its' greatest weaknesses and the largest long-term threat to the world's oldest international sports organization. (The FIG was founded in 1881 which make it a decade older than the International Olympic Committee). The FIG should focus on "service" NOT governance. As I have written in a separate context, the focus should be on "stewardship" not "control" or "authority". We are ultimately and must conduct ourselves as the stewards of the sport.

The Academy program, while providing worthwhile information is NOT a development program, but rather, a small part of what could and should be a comprehensive program organized and orchestrated by the FIG to grow and promote the sport of gymnastics.

Exacerbating my disappointment is that not only am I not involved, but the person currently running the Academies (as a full-time paid FIG employee) is Hardy Fink, the long-time MTC member, who was offered the job by President Grandi in exchange for leaving the MTC. The "politics within politics" is beyond the scope (or point) of this narrative, but suffice to say, not being the head (or even involved!) in what was a "dream job" remains my biggest disappointment.

Even if I wasn't the formal head of International Development, it galls me that Hardy, who stood up with me at my wedding and who knows my work perhaps better than anyone else has never asked me to be involved.

Hardy Fink was the pioneer in the concept of an "open" code of points which was a unique achievement and profoundly significant contribution to the sport. He is by his own assessment, a technician, and the Academy that he runs is exactly like that. The Academy conducts coaches courses. He travels with a group of technical experts (chosen by him) to various countries, and gives lectures to coaches on topics including biomechanics, skill acquisition, physical development according to age, morphological characteristics of high level gymnasts, etc. At the end of the course, the coaches are given a test, receive a diploma, and line up for a group picture. All of which are positive things, but sadly do not address the essential factors which impact growth and development.

Mr. Fink is a highly capable individual, but he's not the person that should be heading the international development of the sport. He is not especially passionate about this topic. He may be enthusiastic, but it is not his "life's work", it's a job. I do not believe he has a long-term vision for the program (except to do more of the same and perhaps do it better).

The disappointing reality of the Academy program is that it could be so much more, it could be unique throughout the international sporting world.

What could a viable "FIG International Development Program" include? More importantly, what is currently lacking? First, it lacks a true mission statement. My mission statement would be: "To plan, organize, and implement the development of gymnastics throughout the world."

At this time the FIG has 130 member Federations. There is no reason that an International Development program shouldn't reach out to countries (or Olympic Committees) that currently are NOT members of the FIG. Who says Mohammed has to come to the mountain? The ONLY thing that keeps me from, for example, getting on a plane, traveling to American Samoa and speaking with the ASOC Secretary General Mac Ane (they aren't part of the FIG) about getting a gymnastics program set up through their Parks and Rec Dept. (run by former Washington State quarterback Samoa Samoa) is funding. Every country in the world, including American Samoa should be pursued by and become part of the FIG! It only takes somebody with the vision or interest in getting them involved.

I know an accomplished female gymnast whose father is Tahitian, but she did not have the opportunity to participate in international competition. Why? Tahiti is a member of the IOC but is not part of the FIG. Where are the officials who could therefore contact Tahiti, meet with their Olympic Committee, and get them registered and included….the FIG (through the IOC) has access to vast financial resources. Money at that level isn't r-e-a-l-l-y the issue. The only issue (maybe this is three issues)is the passion to continue to effect meaningful change, the vision in which a long-range plan can be set up, and the ability to follow it through…..

What else is the FIG Development (i.e.Academy) program lacking?

1. strategic administrative planning

the majority of Federations do not have long-term plans or detailed organizational structures. It would not be difficult for the FIG Development program to assist and encourage Federations in developing organizational charts and planning. The FIG Development program should be closely involved with the member Federation's business models. This would include active involvement in the procurement of sponsorships, television rights, coordinating membership programs, fees, et.al.

The FIG should be available and an active resource for every aspect of member Federation's business plans and activities whenever member Federations request advice or assistance...

If I were in charge of this program I would do everything in my power to encourage and assist (for example) Egypt in coordinating a bid to host a future World Artistic Championships. Some of the issues that this at least 4-year project would necessitate addressing would include infrastructure, transport, accommodations, logistics, personnel(volunteers), government relations, sponsorship, media, marketing, medical, membership, and technical matters, and budget.

2. "new growth"

The FIG is the organization that oversees the health and well-being of the sport worldwide. As such it should be intimately involved in the oversight and support of not only all its' member Federations, but proactive everywhere in the world. The Academy program (or perhaps more broadly) the Development program should be focused on developing the sport in EVERY country and coordinating the formation of Gymnastics Federations in every country that currently does not boast same! It would be part of the mission to develop new FIG members, i.e. Kenya, Uganda, Oman, etc. I would NOT assign technical courses or expend scarce resources on highly competitive and/or wealthy Federations.

3. Technical/competitive planning and oversight

The Academies program as it currently exists could be an integral component of this aspect of development. In addition, FIG should actively encourage its' member Federations to take part in pertinent events and competitions. l would advocate hypothetically that Uruguay (for example) make every effort to participate in Pan American and South American competitions.

4 . Accessable resource:

Why can't the FIG (especially with the proliferation of communication and media currently available!) be a 24/7/365 resource for the sport? If a coach in, Sri Lanka for example, has a question or problem, where is the email list of experts whom he/she can contact to ask questions?

Why doesn't the FIG set up an Academy website where there are forums or blogs for technical (or any other kind) of questions that Academy "experts" (or anybody else who wants to contribute for that matter!). YouTube is a revolutionary tool. Anyone who wants to see, well, virtually anything can do so....there is no reason that the FIG Development can't steer/point people in a given direction. It might be very interesting for a Lausanne university student who would like to work as an intern to attempt to catalog what's available...obviously, there will be "everything" available soon....the Academy/Development Program's role? To channel people's inquiries into a direction that provides answers....

5. Central Data Source

yes, the FIG has a list of the coaches who have taken the courses and passed the tests....now, what are they doing with that? Any follow up? Any extended communication? As far as I know, there's nothing. Which is a shame, because as anyone who has actually worked in development knows, the key is follow up, continued communication, continued interaction, and letting people (your clients, colleagues) know that "you need them, you like them, and that they're doing a good job?"

6. Tracking

related to #5, but as I conceive it (and have done so consistently in my almost 2 decades of independent work in the field), once a relationship is established, it's crucial to continue to explore and communicate....how are the persons you've worked with doing? What are their problems, their concerns? How can you help them? Simply, send an email: "how's everything going? When are your regional/national championships? Is there anything I can do to help?"

I know from personal experience, that receiving that FIG/IOC diploma is a HUGELY important thing for most of the people that go through the courses and receive them....the idea that the FIG traces and tracks them, and includes them as "stakeholders" in a bigger picture is incredibly motivating and exciting....simple to do, but takes vision, obviously....

7. Networking

with a tracking database, it would be simple for the FIG Academies to be a centralized, if not "clearing house", a central networking mechanism whereby any jobs or coaching positions that became available might be channeled to an appropriate pool of candidates. While it is of course appropriate for the various clubs and Federations to advertise for positions, there is no reason that a centralized and connected resource like the FIG Academy couldn't be an additional contact....a simple precedent would be my being able to connect Karim-Abdul Achrani (Algeria) to a coaching position in Zimbabwe a number of years ago, or my involvement with any number of foreign coaches being able to matriculate to the USA for work or study over the last few years.

8. Olympic Solidarity

for at least 20 years gymnastics has lagged far behind many of the other Olympic sports in the number of courses and dollar amount of funding that it has received from the IOC and the Olympic Solidarity program. It is absurd that the most popular Olympic sport annually ranks between 9th and 14th in Solidarity activity and funding.

Year	# courses	rank	#1 Org	# courses
1994	12	14th	IAAF	37
1995	18	13th	IAAF	30
1996	16	10th	FIBA	36
1997	10	10th	FINA	21
1998	5	21st(t)	IAAF	29
1999	12	12th(t)	IAAF	29
2000	3	11th	IAAF	12
2001	7	9th	IAAF	15
2002	10	9th	IAAF	18
2003	6	11th	IAAF	31
2004	7	13th	IAAF	29

The FIG Development program (if it was made a priority) could procure significant funding from the IOC and as a result be able to generate significant amount of activity that would otherwise either not happen or would have to be funded by the member Federations.

Summary

The FIG, even with the progress made by the institution of the Academies program continues to lack a true vision of Development or strategic plan. As anyone who's ever formulated one knows, a plan must include, at minimum, specific and measurable objectives and a timeframe in which it's projected to achieve them.

If the FIG had a leader with vision and a serious passion for the international development of gymnastics, it would rank #1 in IOC funding by 2013 and have 200 member Federations by 2025.

"When you're born you're 3 feet tall....when you die, you're 6 feet tall....it's a helluva struggle for a yard."
Raoul Walsh

Chapter Fifteen

FIG DIPLOMA

Abie Grossfeld who arguably has done and seen more than any other single person in the history of United States gymnastics has cogently argued that there is a fundamental difference between "achievement" and "award"....he points out that competing in the Olympics is much different (accomplishment) than being being given a certificate on the White House lawn (award).

That said, while it's my accomplishments that are of primary importance to me, it would also be nice to be officially recognized for same....

The FIG has what is in essence, a "Lifetime Achievement" award for judges and coaches. The single (the O-N-L-Y!) criteria is that an individual be able to document that he/she have participated in his/her particular capacity at a minimum of 8 (total) Olympic Games and/or World Championships. To date there are fewer than 100 coaches in the history of gymnastics that have qualified for this award.

Perhaps the single most disheartening thing about dealing with "officialdom" at the international level of gymnastics (not that it's exclusive to this particular sport) is what often feels like the "politics of the personal". As described in the preceding chapter, it seems that policy disputes or disagreements so often devolve into "personal" grievances and "one-upsmanships..."

When I originally applied to the Men's Technical Committee (the FIG body responsible for processing the nominations) for the award in 2004 (I'd coached at 9 WCs at the time), I was denied and informed that "in order to receive the diploma, it was necessary to be nominated by a Federation." Even though there had been no previous stipulation, and that many other recipients had gotten the award without their Federation's involvement, I was required to apply "though channels"

I appealed to then-MTC member Hardy Fink asking for clarification; Hardy's response was as follows:

"No vote was called. It was deemed by Stoica (MTC President) to be in the

Office's hands....Norbert (Beuche, then FIG Sec.-General) told him that he wrote you and that was that. This is not a voting issue. It is a rubber stamp- or should be- once the criteria have been met. .... it now appears to have been taken away from MTC recommendation and authority and handed to the Office or the President, or the Executive or who knows what."

So it seemed that even though I had fulfilled the only criteria stipulated, the FIG refused to award me a diploma. Even if it is the work that's of paramount significance, in the face of institutional resistance, I decided to press forward for formal "recognition", and although it was distasteful for me to do so, I decided to try to "jump through FIG's hoops."

I thought long and hard before reaching out to USA Gymnastics as a "sponsor." Twice elected National Membership Representative for the Men's Program (by a national election of professional members), I have not endeared myself to the "office" due to my outspoken (and some believe trenchant) opposition to centralization of decision-making and authority. I believe that the founding fathers of US Gymnastics in 1962 were very wise when they opted for a federated structure and I've long fought against the notion that in order to be successful, the organization had to have a corporate structure. Naturally, this philosophy of governance runs contrary to the interests of the employees of the corporation (i.e. the "office") who self interestedly (not a pejorative, simply a statement) would prefer to be able to act with as little "oversight"(my word) or "freedom of action"(presumably their phrase) as possible. With this in mind, I approached USAG with a certain trepidation, but was hopeful that they could see the merit (and reasonableness) of my request, plus understand that it basically cost them little or nothing in terms of either time of money. I sent an email to the USA Gymnastics office:

(to a USAG official)

Hope all is going well for you and folks in the office.

We exchanged emails a couple months back regarding the FIG Coaches Diploma for which I've qualified. I would very much appreciate it if USA Gymnastics would contact the FIG and request that I be recognized for the achievement and awarded a diploma.

As you know, the ONLY criteria the FIG has set is for an individual to have coached at 8 World Championships and/or Olympic Games.

Through Aarhus, I've coached at 10 WCs (and if necessary can again provide documentation) for the following countries:

1991 BOL

1993 BOL and ECU

1994 BOL
1996 IRI
1997 BAR
1999 NAM
2001 BOL
2002 BOL
2003 BOL
2006 YEM

I hope that USAG feels it is a positive thing for American gymnastics for "one of its own" to have contributed/achieved this in our sport. Thanks,
I really appreciate your help with this.
Regards,

I was disappointed, and frankly surprised at the response I received. I was basically asked if there was a reason why I didn't approach one of the Federations I had represented at the Worlds to sponsor me.

I wrote back and indicated that while I had great affection and respect for all the countries I had represented, as an American citizen and as someone who has had long-time involvement in US gymnastics, my first preference would have been to be nominated by the USA. As I have previously written throughout this narrative, the notion of nation-states as primary identification might resonate throughout much/most of the culture but has secondary importance for me personally…that said, everything being equal, I am an American, and thought it would be both appropriate and appreciated that I apply through the US National Governing Body (of which I'd been an elected Board member and many years athlete and professional member for goodnessake!).

The response I received was disingenuous and disheartening….the USAG representative wrote that:

We appreciate the fact that you meet the criteria to receive an FIG Diploma and congratulate you on this achievement; however, we cannot place this accomplishment ahead of that of the many coaches who have represented the United States at World and Olympic competitions; many who have won medals. This would send the wrong message to those who have served, and aspire to serve, our sport and country at the highest level.

Huh? Given that one has nothing to do with the other, it seemed apparent that either the persons in charge of making a decision to contact FIG on my behalf either didn't understand my request, or that there was some other agenda…..as Hannah pointed out, if they wanted to decline because I hadn't actually represented the USA at one of the competitions, that would be, while arguable, at least a consistent application of policy....but now, the issue of "bad messages" had somehow been broached...I had approached this with trepidation, and now have a serious knot in my stomach....I hate having to ask these people for anything....that said, what the heck, nothing ventured, nothing gained, so I replied, playing the hand out, anticipating that it's going nowhere, and sent the following:

(to whom it may concern)

I am puzzled....perhaps baffled is a better word....regarding the points you express in your email.

How does meeting the criteria for the FIG Coaches Diploma have anything to do with coaching the USA at World/Olympic competitions? Why would it occur to anybody to put a "rank order" on one versus the other....the criteria are entirely different, aren't they?

I'm curious...what is the message that you think would be conveyed to those who want to serve our sport and country at the highest level?

I'd sincerely like to understand your concerns and/or objections regarding this seemingly simple and straightforward matter.

Thanks I appreciate it.

After waiting several days, I called the office and had a conversation with a senior official; it was clear that they weren't going to budge on the issue, and exasperated, I waited a couple weeks before firing off the following:

(to whom it may concern)

Thank you for talking with me a couple weeks ago.

It seems from your email and our talk that you have 3 concerns regarding my specific circumstance.

1. You suggest that nominating me somehow detracts from or trivializes the accomplishments of coaches who have produced athletes for the USA. Surely USAG does not want to convey to its' membership that ... the only measure of achievement for an American is to compete or coach for the US at the Olympics?

2. Your concern for the feelings of US coaches ...is presumably misplaced. It's difficult to believe that any coach who had not met the criteria would begrudge recognition of others who do. The FIG Coaches Diploma is based on the number of appearances at WC/OGs, not competitive results, therefore measures quantity not quality and as such, is an "apples to oranges" comparison.

3. You said on the phone that the "wrong message" you didn't want to send was might inadvertently be encouraging coaches to "run out and find some small country" with which they could go to a Worlds. Two comments:

a. doesn't it strain credulity that gymnastics in the USA could somehow be threatened by a "brain-drain"? Hasn't the USA (for decades) been the beneficiary of the opposite?

b. trying to develop small countries' gymnastics programs isn't as simple or easy as one might think....it is improbable that sending an email to the FIG and the MTC President in this matter will inspire imitators.

Not that it advanced my ultimate objective, but it seems I had hit a nerve. I then received a rather huffy email asserting that I had taken several words out of context and that the person contacting me denied that he had had concerns about having American coaches go to small countries in order to get international opportunities. Understanding that I wasn't going anywhere farther with these folks, I concluded the exchange as follows:

To whom it may concern:

My apologies for any misunderstanding pertaining to context, and perhaps I should not have put quotation marks around "find a small country", but I clearly recall and made a note during our conversation of your concern regarding the possibility of persons doing exactly that....if I have misinterpreted your meaning, would appreciate clarification at your convenience...

Regarding your points:

1. I'm not debating, I simply do not understand why two unrelated "achievements" are somehow being linked and ranked.

2. You also wrote:

"This would send the wrong message to those who have served, and aspire to serve our sport and country at the highest level."

You know, I've aspired to serve our sport and country at the highest level...it disappoints me that you (and/or other Sr. USAG management) do not perceive my work as worthy of the modest support I've requested.

The reader will presumably not be surprised to know that there has been no additional discussion between me and the USAG office.

I did however, feel compelled to share the " fun" with a long-time and highly respected gymnastics friend by sending him the basic gist of the story along and copied him on pertinent emails in the thread....he responded by commenting:

I'm assuming there is more going on than I can glean from these emails. Funny how the rationale changed from 'have Bolivia do it' to 'its about representing the USAG, sorry USA'. ....this looks like the USAG is a dead end. This is a shame.

I told him that of course there was more going on.....I'm not sure of what the exact reasons were, but I know that I'm disliked on some personal level....more importantly I am considered "bad" by the office perhaps most significantly because I've consistently communicated to the gymnastics community that the office works for the membership not
vice versa.

I explained that I don't believe in "dead ends".....while this is enormously frustrating, I had and have 2 things on my side, one of which the
USAG office doesn't care about, the other, they haven't considered the possible ramifications of their "non-action"...
a. I have qualified for the award
b. I have NOTHING to lose by continuing to agitate for recognition and
on a certain level, and I'm being dead serious here, I regarded and continue to regard the matter as "high theater" or "low soap opera".....being so petty over something so insignificant (to USAG or the FIG) is so absurd and over the top that it's funny.......
I sent some further emails and concluded by telling him to: ".enjoy the silliness"...

He wrote back:
Your approach is, as always, proactive and healthy. In the face of, as you say, silliness.

*The following is a bit of a rant. I can't tell you the number of times I have had the rug pulled out from under me for some initiative of mine. There are two ways to pull the
rug; two ways to say the 'administrative no'. One is 'to serve the system' when the real reason is to quash initiative or the initiator. The other is 'to not offend personalities' when the real reason is to quash initiative or the initiator. I talk about the benefits to the organization, they come back with the difficulties this creates for the individuals involved. I talk about the benefits to individuals and they come back with the precedent in the system (established for no remembered reason) that prevents it. I've got a couple of letters around here somewhere that actually do both. Talk about gymnastics (or is it*

contortion?).

USAG has pulled the 'personality' rug. The system is served, you're qualified. "X" acknowledges it. The personalities of the US coaches, many with medals (but who aren't qualified by the system) prevent it and come first. It seems to me that the 'wrong message' they are talking about is that in this area the US guys aren't qualified -- yet. I know the personalities. So do you. Seems to me they could handle it.

"...personality rug..."

I really like that!!

As frustrating as all this has been, it amuses me that USAG does not dispute my right to the diploma..........I will also share one more thing so that the reader can clearly see my point of view.... I can name at least 50 coaches in the US who have achieved more on the competition floor or who can coach gymnastics better than me...probably many more if I were challenged....but the simple fact is they haven't been to 11 WCs or OGs as a credentialed coach and I have..........as Carlos Mencia put it: DUH-da-DUH!!!

I shared this with my colleague, who sage that he is, gets the last word:

You have right on your side. Which in my experience means nothing once either the 'personality rug' or the 'system rug' has been pulled. You are an American (USA! Apple Pie! Truth! Justice! etc!) coach who's qualified for a world level award for which others are not qualified. I'd call that a motivator. Maybe the others guys would all want this award. But then maybe the "office" is afraid there would be a talent drain since our guys aren't getting enough recognition in country. What nonsense.

"A man's reach should exceed his grasp...else what is heaven for?"
Robert Browning

Chapter Sixteen

NASHWAN AND DENMARK

"Unbelievable" is unbelievable even for me....The biggest difficulty with "adventures and craziness" is while you're actually living it, you don't know how it's going to end, and of course, there's always the possibility (maybe even likelihood!!) of disappointment, frustration, and disaster....

Anyway, in the spring of 2006, I had been working with Troy Maillis, a gymnast from the Bahamas for over 2 years, and using every diplomatic technique I could think of to persuade that Federation to inscribe him for the 2005 and then later 2006 Worlds.

Troy had participated in the 2003 event in Anaheim and had actually been instrumental in the development of that Federation, but was unable to retain control of the BFG. Subsequently, officials in 2005, giving him virtually no notice, had decided that he should not participate at that Worlds. Un-friggin-be-leeee-vable....so after a 2 year investment of time and emotional energy, it looks like I'm out and the project is over... Both he and I were devastated. (Coda: happily, Troy was able to compete at the 2007 Worlds and has aspirations for the upcoming quadrennium.)

Well one thing I've come to believe over the years and which has been documented in so many different ways in this book is that "ya never know what's around the next bend…."so while I'm trying to recover from this debacle, of the clear blue, I get an email from a gymnast from Yemen (!!!) who wants my help and is willing to fund himself...

To go back….as described in Chapter 12, in the early Fall of 1996 I conducted an IOC development course in Yemen. As is my usual procedure, I asked about goals, and they gave me a small one (see Appendix)….I then proceeded to tell them that they were aiming too low, and that there was no reason that Yemen shouldn't "shoot for the stars." I remember the circumstances vividly…we were in the main training hall at their Olympic Complex (their National soccer stadium and a modest collection of buildings)....standing by a home-made vault board were a number of young gymnasts. I pointed to one of them, the one who could really twist...."this could be your guy...this could be the first Yemeni to compete at the Worlds...." His name was Nashwan al-Harazi. He was 10 years old.

From that time on, for the 17 days I was in Yemen, Nashwan basically attached himself to me....just about everywhere I/the coaches went, he was right there, usually right at my shoulder. We had kept in touch over the years and he had had some opportunities to train in China, and even competed and medaled at some smaller international events. In 2002 I worked to help him get to the 2003 Worlds, but outside circumstances didn't allow it. In 2004, I urged him to prepare for the '05 Melbourne Worlds, and again, internal Yemeni gymnastics "politics" kept the project from getting to full fruition (in other words, "no go")

I hadn't heard from Nashwan in at least a year and a half, and out of the blue, almost immediately on the heels of the Maillis/Bahamas disappointment, he wrote to me an almost despairing email in April 2006 describing how difficult things were for him in Yemen, and how he was at a crossroads. He wrote: "Mr. Jim, I need to do something amazing in gymnastics or I need to leave the sport. Can you help me?"

Of course....so (as I've suggested in the past) I told him sure, I'll be happy to help, and the project that he should be planning for is to participate in the 2006 World Championships and that he should ask his Federation to enter him and name me coach...."no brainer", right?

The very next email I received was from the Federation President, an old acquaintance of mine, who asked for the information from the international Federation...apparently no one in Yemen knew when the Worlds were, where they were, or how to enter gymnasts. Yeesh! Sooo, I sent this information along and explained exactly what the dates for deadlines were and which forms to request, how to fill them out, what information to include, and web links to information pertaining to the Championships. Even though I have met many officials from various Federations around the world and understand that they don't all necessarily have a background in the sport, I found it a bit disconcerting that the President of a Federation would have no knowledge of a Worlds Championships taking place in the same year.

That said, I was gratified when I learned that they had, indeed processed and sent the Provisional (first) and Definitive (second) inscriptions (go back and review the process as outlined in the Bolivia chapter) well ahead of the deadlines

My next issue, while directly related to participation in the Championships was of a domestic nature. By domestic in this sense, I do not mean confined within the boundaries of the United States, but rather within the boundaries of my house. When I received word that the inscriptions had been received by

FIG, I basically (as I always do in these instances) bounded into the house and exclaimed happily to Hannah: "Guess what, the inscriptions have been received and processed by the FIG and we're going to the World Championships!!!" She turned and looked at me coldly...."What do you mean WE are going? You are the one that's going to be going." "No, no, no!", I responded, "it's gonna be great, we're going to go, you'll be credentialed at the medical person and we're going to have a blast working with Nashwan!" She remained profoundly skeptical (and obviously not very happy!)...."Yemen is a conservative Islamic country...there is no way that they are going to allow a woman, especially an American woman represent them at some international event!" I tried to convince her: "Hannah, you don't understand the place...there are restrictions within Yemen and the culture certainly, but I've explained to the Federation in detail how much you will contribute to the project, and I'm confident that things will work out." Hannah remained dubious..."I doubt it."

One thing we've learned through repeated experience over the years is that (among other things) in dealing with gym programs in developing countries that the principals involved usually have no sense of (or do not care about) differences in time zones. After a few weeks of Hannah being grumpy about (presumably) not being included, we were in bed when the phone rang at approximately 4:30 am one Sunday morning.....a phone call that early in our house means one of two possible things...either there has been a family emergency and we are being notified, or there's some either "catastrophe' in some 3rd World gym program, or something marvelous that's about to be communicated. "Madam Hannah? Madam Hannah?" a distant voice on the other end of the phone inquired..."yes, this is Madam Hannah" she replied groggily...."this is <unclear, I mean the woman was half-asleep!> from Yemen....
Madam Hannah, please tell Mr. Jim that the Nominative inscription has been sent to FIG and that we are so happy and honored that you and Mr. Jim will be our medical person and coach for our dear gymnast Nashwan at the Worlds!" A few more pleasantries were exchanged and the phone was hung up. What could I say? "TOLD YA!" So Hannah was going to be the medical person at the 2006 World Championships for the debutante country of Yemen...life can be difficult at times, but it sure is almost never dull in our house!! Onto Aarhus!

It get's better (or worse depending on your point of view)... I'm totally excited, psyched, and ready to rock and roll with this new project and opportunity, and the gymnast is ecstatic, then....wham!!!!

Up pops a NEW problem...did I mention the 2006 World Championships was in Denmark? Hey, remember how absurd (and tragic) the news was a couple years ago when all those Muslim countries got upset because of some cartoons in a DANISH newspaper? Well, apparently, even though nobody else in the Islamic world has thought of it, some idiot bureaucrat in the Yemen Sports Ministry had decided that those cartoons were so offensive, that Yemen (!!!) was going to punish the Danes by prohibiting Nashwan from participating in the Championshiips....oh in case it wasn't already obvious, there had NEVER been a Yemen gymnast at the World level....un-be-leeeeeee-va-bul.....so what to do?

My very first step was to contact the Yemen Federation and explain to them that it was necessary to be extremely proactive regarding this issue...my communication was as follows:

Dear friend Eyhab,

The Neshwan/Sports Ministry situation has potentially profound international political consequences.

If Neshwan becomes the first Yemen gymnast to participate at the World Championships in Denmark, it will be a positive, but relatively small story in the world gymnastics community and may possibly be noticed by the general media.

If, however, the Yemen Sports Ministry forbids an athlete to participate for the sole reason of the Danish/Islamic misunderstanding of several months ago, it could generate huge international media attention and condemnation directed at the nation of Yemen.

THE POLITICAL CONSEQUENCES OF SUCH AN ACTION COULD BE LARGE AND VERY SERIOUS.

As far as I know, there is NO other Islamic country that is planning on boycotting the Denmark World Championships.

I do not know specifics of Yemen politics but I do understand bureaucrats. A strategy of "personal relationships" (as opposed to pressure) can create a positive outcome.

In addition to persons in the Olympic Committee, which other influential individuals in Yemen might persuade the Ministry to not take this drastic step?

If President Ali Abdullah Saleh did not suspend diplomatic relations with Denmark, how is it possible that the Sports Ministry can state a policy in contradiction of the government's?

I fully understand that this is an internal Yemen problem, but the Ministry must be made to understand the gravity of the matter, and that the best action is sometimes to take no action.

I eagerly await your thoughts on this matter. Ensha Allah, all will be well.

IMPORTANT: please complete and send into the FIG the 3 inscription forms; I respectfully wish to emphasize the importance of optimism and preparation.

Warm personal regards,

Additionally, I believed strongly that international pressure might make a difference in the Sports Minister's perspective pertaining to the issues. As I have discussed in detail previously, there are some significant philosophical and "temperamental" differences between me and the FIG establishment. Regardless, we were in a fix. Loathe though I was to do so, I invoked my inner Emerson who once famously observed that "....foolish consistency is the hobgoblin of small minds." I therefore held my nose and sent an email to Bruno Grandi asking him to personally intervene. I definitely "laid it on pretty thick" ....

May 30, 2006

Dear Bruno,

Your belief in the concept of "Separation of Sport and Politics" and your commitment to the development of our beloved gymnastics is known worldwide.

As you may be aware, Yemen has inscribed a gymnast to the upcoming 2006 World Championships; this will of course be Yemen's first ever participation at the World level, and will be an unprecedented and heretofore unimagined boost to the growth of the sport in Yemen and the region.

However, a deputy minister in the Yemen Sports Ministry recently informed the gymnast Neshwan al-Harazi of the Ministry's opposition to participation on the grounds of the recent Danish/Islamic "controversy", and recommendation that the gymnast be barred from competing in Denmark.

While a final decision has not been made, this policy in direct opposition to the Olympic creed, and contradicts the philosophy of humanity that you have expressed in the numerous essays you have published on the subject.

Bruno, I'm sure that you see the magnitude of the issue, and hope that you might directly intervene in some appropriate manner. In no way do I presume to suggest specific actions, but I believe that this unfortunate situation can be a wonderful opportunity for the FIG to reach out and create better communication and understanding between peoples.

I am profoundly grateful for whatever you might be able to do in working towards a successful conclusion of this matter. If I can provide any additional information, please contact me; the email address of Yemen Federation President Eyhab al-Salami is:

eyhab_gym@hotmail.com

With great respect and
Warm personal regards,
Jim Holt
Yemen Coach
2006 World Gymnastics Championships

There was a two-fold message in the response I received from the FIG office. The first (and extremely welcome!) was (regardless of it was actually true or

not), that Bruno would look into the matter. The second (and extremely predictable!) was that messages should proceed "through proper channels".
From: Andre F. Gueisbuhler
Subject: World Championships Aarhus
Dear Jim
Thank you for your e-mail of May 30th to our President Burno Grandi.
Our President wishes to discuss this matter with the Executive Commission which will meet here in China at the beginning of next week. We will come back to you after this meeting.

We kindly ask you to address any further correspondence not to the Presidents personnel e-mail address, but to the official address of the FIG (info@fig-gymnastics.org or agueisbuhler@fig-gymnastics.org) and strictly through the Yemen Gymnastics Federation.
Kind regards,
Fédération Internationale de Gymnastique
André F. Gueisbuhler

I subsequently received an additional email which stated that Bruno was indeed vitally concerned about this issue and would take steps to address it...further, the FIG office sent a second saying that the issue was an agenda item on the FIG (international federation) Executive Committee meeting for thc following week....

In addition, I sent correspondence to the gymnastics Federations of Morocco, Algeria, Egypt, and Saudi Arabia and Denmark (host country) asking for their support and requesting that they send correspondence to the FIG and (Denmark excepted) to the Yemen Olympic Committee.

It is unclear to me to this day what the exact levers were that induced the Minister of Sports to reconsider and change his position. I understand that the topic was discussed by the FIG Executive Committee but I have no knowledge that they actually contacted officials in the Yemen Sports Ministry or Government. I do know that Yemen Gymnastics Federation President Eyhab al-Salami along with Nashwan and Nashwan's uncle Ehssan met with the Minister and presented a "case" for Nashwan's participation based in part on several arguments and points including someI had suggested. I also heard from Nashwan that there was some possible pressure from the Yemen Government, and in particular from President Ali Abdullah Saleh....supposedly Nashwan has a relative who's wife is a blood relation to the President's wife....after having to deal with this issue (and many of the one's prior as described in the book), NOTHING would surprise me......oops, not quite true:

Oh, in case you missed it (and sorry for stating the OBVIOUS that everyone seemed to have overlooked)....these Yemeni bureaucrats are so upset about Danish cartoons, but the notion of an American, a gringo as coach of Yemen gymnastics didn't seem to bother anybody......unbelievable......ON TO AARHUS!

Fast forward 6 months….Nashwan, Hannah, and I rendezvous in Aarhus after exchanging training suggestions, ideas, and comments via voluminous emails and a couple videos. His technique on pommel horse was and is extraordinary and during podium training caught the eye of long-time German expert (and former National Coach) Dieter Hoffman who wrote him up as an athlete to be watched on the FIG website. He competed solid sets on floor and pommels, and hit two wonderful vaults to finish 27th in the competition on that event; not bad for a World-level debutante! Nashwan proved so impressive, that International Gymnast magazine sought him out for a feature piece which appeared in their 2006 World Championships report issue.

So, a dream which began in the training hall in Sana'a in 1996 came true in Denmark a decade later…..on to the next incredible/impossible dream!

"Hey, now you pay attention to something here. These kids ain't the same anymore. And you know what's behind it all? Rock 'n' roll. That music is turning the kids into a bunch of sex hungry, beer drinking, road racing werewolves."
William Sadler (Roadracers, 1994)

Chapter Seventeen

NASHWAN COMES TO AMERICA

This chapter is a valentine to Pam Cowan and Steve Miller. They are immigration attorneys who managed to get a young man from Yemen into (the then) George Bush's America.

Here's the story:

After Nashwan's success at the 2006 Worlds, it was clear to us all that we needed to continue our collaboration. Hannah, Nashwan, and I were a very efficient and effective team, and moreover, she and he had bonded easily during the (too) short time we had shared together in Denmark. Upon arriving home, I pondered the future, and decided that in order to get to the next level, Nashwan needed to come to America.

My first step was to send to the Yemen Gymnastics Federation and Olympic Committee a report about the World Championships. In it, I not only recounted what Nashwan had accomplished and the enthusiasm with which his participation was received, but (as is my usual wont) articulated a new objective and a plan which would potentially enable us to accomplish the goal. I explained to the Federation and OC that it was now appropriate that Nashwan train seriously to achieve an international ranking (his best ranking/result in Aarhus on the 3 events he competed was 27th on vault) in order to position himself for future high-level successes (including, although even to me it seemed an "impossible dream", the Olympics). In order to do so, I argued, it would be necessary for him to train outside Yemen, and with someone he knew, trusted, and with the experience that would enable him to achieve these projected goals. In other words, and I spelled it out explicitly, it was time for Nashwan to come to America and live and train with me.

The response was both immediate and very very (happily so!) surprising to me...the YOC emailed me back within the week and asked for a financial proposal or budget. Wow. I pondered the specific requirements for a few days and submitted as per their request, a budget. After a week of silence, I received an email from Mohammed al-Ajari the President of the Yemen Olympic Committee and the short version of his answer to my proposal was: "ok."

Wowwwwww.......

Now came what I thought (little did I anticipate some of the pitfalls ahead) would be the hard part. Yemen had said yes! Now, how do I go about getting a 20 year-old Yemeni male into the USA? Not to belabor the political aspects of this, but I remind the reader of the reactions of the United States government and the modification(s) of it's "open-door" visa and immigration policies in response to the events of September 11, 2001. In addition, our particular circumstance was exacerbated due to the origins of a certain uber-criminal mastermind who was the organizer of the tragedy that befell the US on that date. Osama bin-Laden's parents were Yemeni, ergo the Bush administration was particularly sensitive to Yemeni requests to enter the US to visit.

Anytime I've had any issues pertaining to immigration or foreign athletes or coaches, I turn to Pam and Steve. They have had 100% success rate in the cases I've brought to them, and it is my opinion that they were particularly intrigued with this particular challenge. They gave us a comprehensive list of documents required by INS, proposed modifications to language used in applications, and were tireless negotiators after the documents had been submitted to INS. Nashwan was applying to come to the US on a B-2 visitors visa and had to show (beyond a reasonable doubt) that he was here for a reasonable reason, had a US citizen (me) who would vouch for him and be responsible for him while he was in the United States, and that (most important to the Federales) would leave on or before the expiration date of his visa.

In addition to the submission of paperwork, Nashwan was required to make an appointment for an interview at the American Embassy in Sana'a Yemen where an Embassy official would be making the determination whether to grant the visa or not. Pam and Steve provided a list of likely questions that would be asked, and coached Nashwan, via email on his answers. A key component of our case is that Nashwan was coming to the US to prepare for a specific event; we were preparing for the 2007 World Championships in Stuttgart Germany, and since he was scheduled to compete on September 4, we were projected a departure from the US on the 26th but certainly no later than the 27th of August of that year.

Our paper documentation was as airtight as Cowan and Miller could make it. Nashwan apparently passed his interview with favorable impressions on the part of the US officials. Two, then almost three weeks went by without communication. Both Nashwan and I were approaching "frantic" on our scale of worry. Pam had several discreet and diplomatic exchanges with the officials in the US Embassy. Ultimately, it became apparent that they were reluctant to "pull the trigger" due to concerns about the reliability of everything we had provided.

Pam forwarded me the following email:

Dear Ms. Cowan,

In the process of reviewing Mr. Al Harazi's application, it would be helpful to know some information that he was unable to provide at the interview, and perhaps we could enlist your cooperation on that matter. Namely, has Jim Holt ever been affiliated with any other visa applicant in the past, for similar gymnastics training purposes? If so, please provide their names, nationalities, date applied, and current whereabouts.

Consul
US Embassy
Sanaa, Yemen

Oh baby….talk about having a softball question lobbed up to me….no guarantee that they'll listen to reason, but the folks in Sana'a are r-e-a-l-l-y nervous about signing off on this and need their hands held/reassurance that everything is going to be ok…..slam dunk, I can give them puh-lenty of reassurance….after consulting with Pam and getting her approvial on the tone and wording, I emailed the following off to the US Embassy:

Dear "x"

... I have been involved in gymnastics for most of my life. For the last fifteen years, I have specialized in the growth of this sport throughout the developing world. My particular expertise is in helping young Gymnastics Federations and their athletes compete at the international levels including the World Championships and Olympic Games... Many of them have gone on to have successful gymnastics and post-gymnastics careers.

These individuals include in rough chronological order:

1993 - Manuel Rojas from Ecuador, who came for training on a B-2 visa. Manuel competed at the 1993 World Championships for Ecuador and currently owns a gym school in Quito, Ecuador.

1994 -Cecelia Mass Porras, from Bolivia, who came for training on a B-2 visa. She competed at the 1994 World Championships. Cecelia currently lives and works for a Natural Gas company in Santa Cruz, Bolivia.

1997 - Brooke Bell, from Australia. Brooke was on a student visa, and participated the USA Gymnastics age-group optional program. He qualified on to the State and Regional Championships. Brooke returned to Australia at the end of school year, and ...is living in Cairns, Australia.

1998 - Khumbulani Moyo, from Zimbabwe. Mr. Moyo came to the United States on an H-1B visa Khumbulani was a Silver Medalist at the All-African Games, worked for almost six years in H-1B status, is now a

permanent resident of the United States working as Head Coach of Umpqua Valley Gymnastics in Roseburg, Oregon.
1999 - Stanley Chinyerere, from Zimbabwe. Mr. Chinyerere came to the United States on an H-1B and worked as a Gymnastics coach, while also receiving training, and was the Zimbabwe team captain at two All-African games. Stan is the Head Coach of a Gymnastics school in Indianapolis, Indiana.
2001 - Nirvana Zaher, from Egypt. Ms. Nirvana came to the United States on a student visa, the first and only Egyptian to date to receive an athletic scholarship for gymnastics... for Sacramento State University from 2001 to 2005. Ms. Nirvana received her Masters in Exercise Physiology last spring, and currently lives in Cairo, Egypt.
2003 - Jorge Pedraza, from Bolivia. Jorge came to the United States on a B-2 visa to train with me prior to the World Gymnastics Competition in Anaheim, California. Jorge competed at the 2001, 2002 and 2003 World Competition with me as his coach. He currently lives in Japan where he teaches at a private sports club.
With respect to all of the above gymnastics students that I have trained, NONE of them have ever broken any U.S. immigration law or regulation.... Mr. al-Harazi has great gymnastics potential, and the 2007 World Championships take place in Stuttgart Germany in early September, 2007... As indicated...Mr. al-Harazi will be completely supported by the Yemen Olympics Committee, and he will leave the United States at the conclusion of the training to fly to Stuttgart, Germany for this competition. His plans are then to return to Yemen from Stuttgart...
We will deeply appreciate your immediate attention to Mr. al-Harazi's visa application, etc.

One funny thing is, after the fact, I realized I had omitted 2 other individuals I could have sited. It didn't matter. Two days after submitting this to the Embassy Nashwan was given his visa.

Meanwhile, broadly related to the possibility of Nashwan coming to live with us, but primarily because it had been 15 years since we had done anything, Hannah had planned a detailed revamp/remodel of the upstairs living area in our home. This consisted of a complete replacement of carpet for two bedrooms, a foyer area, hallway and stairs, as well as a new paint job for the entire area.

We had just started moving furniture and 15 years of assorted bric-brac out of the area on the Saturday morning I had sent the email to the US Embassy in Sana'a. On Monday, I learned that Nashwan's visa was approved, and sure enough, I received a confirmation from an extremely excited Nashwan who also happily informed me that he would be arriving on Friday. For those who haven't traveled extensively in the Middle East, they don't bother with those

14-day advance tickets….people can purchase right away…and they do. So, I had the happy task of approaching Hannah and letting her know that "Honey, Nashwan's visa has been approved and he's arriving on Friday."
Hannah was just now making sure I'm taking books and bookshelves downstairs to clear the upstairs for our remodel.
"Which Friday?"
"This Friday."
"Which this Friday?"
This Friday."
"Which this Friday?"
"Friday."
You mean THIS Friday? Four days from now???"
"Yes."
"WHAAAAAT???"

In any event, we spent the next few days getting things cleared away, picked Nashwan up at the airport on Friday, and over the weekend, the 3 of us spent a long couple of days doing a "crash-course" in getting the place painted and furniture put back in so that he could have a livable living space.

We have exactly 26 weeks until the World Championships. Nashwan informs me that the Olympic Committee has decided that in addition to my projected objectives, they would like to see two additional things happen as a result of our collaboration. Not only do they want this 3 event specialist to do ALL-AROUND in Stuttgart, but they think it would be a good idea to see if we can't manage to qualify to the Olympic Games!!!! Great. Nothing like dropping a couple impossible goals into an impossibly short timeframe.

Nevertheless, we got into the gym and started to work. Yulia Hancheroff and Guennadi Komissarov, the owners of Metropolitan Gymnastics could not have been more supportive; they graciously provided free gym time for Nashwan to train. The details of Nashwan's training and the specific elements and compositions of his routines are not of significance (with respect to this narrative!)….what is astonishing, and I'm certain unprecedented anywhere in the world at this level is that a three event specialist who had basically never worked rings, parallel bars, or horizontal bar was able to learn sufficient skills to be able to put together exercises in only 6 months time! Nashwan is a true physical phenomenon….in 26 weeks of training, he learned 24 NEW elements, and was able to put together exercises on the three events (Yemen does not have modern rings, p-bars, or high bar). Again, I suspect it was the first time in the history of gymnastics that the first time a gymnast performed a routine in competition was at a World Championships. Nashwan debuted his rings and parallel bar routines on the competition floor in Stuttgart. (Note: A sore wrist prevented him from competing on the horizontal bar.)

Having Nashwan as part of our household was a joy; in the days and weeks we shared together, Hannah and I came to love him as a surrogate son.

As we approached mid-summer, I was eager to get approval for his entry visa into Germany resolved in an (early) timely manner. Unlike the United States, Yemenis are among the peoples that are required to apply for a visa when entering member nations of the European Union. Unlike some countries' policies, applicants for the "Shengen" (EU visitors) visa must apply in person to an Embassy or Consulate. I received all the pertinent information from the German Embassy in San Francisco, and was provided address and phone number to the nearest German Consulate, located in Portland Oregon approximately 180 miles (350+ kilometers) from Seattle. We made an appointment, and on a July morning, filed our paperwork, application fee, and had a very nice interview with Counsul Hallen and his secretary. I was mildly amused that the Consulate did not have access to email as a means of communication, but rather relied solely on telephone and fax. We were told at the end of our interview that the visa would be processed within 2-3 weeks.

A recurring theme throughout this book (and my life!) is that one should "never say never", and conversely, NEVER assume that anything is truly finalized until (in the sense of projects like these) the gymnast is actually on the competition floor on "game-day" and saluting the judges to mount the apparatus.

An earlier chapter described "fun with passports" How 'bout the obverse, "nightmares with visas". We got home from training, looked in the mail, no the visa had not been returned, and there was a message on my answering machine....it turns out that we were misinformed by the Embassy in San Francisco and that according to "Shengen visa regulations and procedures", the

Oregon Consulate was not the appropriate place for Nashwan to interview and process his visa, but rather he was REQUIRED to submit his application IN PERSON to the German Embassy in Yemen!!!! I just about had a heart attack and expired right then and there.

If in fact, there was no way around this, or if we couldn't convince the Germans to make an exception, we were, at least at first glance, "screwed". Among the problems this brought up:

1. Nashwan would have to leave the United States; because of the conditions of his B-1 visa, he would not be permitted to re-enter the USA without applying for a new visa. There was not adequate time remaining (about 7 weeks until the competition) to accomplish this.
2. He would therefore have his training interrupted/stopped at the most crucial phase of training.
3. the unanticipated/extra airfare/transportation costs would blow a hole in our budget.

4. so on and so forth……

After the initial shock, I decided we needed to try and contact the German Embassy in Yemen and speak to someone directly about the matter. I send a preliminary email outlining our problem and requesting a "waiver", then started phoning them….two challenges with the telephone…..Embassies are notorious in their lack of having a "live" person answering the phone; in my experience, they rely overwhelmingly on "voice messaging", or in many cases (German Embassy in Sana'a Yemen as a case in point), not answering the phone at all.

Remember, Sana'a is eleven time zones ahead of the west coast of the United States…. we must have, over a 4 or 5 day period made 79-100 phone calls in 15 minute increments (in addition to email) trying to make contact with the German Embassy in Yemen.

About 02:15 on a Monday morning, (in what seemed almost like a miracle), a

"real live" person answered the phone…."could we please be put through to the person who handles 'Shengen' visas?" "Yes, of course…" two rings, and (again almost miraculously), a "live person" on the end of the phone….I explained our situation/dilemma in detail, and Ms. Anja Zougourari informed me that she would look into the matter and respond at her earliest opportunity. She asked me to document/recount our conversation in writing…

I responded:

Dear Ms. Zougouari,

It was a great pleasure to speak with you today!

In summary, I am writing on behalf of Mr. Nashwan al-Harazi, a citizen of Yemen who has been in the USA for the last 4 months...

a. Neshwan is sportsman traveling to Germany on Sports/Cultural matter with invitation from Stuttgart World Championships organizing committee (attached) and is financially supported by the Yemen Olympic Committee. He has documentation proving he will return to Yemen immediately after Championships.

b. he has twice before received visa from German Embassy to EU countries for sport and has returned to Yemen without incident (2004 Germany, 2006 Denmark)

c. prior to flying to the US, he apparently contacted persons in the Embassy in Sana'a and was informed that he could apply for and receive his visa while in the USA.

I am Nashwan's coach and last year accompanied him to the 2006 World Championships in Denmark where he became the first Yemeni in history to participate at that level.

Your help is profoundly appreciated;

SHUKRUN!!! (danke shoen in Arabic as you know!)

warmest regards,
She, in turn, responded in kind:

> *Dear Mr. Holt,*
> *I assume that we are talking of Nashwan Haidar Al-Harazi, DOB 29.11.1986 in Sanaa, Passport N° 02118977, issued on Nov. 19.2005 in Sanaa, valid until Nov 19, 2011 - this is at least what our visa database tells me.*
>
> *The Embassy has no objections against authorizing the visa issuing by the Consulate General San Francisco, I suggest that upon receipt of the attachment I will contact my colleague in San Francisco and inform him about the upcoming application.*
>
> *Best regards*
> *Anja Zougouari*

YESSSSSS!!!!!!!!!!!!!!!!!!!!!!!!!!

Now, the only thing (pertaining to this particular issue!) remaining was to ensure that the German Embassy in San Francisco was aware of the decision taken by the German Embassy in Yemen, and it turns out, according to German diplomatic (or possibly) European Union procedure, to repeat all our steps and resubmit our application in person to the German Consulate in Portland.

As per our previous experience, we drove to Portland, submitted our application with (appropriate duplicate and non-refundable) fees!. The Consul apologized profusely for the mis-communication which had made it necessary to repeat our steps, but Nashwan and I didn't care….the only thing that mattered was that the German Government had (basically) approved his request for visa, and that we were, unless the unthinkable happened, on our way to Germany and the Worlds.

As recounted elsewhere in the narrative, we did indeed receive the visa and Nashwan participated successfully at the World Championships in Stuttgart.

Have I mentioned throughout the narrative that one's wildest and most impossible dreams can come true?

A few months after the competition, we received word, well, the International Gymnast magazine and website captures it perhaps better than I could….they published the following:

Al-Harazi "Still in Shock" Over Olympic Berth

Jim Holt and Nashwan Al-Harazi

Yemen's **Nashwan Al-Harazi** told IG he is "still in shock" after recently receiving a wild-card berth for this summer's Olympic Games in Beijing. Al-Harazi will be the first gymnast from Yemen to take part in Olympic competition, after a tripartite commission selected him and female gymnast Thuong Di Thi Ngan (Vietnam) for the two available wild-card berths for Beijing.

The tripartite commission consists of the International Olympic Committee, the International Gymnastics Federation and the Association of National Olympic Committees. Geographic representation at the Olympics is one of the factors for designating wild-card berths.

"I know that there are gymnasts with greater accomplishments than me who have not been invited to Beijing," Al-Harazi told IG from Yemen this week. "I feel a great responsibility to them and to the international gymnastics community to perform my best, and to be a worthy example of what the Olympic spirit is supposed to mean."

Al-Harazi got the news of his wild-card berth at home, where representatives of the Yemen Olympic Committee telephoned him. "I am still in shock," he said, noting that officials from his country's gymnastics federation are equally enthusiastic.

"They are very, very pleased and hopeful that this will help gymnastics develop in our country, so that we might have a full team compete at some point in the next quadrennium and beyond," Al-Harazi said.

At the 2007 World Championships in Stuttgart, which served to qualify gymnasts for the Beijing Games, Al-Harazi competed on five events only because of a sore wrist.

Al-Harazi said that, prior to the start of his U.S.-based training under coach **Jim Holt** in Seattle, Wash., he had never trained on rings, parallel bars or high bar. In Stuttgart, he competed for the first time ever on rings and parallel bars.

As Al-Harazi awaits approval of his visa to return to the U.S. for pre-Olympic training under Holt, he said his training plan has shifted "from the 'long-term' to 'competitive preparation' phase." He intends to compete in the all-around at the Beijing Games.

"I'm looking to have my floor, pommel horse and vault Start Values in the top 15 in the competition," said Al-Harazi, who placed 27th on vault at the 2006 Worlds and 21st on vault at the 2007 Worlds. "*Ensha Allah*, my goal is to perform my exercises cleanly!"

Holt said Al-Harazi's 2007 Start Values were 6.3 on floor exercise, and 6.2 on pommel horse and vault. "We're trying to do a little better, yet be clean, clean, clean," he said.

Al-Harazi credited Holt and his wife, Hannah, for their support of his career. Under the Holts' partnership he became Yemen's first gymnast to compete at a World Championships when he competed in 2006 in Aarhus, Denmark. Al-Harazi trained briefly under Holt at Metropolitan Gymnastics in Seattle prior to Aarhus, and spent eight months training with Holt prior to Stuttgart.

"Jim started me on the path that led to Beijing," Al-Harazi said. "It was a dream come true for me to be able to live and train in America with him and Hannah this past year, and to be at Worlds with 'my second parents.'"

In 1996 Holt conducted an IOC Solidarity Course in Sana'a, Yemen, where he asked a group of 40 Yemeni coaches and gymnasts to define their goals.

"They said, 'We'd like to be competitive with the Arab countries,'" Holt recalled. "I responded, 'That's too small. If you're going to do this, you need to pick an impossible dream and chase it. There's no reason that Yemen can't have a gymnast compete at the World Championships or even qualify for the Olympic Games.'"

Al-Harazi, then age 9, was among the group of gymnasts standing on a mat next to a homemade vault board. "I pointed to Nashwan and said, 'This could be your guy. This could be the first gymnast from Yemen to compete at Worlds,'" Holt said. "And as Nashwan told you, he believed me." — *John Crumlish*

Although regrettably, I was not nominated by the Yemen Olympic Committee to accompany Nashwan to Beijing, I am enormously proud and was so very happy that he was in fact able to realize his "impossible dream" and compete in the Olympic Games. Nashwan competed on Pommels, Floor, and placed 16th on Vault.

As of this writing, we are working on acquiring him a "work-visa" in the United States, so that he can coach, continue to train and compete, and advance his education here in America.

"Dum vivimus vivamus!"
Robert Heinlein (Glory Road)

Chapter Eighteen

CONCLUSION

I've wandered and traveled the world working to make a difference, and have utilized the sport of gymnastics as my platform.

I've had many disappointments and projects that have failed or failed to materialize, but have been blessed with the opportunity to do some things that even now, seem preposterous....but very special.

Hopefully, I've made a positive difference in the lives of the individuals I've touched along the way, and, regardless of the defeats, I've always had an amazing amount of joy and fun doing whatever it is that I've done.

Like Erasmus, I've smiled, often sardonically, sometimes ruefully at the oddities and craziness of the human condition and at our (including my) conceits. At my absolute finest, I'd like to think, that like the motion picture pioneers that Kevin Brownlow so admires, I've achieved or built something that, if not for me, might not have come into existence. Finally, like Odysseus, I've been a restless soul on a quest....and ultimately, I think, would like to be considered as a tenacious and resourceful survivor.....who knows? It is for others ultimately to evaluate whatever it is I've managed to accomplish; for myself, I'm satisfied that to date, I've tried my best.

What's next? Who knows? I can tell you this....if you're involved with gymnastics in any developing country and want a quixotic, passionate individual who is convinced that the impossible is possible, and who is certain that dreams exist in order that we strive to make them real, you need to contact me. My bags are packed and I'm ready to go.....

Chapter Nineteen

THE "HONOR ROLL"

Athletes who Hannah and have had the privilege of coaching internationally:

Worlds: (chronological order):

Igancio Morales(BOL)- WC 1991, 1993, 1994
Iggy is Vice-President for Logistics for Central America for United Parcel Service

Manuel Rojas (ECU)- WC 1993
Coaches at a gymnastics school in Iowa.

Cecelia Maas Porras(BOL): WC 2994
Bolivia's first woman to compete at Worlds, Cece is in management for a major petroleum country in Bolivia

Farhad Behahin (IRI): WC 1996
Freddie graduated from Medical school and currently owns and operates Gymnastics World gym school in the San Fernando Valley in California.

Sean Grosvenor (BAR): WC 1997
Police officer in Chicago Illinois, husband, father of four

Jorge Pedraza (BOL): WC 2001, 2002, 2003
Jorge teaches ballroom dance in Japan, is married to Izumi and they have a daughter named after my wife Hannah

Maria Jose de la Fuentes (BOL): WC 2003; OG 2008
Attending University in Bolivia

Nashwan al-Harazi (YEM): WC 2006, 2007
OG: 2008
Nashwan is currently living in Yemen, is planning on getting a work visa to work and live in the USA and attend university in same.

"The Class of '95"- Zimbabwe Men's Team, All African Games:

Ricky Batista (ZIM): AAG 1995
Rick is the program director and head coach for the women's and girls gymnastics program at University of Zimbabwe in Harare.

Warren Blumears (ZIM): AAG 1995
Warren coaches at a gymnastics school in Los Angeles California, is a husband and father

Stanley Chinyerere (ZIM): AAG 1995
Stan is married and coaches at a gymnastics school in Indianapolis Indiana

Wesley Chirema (ZIM): AAG 1995
Wes coaches boys gymnastics at a club in Saskatoon Saskatchewan Canada.

Erasmus Garakare (ZIM): AAG 1995
"Mario" runs a gymnastics program for children in one of Harare's "high density townships"

Khumbulani Moyo (ZIM): AAG 1995, (WC 1997)
Khum is a coach in Roseburg Oregon is married and has an infant daughter

Lucky Mutare (ZIM): AAG 1995
currently living and working in Denmark

Exceptional Merit:

Mike Williams(USA)
only American in history to perform triple salto on floor exercise, Mike is a pharmaceutical rep and his wife Beck and he have 3 children in Anchorage Alaska

Nirvana Zaher(EGY)

only Egyptian to receive gymnastics scholarship to US university, competed 4 years for Sacramento State, received Masters at Lonerbaugh U. in England, currently working as Physical Trainer in Cairo

Honorable Mention:

Augustin Eraghebe(NIG):CG 1994
Augustin relocated to Canada shortly after the Commonwealth Games

Kingsley Eraghebe(NIG): CG 1994
Relocated to Canada shortly after the Commonwealth Games

Smart Idahosa (NIG): CG1994
relocated to Canada shortly after the Commonwealth Games

Cletus Okhpoh (NIG): CG 1994
Relocated to Canada shortly after the Commonwealth Games

Index

C

D

I

J

K

L

M

Q

R

S

ABOUT THE AUTHOR

Jim Holt has spent most of the last two decades passionately pursuing his dream of developing and growing gymnastics around the world. He has coached (to date) in 11 World Championships, including 1991- Bolivia; 1993-Bolivia & Ecuador, 1994-Bolivia, 1996-Iran, 1997 Barbados; 1999-Namibia; 2001-Bolivia; 2002- Bolivia; 2003- Bolivia; 2006-Yemen; 2007- Yemen. He was the National Coach for Zimbabwe at the 1995 All-African Games where he also served as Gymnastics Competition Director, and was Assistant Coach for Nigeria at the 1994 Commonwealth Games. Jim also filled the role of advisor and personal coach for Paul O'Neill (Silver Medalist-Rings) for the 1994 Worlds. He has met criteria for FIG Coaches Life-time Achievement Diploma by virtue of coaching at 11 World Championships for 6 different Federations. It is believed that the latter is unprecedented in the history of the sport.

Holt has been an IOC Olympic Solidarity Technical Expert and has conducted courses for Bolivia, Chile, Egypt, Mexico, Namibia, Nigeria, Swaziland, Yemen, Zimbabwe. No neophyte at organizing events, Jim has been Competition Director at the 1990 Goodwill Games, 1995 All-African Championships, and was on the staff of the 1996 Olympic Games in Atlanta.

Prior to his intensive involvement internationally, Jim was the Head Men's Coach at the University of Washington, and Assistant Coach at Portland State University. A prolific author prior to this work, he has co-authored *Coaching Women's Gymnastics for Clubs and Schools* (2002); Holt &Dowdell, edited *International Development Systems* (1994)and contributed 100+ articles for a variety of periodicals (IG, FIG-WOG, etc. on sport) throughout the world.

He was an invited guest to 1998 FIG Congress and was twice elected National Membership Director (Men's Program) to USAG Board of Directors. Jim was also a member, USGF Hall of Fame Selection committee (1989-1996)

Jim lives in Seattle with his wife Hannah, another life-long gymnastics professional who has accompanied Jim around the world contributing to the development of gymnastics internationally, and with two energetic dachshunds. He is an avid collector of antiquarian books and is keenly interested in film history, particularly the Silent Era, early rock n' roll and its' roots, and is a voracious reader of virtually anything pertaining to culture or history. Jim received his J.D. from Lewis & Clark (Portland, OR) subsequent to his batchelor's degree from Washington State University.

Made in the USA
Charleston, SC
03 December 2009